Devas Sees The Light

(Grandpas Tell The Best Stories)

To Jeanne,
To my fellow
Beach Tone.
Hope you enjoy
Don Alcorn
2/11/13

By
Donald Alcorn

Devas Sees the Light

Copyright ©2012 by Donald Alcorn
All Rights reserved.

*This book may not be reproduced or transmitted
in any form by any means, electronic or mechanical,
including photocopying and recording, or by
any information storage or retrieval system or
utilized in any educational program
without the prior written permission
of the copyright holder.*

*Further reproduction by any means may make you civilly
and criminally liable for violation of copyright laws.*

Table of Contents

Chapter 1, Gone Fishing 1
Chapter 2, The Storm 5
Chapter 3, Home Coming 9
Chapter 4, The Village 13
Chapter 5, Rabbi Abdon's Replacement 19
Chapter 6, The Sabbath 29
Chapter 7, Sailing to Capernaum 35
Chapter 8, Not the End, The Beginning of Other Stories 43
Chapter 9, Ezra and Merchant Return Home 47
Chapter 10, Continuing Walk Home From Capernaum 49
Chapter 11, Back in Hippos At the Tax Gate Near the Pier 53
Chapter 12, The Great Escape From Hippos 59
Chapter 13, Back At The Sanhedrim In Jerusalem 71
Chapter 14, Back In Capernaum 75
Chapter 15, Bird Headed To 3653 81
Chapter 16, At the Caravan 91
Chapter 17, Family Reunion at Caravan Camp 93
Chapter 18, Bird's Hidden Valley 95
Chapter 19, Back at the Roman Outpost In Hippos 101
Chapter 20, Commander Walked Through Hippos 115
Chapter 21, To the farm And Back to Hippos 133
Chapter 22, Back in Hippos 139
Chapter 23, Rabbi Abdon arrives At Synagogue 143
Chapter 24, Back in Hippos Waiting For Devas'
and Ezra's Family 147
Chapter 25, Grandfather on His Way to Protect His Family 151

Chapter 26, Grandfather Back at The Marketplace 155
Chapter 27, Campsite In Hippos 161
Chapter 28, How Grandfather Got to Hippos 169
Chapter 29, Back at the Synagogue Compound 181
Chapter 30, Commander Back At The Outpost......................... 189
Chapter 31, First Full Day After Devas' And Ezra's Families Returned Home.. 193
Chapter 32, The High Council Of The Temple of Jerusalem .. 197
Chapter 33, From the Base To the Hide and Seek Trail 203
Chapter 34, The Play.. 215
Chapter 35, Day after the Play... 225
Chapter 36, What the Historians and Scribes found 229
Chapter 37, Meeting with Herod At Fort Machaerus 237
Chapter 38, Hippos 251
Author's Note 255

Introduction
The Beginning

    Did you see the little statement on the cover of this book? **Grandpas tell the best stories.** This story is written just as a grandfather would tell it to his grandchildren and their friends. The book is not likely to win any literary awards but if it brings a smile, a laugh or if it encourages anyone to read the wonderful stories in the Bible, that's the best reward this grandfather can receive.

    I wrote a shorter version of this book in 2003 and had a little over two hundred books printed for my family and friends. Chapters One through Eight of this book are similar to that book. That book was printed just after Hurricane Isabel roared through our little village of Kempsville. We are a subdivision of the city of Virginia Beach, Virginia.

    Most of the stories in this historical novel occur in the small town of Hippos, Israel, between 168 BCE and 30 CE. This is the period of time from when the Roman Empire defeated the Greek Empire and when Jesus began His public ministry. Kempsville is larger than the little town of Hippos but not long ago we were much smaller than we are today and many of us old timers can still remember dirt roads and fields with crops or livestock as far as you could see. We now have our share of shopping centers, strip malls, homes and busy surfaced roads. The most important ingredient in a story, is the people. How they act and react to situations that affects their lives. I hope this story will remind you of your neighbors, friends and other people you know. The first few chapters of this book are about a storm and how the storm affected the people that lived in Hippos. If you have lived through a hurricane in Kempsville, you can envision the storm in this story. I included the following comment on the back of the book I wrote in 2003:

    Hurricane Isabel came through with such destructive power that many of our lives and property will never be the same.

Trees downed, electric power off, homes, fences and cars under huge old trees and the children went without TV for the first time in their lives. Isabel was much like the storm I tell about in my book. The quick helpful reactions of neighbors and friends were also like those told in "Devas Sees The Light".

My original book contained more information about my grandchildren and family. In "this edition" you won't have to read about my family. -----You'll have to wait for my Christmas newsletter. (I'm kidding) Even though I have removed some of the personal references about my family and friends, they and hopefully you, will recognize some personal traits of the characters in this book.

While I was updating and expanding my original book, I was truly amazed how much had happened in those eight years. A baby born eight years ago is now in the third grade of one of our village schools (Arrowhead Elementary or Point O View Elementary) and a child graduating from one of these elementary schools is now in or recently graduated from Kempsville High School. We have new villagers and we have lost some of our oldest and dearest villagers. In short, life has moved on and we have all been affected by the passing of time.

The beginning of a story is usually just the continuation of other stories. For example, if I were to write the story of your life, I would start by telling about your parents, grandparents or maybe your great grandparents. Your story would include such things as why you live where you do, where your parents were born, how they got to this country and many other facts that lay the groundwork for your life story. Somewhere in your life story you would mention persons or events that could be the beginning of a whole new story or a series of stories. Part of your life story would become a part of someone else's life story and on and on.

The Bible is the only book that starts at the beginning. All other stories have their beginning after some event has laid the groundwork for the beginning of the story. Now I make no claim that my stories are anything but an attempt to view some of the most beloved stories of the Bible through the eyes and ears of imaginary observers.

I announce very boldly that this story is based on research of the scriptures and information about the area and people during the times these wonderful stories were recorded in the Bible. I claim no divine inspiration other than the same Holy Spirit that Jesus promised we would receive as Christians. I also confess that I love the expressions on peoples' faces as a story takes them on a journey through time to view a truth or promise from our Heavenly Father.

Most stories, like a river, start at many locations and funnel into what we call the beginning. Once the main story is told, the ending branches back out to form the beginning of a whole group of stories. This book has many beginnings and I hope you will journey with me through the streams that form the branches that form the flowing river that will carry you through our story.

The Bible tells us that Peter, James, Andrew and John were fishermen before Jesus called them to be His disciples. He was teaching them how to be His disciples and to lead others to be His followers. Jesus sent His disciples out into the area around the Sea of Galilee in groups of two and he gave them power over unclean spirits. They set out on their journey and performed miracles, healed the sick and taught God's plan of salvation. When they returned to Jesus, they were anxious to tell Him about all the wonderful things they had done in His name. Jesus wanted to spend time with them and to hear all about the wonderful things they had done and seen, however, the crowd grew so large around them that Jesus and His disciples decided to go to a quiet place. So at Jesus' command, they got into a boat and departed to a deserted place to be by themselves.

Now is a good time to set the scene for this story and many of the other stories that occurred in this region. The Sea of Galilee is in the northern area of Palestine. The Sea is really a lake that is fed by waters from the Jordan River. The Jordan River enters The Sea of Galilee at its northern-most area and discharges back into the Jordan River at the southern-most area. Jesus grew up around the Sea of Galilee, then spent much of his adult life in this region and began His ministry around the town of Capernaum, which is located on the north western area of the Sea of Galilee.

Chapter 1
Gone Fishing

Our story begins in the little town of Hippos, located in the southeastern area of the Sea of Galilee, with Devas, a fisherman, saying to his brother, Ezra, at the end of a hard day's fishing.

"So few fish..... So much work... Fishing these waters is not what it was when we were children. Our father and grandfather would fill this boat with fish, then clean and salt them before the sun went down. Now we fish for two days and are lucky if we get half a boat load and then that greedy Roman tax collector takes a fourth of what we catch."

"Now Devas, settle down," came the ever calming voice of Ezra. "You and I have fished these waters all our lives. We have had hard times before. This old boat has fed and provided for our families and given us a good living. Fishing is going to get better, you'll see.... You know, I've been thinking ...there are so many new settlements and towns springing up around the sea that the increased noise and lights may be causing the fish to go farther out where it is quieter and there are fewer lights."

"My brother, you are absolutely right. I remember the many times when we were young and playing on this same old boat, our father would whisper in a stern voice, 'Be quiet and put out that lantern... you are scaring the fish away'. We should sail to a deserted area I know on the other side of the sea where there are no lights and no noise. We can catch a boatload of fish. Joshua and Sam have been asking to go with us someday, so let's take them with us tomorrow."

Devas and Ezra lived a short walk from each other. The news about the trip and who was going, received the same welcome at both homes. Ezra's child, Joshua, and Devas' child, Sam, reacted to the news with big smiles and excited hugs. Mothers were not quite as happy about the news as the children were.

"They are too young.... They have chores to do.... Where

will they sleep?... Food?... What will they wear? No, it's too dangerous." The mothers had only begun to recite the list they had been preparing for the last year. Mothers have a way of knowing when it is time for adventures outside of the secure realm they have so lovingly created for their children. "Can't you wait until you go out for a one day trip?"

"You mean within your sight."

"No, I mean I worry about you when you go out, but now I will worry even more."

The fathers knew the mothers wanted to share in this happy moment of their children. They also knew how hard it was for the mothers to accept that their children needed a bigger world.

The next morning, before the sun was up, there were Devas and Ezra on their boat as usual, but this time they had two new, excited helpers.

"Sam, you steer.....Joshua man the sails while your father and I get the nets ready."

On the pier were two, apprehensive mothers, waving and shouting, "I love you." None of which was aimed at the grown men.

At the same time, across the sea, Jesus and his disciples were getting into a boat that was departing to a deserted place where the disciples could tell Jesus about their mission to heal and to spread His word.

We now have two boats from different places headed to the same location for two different reasons. One was to get away from people and lights so they could catch fish. The other group wanted to get away from people so they would be able to rest and tell Jesus about the events of the last several weeks.

The crowds that had been following Jesus and His disciples began to run along the shore, telling everyone as they went, that Jesus was in that boat. The crowd grew and grew to over 5,000 men plus the women and children. The crowd arrived, at the ordinarily deserted place, Jesus had selected as a place to rest and spend time with His disciples.

As the two boats neared their destinations, Devas said, "Sam, turn to the right a little and follow that boat ahead of us. Joshua, pull the sails tight so we can catch up to that boat. I want to see if they are fishing these waters."

The young adventurers worked the sails and rudder and brought their boat within a short distance of the boat ahead of them. Then Devas recognized Peter.

"Peter! Peter! Are you fishing these waters?"

"No, Peter replied, I'm no longer a fisherman of fish." With that remark Peter's boat began to pull away.

"That is strange. I've known Peter all my life and there is no better fisherman. Stay on this course. We should be getting near to where we can drop the nets."

As the fishermen sailed on, a strange sound began to be heard over the gentle rush of the water beneath the boat. "What is that sound?" Devas asked more to himself than to anyone else.

"Joshua, let some air out of the sails. Sam, hold this course while your father and I put out the net."

With the net set, the boat drifted slowly to the selected area. "Now don't make any noise. You don't want to scare the fish away."

Ezra said, "I can't make out what that noise is. I think my mind is playing tricks on me, but that sounds like a lot of people shouting on the shore. Look up there where Peter's boat has landed. I can see hundreds, maybe thousands of people."

"All right Joshua, drop the sails and you and Sam help your father and me pull in the net." Each pull brought in more net, but no fish.

"It's all that noise and light coming from the shore. The fish are gone and we have wasted a trip."

"Devas, we have come this far and we are prepared to stay three days. So settle down. These people will have to be leaving soon, because there is no place for them to get food. The nearest town is a long walk away. Let's pull in closer to Peter's boat and see what is going on. Who are all those people and what are they doing in this deserted place?"

While Devas and Ezra were trying to figure out what was happening, two small voices were saying, "Father that is Jesus. Some people say he is the Messiah. A man coming through town said that he saw Jesus restore a blind man's sight and that a man born lame can now walk because Jesus told him he was healed. All the kids in our village are talking about him."

"Well if those people don't leave soon, they are going to get mighty hungry and we aren't going to catch any fish. Turn this boat around. We will go farther out and set our net and wait for this racket to stop."

With the net set and a calm breeze, the four ate their dinner and rested as they waited for the noise and lights to go away. Sleep fell on all but Devas who was pacing the deck, growing more impatient as darkness consumed the last rays of day. "What bad luck. Why did this man, called Jesus, pick this, of all places to have a meeting?"

The pacing continued and the time crept by. Finally, Devas began to see some lights moving down the beach. Now more lights followed them. The loud noise became a rumble....Then a whisper, and then the lights and the noise were gone.

A weary Devas watched as complete darkness and total silence engulfed their boat. Checking the lines and holding the net to make sure all was well for the night, Devas felt a jerk....then more jerks.

"Ezra....Joshua....Sam... Wake up! Wake up! Feel these lines....Pull.... Pull...." There were fish and more fish. The fish began to fill the bottom of the boat. The morning sun found four tired but happy fishermen and a boat filled with fish. They were so occupied with removing the fish from their net that they did not see a boat approaching them.

"Devas," Peter shouted. "I have never seen a boat riding so low in the water. Fishing must be good."

"Fishing was great once all that racket you and those people caused last night finally stopped. The children said they thought they saw that fellow called Jesus in the crowd."

"Yes. That was Jesus. He told us to go to Bethsaida and he will join us later. I'd like to stay longer and talk with you, but the winds are picking up. I think you had better follow us until we reach Bethsaida and then you can stay with us or you can follow the coast south to your home, if the weather improves. I'll see you there soon. I have so much to tell you."

"Set the sails. Joshua, you steer this time....Sam, man the sails. Follow Peter's boat. This has been a great fishing trip. Pull those sails tight, with this load of fish we need all the wind in our sails we can get."

Chapter 2
The Storm

"What a trip. It looks like we have another generation of fishermen in our families," Devas said to his brother Ezra. "Joshua, stay as close to Peter's boat as you can. Sam, pull harder on those sails; with this load of fish we need as much wind in the sails as we can get to keep up with Peter's boat."

Sam knew how well Joshua had done manning the sails yesterday and here Joshua was steering the boat as well as any grownup could. 'I can't be shown up,' Sam thought. Pulling as hard as a small body can pull... Pull....Pull...Pull, hands aching. Then almost a whisper, "Father, I need help. The winds are too much for me to hold the sails."

"I've been watching you," Devas said. "You have done a great job. I'll just pull with you until the winds let up a little."

There was no let up. The winds tore at the sails. The waves came from all directions and they kept growing bigger. By now both men were helping to hold the fish laden boat on a course that would take them home. The thrill of the catch had faded into fear for the very lives of those on board. There was no time for words but each father found time for a reassuring, firm grip on his child's shoulder.

"Devas, I have tied a line around Joshua and me. I suggest you do the same with Sam."

By now the men were steering and manning the sails. The children knew the boat was in danger of sinking and had found buckets and the strength to bail with all their hearts. Thoughts of dropping the sails and rowing the boat or throwing the fish overboard, flashed in the minds of both fathers. With only two men, however, rowing this boat in these seas was out of the question. There was no time to throw the fish overboard. The sails began to rip.

A little rip at first and then a large part of the sail flew past Devas' head. The boat slowed, but with the remaining sail the little craft was able to maintain a heading into the waves.

"Hold what you've got, Devas. If I can just steer into the waves until the storm lets up, we can make it."

Now it was late evening. Signs of night were on the horizon. Four exhausted sailors clinging to life on a boat that had seen many a storm, but could it sail through the night? All thoughts of keeping up with Peter's boat had vanished. The little light left in the sky was seen only as the struggling boat reached the top of another huge wave and then quickly disappeared as the boat fell into the foaming sea.

A faint voice, ... A lantern...... A boat off to the left. Then the voice grew louder. "Devas....Devas, this is Peter. We knew you were in trouble. We have been looking for you for hours. The sea is too rough for us to come any closer. We will stay with you as long as we can, in case we can help you."

Comfort sometimes comes in small doses. To Devas and Ezra, seeing Peter and his friends, was a big gulp of relief. Knowing that if their boat went down, there was a good chance the children could make it to Peter's boat. Both boats were fighting to stay afloat. Hope faded into despair only to return again as the boats lunged for shore and then were dashed back into the rough sea.

Holding the remaining sail, steering into the waves and bailing took every drop of energy remaining in the four, frightened, aching bodies. Time passed slowly, energy went quickly. Their minds   focused only on survival. Steering.... Pulling ... Bailing ...Steering...Pulling....Bailing. Ezra watched each wave. His mind was plotting a course that would keep the boat afloat while also looking for any sign of light on the shore. No time to look behind, except for a quick look for assurance that Peter's boat was still there. Peter was there in the bow of his boat straining to see Devas and his crew. With each glance Devas could tell that Peter and his crew were in as much danger of sinking as they were. What could they do if Peter's boat sunk? A large wave hit their boat and Ezra's mind was snapped back to keeping his boat and crew afloat.

A sound, a thought or just an awareness that something had or was about to happen caused Devas to look back. Peter had moved from the bow to the side of his boat. His crew had stopped rowing. Devas sensed the fear that grasped all on board Peter's boat.

Devas shouted, "What has happened? How can we help? Has someone fallen overboard?" The roaring of the sea, the howling of the wind, the clap of thunder and the flash of lightening concealed all sounds from Devas.

By now Ezra and the children were watching, the same questions racing through their minds. Then as before, two little voices were saying, "Father, that is Jesus."

Devas said, "That can't be Jesus, Peter said He stayed on shore and would join them later."

All eyes were on Peter's boat. A wave raised their boat to just the right height for all onboard to see Jesus walking on the water and after a while Jesus stepped onto Peter's boat.

Devas' mind quickly dashed back to the need to battle the storm," Pull,...Bail,.... Pull, ...Bail." All shouts were intended to encourage, not to scold, for they all knew that if they were going to live through this storm, there were many more hours of struggle. Each man lovingly checked the rope tying him to his child, and then the wind stopped.... The waves were gone.... Fear turned to amazement. Had they seen a miracle? What kind of a man was this Jesus? All eyes were fixed on Jesus as He moved about on Peter's boat. Devas and Ezra stood in disbelief. The lifeline connecting child to father slacked as small arms found comfort in touching their father. No one spoke; reassurance came from a hand on a shoulder pulling each child closer.

A gentle breeze began to fill the tattered sails. Had they survived the storm? Soon Peter's boat came along side. No need for talking, Jesus' gleaming eyes told all on board that all was well and that they should not be afraid. There would be time for talking when they were home. Shining stars, gentle breeze, calm sea and a battered boat effortlessly carried four exhausted sailors to where they longed to be.... Home.

Chapter 3
Home Coming

Back home, there were two mothers and Cara watching, waiting and worrying. The storm at home had been as fierce as it had been at sea. The pier was still standing but keeping the signal light burning had been a challenge. They had been there for most of the night, with each taking their turn standing on the lookout platform tending the signal light. One short flash of light....a short wait....then a second short flash of light, followed by a longer wait then a longer steady light. The cadence then changed to a rhythm that beat out the words to a song. Each family had its own signal that guided their loved ones home. A fire container is raised to the top of a 15-foot tower that sits on top of a shelter at the end of the pier. Then at the proper time, the fire container is lowered to where it stops behind a shield that hides the light from the seaman and at the proper time the light was raised back to the top of the pole. One of the first things a child learned was a song that sets the rhythm for raising and lowering the fire.

> Shine the light for father to see.
> Bring him home for mother and me.
> Keep him safe while he's away.
> In his strong arms I want to stay.

The entire neighborhood knew each neighbor's signal and when the signal was seen, would wander over to provide comfort, help and encouragement.

Joshua and Sam began to wake from their deep sleep. The weariness that had called them to lie down on the deck five hours earlier was almost gone. There was no special noise or movement of the boat that caused them to stir at the same time. There was no morning light on their faces, telling them it was time to start a new day. There was not a glimmer of light, but there was less darkness. Rubbing their eyes and peeping through half opened eyelids, they saw their fathers. Devas was steering and Ezra tended what was left of the sail.

"Well, it's about time you woke up. Come give us a hand. Sam, you steer. Joshua you tend the sail. Your father and I will start preparing the fish for unloading. We'll be home soon." Devas gave his nephew, Joshua, a pat on his back. Ezra gave Sam, his niece, a big hug.

"I see the signal! I see the signal!!" Sam yelled. Soon all on board the battered boat were watching the tiny flickering light on shore and they began to sing:

> Shine the light for Father to see.
> Bring him home for mother and me.
> Keep him safe while he's away.
> In his strong arms I want to stay.

Cara had no way of knowing the returning fishermen had seen the signal so she continued sending the signal out over the dark sea. Keeping the signal fire going and flashing the message, kept her busy all night. There was little time or reason to look out over the dark waters, but with the morning light, she glanced over her shoulder for a quick peak. For a moment she thought she saw something but there was no time to continue searching. She kept the fire burning and continued flashing the signal. Halfway through the next signal, she took one more peak. The spot, she saw before, was still there, only this time she could tell it was a boat.

Most of the neighbors had gathered at the pier. Everyone, waiting and watching, was surprised when Cara stopped halfway through a signal. Had she seen something? They had feared the worst, for all had been accounted for except Devas, Ezra, Sam and Joshua. It had been a long time since anyone could remember a storm like the storm last night

Cara could see it was a boat that was headed for the pier. Now she could see the sails were almost gone. Cara wanted to yell, "It's them." But she waited. By now she was sure it was the family boat but she could not see anyone on the boat. Then she saw Joshua and Sam waving and then she saw her father and uncle. "It's them! They're here!"

The children were first off the boat and into the arms of their mothers. They had so much to tell and everyone had questions, including their mothers. The mothers wanted to get the kids bathed, fed and into dry clothes. There would be plenty of time later to hear about their adventure.

Some of the neighbors helped secure the boat and removed the fish.

"Go home with your families, we can finish up here." Devas and Ezra were exhausted and agreed. Little was spoken on the way home, but a little song kept going through their minds.

> Shine the light for Father to see.
> Bring him home for Mother and me.

Chapter 4
The Village

A little village, like Hippos, seemed to take on a life of its own. Sometimes the village is happy, sometimes worried, sometimes excited or like today there is a feeling of thankfulness that all had survived the storm. We know the village can only reflect the feelings of the people that lived in and around it, but how nice to have friends and neighbors that shared such concerns for each other that these feelings become the life of the village.

In days past, some boats would bring in fish and some boats would be going out to catch more fish. The fish merchants would be loading their wagons to take the fish to markets. Some of these markets were as far away as Jerusalem or Damascus. Before the merchants could load the fish, they had to empty the cargo they were carrying from faraway lands. The ever-present Roman tax collector would be demanding more and more from the fishermen and the merchants. Today was different, the only fish leaving were the ones caught by Devas and his valiant crew.

The storm had damaged the pier, some boats had sunk and all boats bore scars from the storm. Gardens had been flooded, roofs damaged and parts of the roads had been washed out. The fishermen were repairing their boats, carpenters were working on the piers, older children were helping rebuild the roads, even the tax collectors and Roman soldiers were mending gates and helping with other repairs. Jose, the roofer, was repairing damaged roofs. With all the hustle and scurrying to mend their own property, people still found time to gather at the synagogue and community building to join their neighbors and Rabbi Boni in whatever was necessary to get each building repaired.

There was little activity in Devas' or Ezra's homes until noon. Neighbors had already done as much cleaning and repairing to their homes as they could without disturbing the sleeping occupants. Mother instinctively knew that clean clothes, warm beds and hot food would mend tired, worn bodies and minds. Now the smell of simmering soup, sometimes known as "Jewish cure-all, was beginning to tickle noses.

Devas was the first to join Mother for the morning meal, followed by twelve year old Lydia. Sam was up, but as always, she went straight to her brother, Delaeh's room, at the foot of the ladder.

Delaeh, who is eighteen years old, has been frail since he was four. His legs were too weak for him to stand or walk without crutches and he tired quickly. He seemed to grow weaker with each passing year. From the time Sam (short for Samantha) was born fourteen years ago, she and Delaeh shared a friendship that went far beyond being brother and sister. They seemed to feed off of each other's personalities. Delaeh's outgoing nature, always positive outlook and physical limits, meshed well with Sam's shy, sometimes worried outlook but adventurous spirit. In spite of Delaeh's weak body, he had an analytical mind that could figure out weather patterns, tides and fishing conditions. He could also tell you when all the merchants were due to carry the fish to market and what they would be bringing to offload. To make good use of his abilities, the village elders had built a shelter at the end of the pier where he could sit protected from the weather.

In days past, all the fishermen would go to sea at the same time and all would bring their fish back at the same time, only to find that there were not enough merchants to carry their fish to market. This meant many of the fish had to be taken back to sea and thrown away. With Delaeh's mind and the help of his father, uncle and Rabbi Abdon, they were able to schedule the departure and arrival of the fishermen and the merchants so that everything began to run smoothly. In addition to his abilities and in spite of his health, Delaeh smiled and used his natural way of dealing with people that won the hearts of all the villagers. His mind, smile and attitude remained strong, but his legs and body grew weaker each day. He now had to squint to see the horizon and to recognize the fishermen's boats that were far away and the trip to and from the shelter required more and more of his strength.

Sam, from the time she could walk, had been her brother's constant companion. She would go down the ladder into Delaeh's room, get his crutches, help him up and see that he had his morning meal.

When Delaeh began to go to the shelter at the end of the pier, it was Sam that carried his notes, records, schedules and charts he had prepared and worked on way into the night. Now it was necessary for Sam to make two trips, one to carry the charts and records and one to help Delaeh struggle to the shelter. Everyone in the village knew it would only be a short time before Delaeh would not be able to reach his shelter on the pier and no one really wanted to think that far ahead.

When they were young, Delaeh was confined to their yard and Sam and Lydia stayed with him. Most of the time they were joined by their fourteen year old cousin, Cara, and twelve year old cousin, Joshua. On occasions, Sam, Joshua, Lydia and Cara, when allowed, would wander down the road a little way and return with the most wonderful stories about their adventures. They would sit and talk for hours. Occasionally, when their mothers allowed them to, they would wander up the road toward the marketplace, but only as far as the home and business of their grandparents.

When their grandparents could leave their store, they took the children into the marketplace. The marketplace was full of exciting things to see. There were story tellers, musicians, magicians, plays, singing groups and debates about important issues that concerned all the people that lived in this little village. There were merchants from faraway places like Egypt, India, Rome, China and many other countries. These travelers wore different clothing and spoke strange languages. On one of the days the children were in the marketplace with their grandmother, the village elders were meeting. There was much talk about how busy and congested the center of the marketplace had become. One elder shouted, "We need to stop all these foreigners from bringing their carts through the center of the marketplace." Another elder would shout that, "We need better roads around the marketplace so the outsider can go around our marketplace."

Each elder took his turn shouting down the other elders. When grandfather stood up and raised his shepherd's staff over his head, all the other elders stopped talking. He would say. "My fellow elders and neighbors, you are correct. We need to reduce the traffic through our marketplace without driving away those that buy and sell here. We need to provide a better way around our marketplace and a place where merchants can safely leave their wagons and animals outside the marketplace. The marketplace is not safe to walk because of carts and animals and we are losing the battle to cleaning up after the animals. The roads around the market place are too small to handle the traffic if we make all the merchants go around the marketplace. Two things have happened in the last couple of years that have caused so many new people to want to become villagers and have drawn so many travelers and merchants to our area. The first is the aqueduct that brings fresh, clean and dependable water to us. Many of the older villagers remember how hard it was to get good water for our families, animals and crops. Just look at that water fountain in the middle of the square. The second is the roads that the Romans have built throughout their Empire. Not only are they good to travel on, they are safe to travel on. For those that are Jewish, we can safely make our pilgrimages to Jerusalem and back without being robbed or killed. I would like to be free of Roman dominance, but we have not had better living conditions since King David and King Solomon. I believe the elders should consider increasing the size of our marketplace and work with the Roman authorities to expand the roads around our a new and bigger marketplace. The Romans know the more traffic, the more taxes they can collect. The marketplace should be laid out to provide space for local and foreign merchants. There should be areas for keeping and taking care of their animals near the marketplace and where merchants and travelers can rest while visiting our village."

  When grandfather sat down all the elders shouted their approval.

  Grandmother looked at the children and said, "There he goes again. He gets all those elders all fired up then he has to do all the work."

  "I thought Grandfather looked like Moses parting the red sea when he stood and held up that staff," Cara said.

  "That's your grandfather; he knows how to work a crowd."

  On the day after the big storm, the table was set at Devas' home. Three of the spaces were occupied and one waited for Mother."

  "Come Mother," said Devas, sit with us while we each give thanks to God for allowing us to all be together again. We also want to thank God for this wonderful meal. We are also thankful that there are no fish on this table today. What a meal!"

Sam talked on and on about the fishing trip; the crowds that followed Jesus, catching the fish, the storm, seeing Peter's boat following them, how Jesus came walking on the water, how the sea calmed, how strong father and Uncle Ezra were and how good it felt seeing the signal. Sam began to sing:

> "Shine the light for Father to see."
> Then they all began to sing.
> "Bring him home for Mother and me.
> Keep him safe while he's away.
> In his strong arms I want to stay."

Mother was so pleased to have her family safely back together that she hardly noticed the water dripping from their damaged roof. Father assured her that he would find Jose and have the roof fixed before dark. Mother was not going to have anything to do with Devas fixing the roof. She had tried that before and still remembers the mess he made. As far as Mother and most everyone in the village was concerned, no one could repair a roof like Jose. Everyone called him Bird even though he preferred to be called Jose. He could take straw, mud and tar and fix a roof as well as a bird could build a nest.

Chapter 5
Rabbi Abdon's Replacement

Rumors had been circulating for several months in Hippos that the Sanhedrin was very concerned about what was happening in the region around the Sea of Galilee and Hippos was part of that region. The disturbing stories the Sanhedrin were receiving from this area were about a fellow called John, the Baptist, who was the son of a priest and Jesus, the son of a carpenter. Rabbi Abdon's new assignment in Jerusalem was to search the scriptures so he could advise the Sanhedrin how they could confront these two radicals and their followers. In short, he was to find out all he could about John, the Baptist, and Jesus and refute their claims that they were fulfilling the scriptures.

A year ago, a Roman courier rushed into the Synagogue compound and stopped when he saw a lady hanging clothes on a clothes line.

"Can you tell me where I can find Rabbi Abdon?"

"Yes I can, after you take that poor horse over to that stream and give it some water. You look like you could use some water also."

Now Mrs. Ruby was concerned about the wellbeing of the horse and its young rider but she was more interested in what was in that courier's pouch.

"This is Rabbi Abdon. Now give him the message."

"Are you Rabbi Abdon?"

"I told you he was, didn't I?"

"That's all right, Mrs. Ruby. The courier is just doing his job. Yes, I am Rabbi Abdon."

The message was from the High Council of the Sanhedrin that informed Abdon he was being replaced by a Young Rabbi named Boni and he was to report to the High Council of the Sanhedrin in Jerusalem. His replacement was to arrive in three days. The message gave a brief resume of the young Rabbi that would be replacing him. He had done well in his studies and came highly acclaimed by his professors, but he was so young. The message concluded with, "Rabbi Boni left Jerusalem this morning and should arrive in Hippos in three days. You are to stay in Hippos to help Rabbi Boni get started in his new position. You are to report for your new assignment in forty days from the date you receive this message."

Rabbi Boni had not quite completed his Rabbinical Training in Jerusalem but the Sanhedrim needed someone to replace Rabbi Abdon so they decided to proclaim him a rabbi and let him finish his studies at his new assignment. The many years of training he had already completed had exhausted all of Boni's and his family's money. He knew he needed manuscripts so that he could continue his studies and teach the scriptures at his new assignment and his clothes were old and tattered. He didn't know what to do, so he went to his mentor, an elderly Rabbi that had taken him under his wing. He explained his concerns about not having funds to purchase the necessary scriptures and suitable clothing and he needed money to get to Hippos. The kindly old Rabbi told Boni he had recently received word that his dearest friend, a Rabbi in Jericho had just passed away. His friend's congregation had sent a message telling him that his friend's last wish was that all his rabbinical belongings should be given to him along with a note. The note said, "You are too old to use these things so see that a young deserving Rabbi gets them. You and I know what it's like to get started unless you have a rich family. Use this money to help some deserving young rabbi get started." The note from Jericho concluded by saying, "There are so many papers, scriptures and clothing that we have stored all of them, so that someone can pick through them and take what they want. Your dear friend also requested that we send the enclosed money for you to use as you see fit."

Rabbi Boni did not have a formal send off from Jerusalem. He was handed a parchment, stating that he was officially a Rabbi and a note saying that he was to replace Rabbi Abdon in Hippos. He received the parchments along with a letter of introduction and more money than he needed to buy new clothes and sandals. He also had enough money left to get him to Hippos.

The new, excited Rabbi was off to Jericho to select items he might need in his new assignment.

Jericho was a full day's walk from Jerusalem, but by the time he had finished his business at the temple and bought new sandals and clothes, the sun had already passed overhead. His mind told him to wait until morning to start his trip, but he was anxious to get started on his journey and his youthful thoughts of invincibility told him that he could make it to Jericho, if he just walked faster. After an hour of fast walking, his feet began to tell his head that new sandals were not like a new hat. You don't have to break in a new hat before wearing it on a long walk.

He was little more than half way to Jericho. His feet were killing him and the sun was fading behind the hill in front of him. The more the fading sun went down, the more the hair on the back of his neck stood up. He sensed that he was being followed. He quickened his pace over the objections of his feet. He now had no doubt that he was being followed and the person was getting closer. He started running as fast as he could. He turned his head for a quick look behind him. When he turned his head in the direction he was running, he saw a large man standing inches in front of him. There was just time to see the man raise his right hand and to feel something cold touch his side. The large man grabbed him by the neck and held him until his partner ran up.

"It looks like we caught a good one. Search his pockets. He must have some money. Take those new clothes and don't forget his sandals."

Once they had his clothes, all his money and his sandals, they beat him and left him for dead on the side of the road. As they started to leave the large man said, "Grab those papers, there may be something in them we can use."

Rabbi Boni laid there unconscious until morning. He vaguely remembered calling out to a priest and a Levite, when he saw them walk past him on the other side of the road. He saw several people stop for a moment and then go on by. Some stopped to see if he had anything of value on him and just left him there to die.

He had given up when a man stopped and seeing his wounds took pity on him. The man bandaged his wounds and poured oil and wine on them.

He remembered trying to thank the man but his jaw and mouth were so badly beaten, he could not talk. The man brought his donkey and cart over to where the young Rabbi was lying and was able to get him into the wagon.

For the next couple of days the young Rabbi was pretty much out of his head. When he started feeling a little better and things made a little more sense, the innkeeper told him about the man that brought him there and that he had left money for them to take care of him. He said he would be back in a few days to see how you were doing. If we needed more money, he would pay when he returned.

Back in Hippos, Rabbi Abdon was busy preparing to meet his replacement. There were so many things he wanted to go over with him and thirty days was not enough time. Now that his replacement was two days beyond the date he was scheduled to arrive, Rabbi Abdon was getting very concerned. His biggest concerns were that his replacement was too young, too inexperienced and now maybe too irresponsible to be trusted to handle the responsibilities of a Rabbi in Hippos. He knew he had to get a message to Jerusalem telling them that his replacement had not arrived. He also needed instructions on what to do and to ask for more time before he reported to his new assignment.

The following day, Bird, whose real name was Jose but everyone called him Bird, came to the synagogue and told Rabbi Abdon that he received word last night that his replacement had left Jerusalem as scheduled. He was to stop in Jericho to pick up some information and this might have delayed his arrival in Hippos by one day at most. The message I received this morning said they had sent someone to the place the young Rabbi was to have stopped and he had not arrived. They are requesting that we ask anyone that is traveling from Hippos to Jerusalem to inquire if anyone has seen a young man traveling alone.

Rabbi Abdon thanked Bird and then headed to the marketplace to try to find out what happened to his replacement. His next stop was at the fishing pier and he repeated his request there. As the Rabbi started to leave, he saw Merchant chatting with the Roman guards at the tax gate. The rabbi walked over to say hello and to ask the guards to spread the request to any travelers that came through their gate headed toward Jerusalem.

Merchant said, "I'm sorry to hear that you are being transferred."

"Right now I'm more concerned about what has happened to my replacement."

"What happened to him?"

"He's four days late and we are beginning to fear that something may have happened to him on the road shortly after he left Jerusalem."

"The Romans have made the roads safe to travel during the day but unless you are traveling with a large group, you don't want to travel after dark. Just the other day I saw a man lying alongside the road. He had been robbed and badly beaten."

"Was he dead?"

"No, but he was in mighty bad condition. I was able to help him a little."

"You're a good man, Merchant. I hope the man pulls through."

"Thanks Rabbi, but I only did what anybody would do."

"No, I think you did much more than most people would do. I always enjoy talking to you. Now, don't forget to ask around about my missing replacement."

Merchant headed to pick up a load of fish and the Rabbi headed home.

"Wait!" Both men yelled. "Are you thinking what I'm thinking?"

"Where is this man now?"

"I have an innkeeper in Jericho taking care of him. I plan to pick up my load of fish and stop by the inn to check on him and to give them more money for caring for him."

"How long will it take to get loaded and arrive in Jericho?"

"Two and a half days."

"How long will it take, if you get someone to take your load for you, so we can leave right now?"

"If we travel all night, we can be there tomorrow by midafternoon."

"You check with Delaeh about someone taking your load of fish and I'll get Cara to tell Mrs. Ruby where we are going."

Ezra saw Cara running from the pier. "What's your rush?"

"I'm going to tell Mrs. Ruby that Rabbi Abdon is going with Merchant to Jericho. They think they may know where that missing rabbi is."

"Tell mother that I'm going with them."

A few minutes later, the guards had the gate open before the rushing duo got there.

"Wait! Wait! I'm going with you."

Ezra jumped on the wagon and away they went.

The trip to the inn was hurried but uneventful. The owners took Merchant, Ezra and Rabbi Abdon to the room, where they had been nursing the young man back to health.

The young man's eyes were black, his lips and jaws were swollen, his voice was coming back but his neck was swollen and talking was painful.

His caretakers told their patient that this man had found him alongside the road and most likely saved his life.

A painful smile came to the young man's battered face and with a very weak voice whispered, "Thank you." He tried to stand, but the self-inflicted damage to his feet was taking longer to heal than the beating the robbers had given him.

"This is Rabbi Abdon from Hippos. He has some questions to ask you."

Rabbi Abdon began, "I know it must hurt you to talk, but please take your time and try to answer a couple questions. Do you know a young Rabbi named Boni?"

There was a long pause, the young man tried to speak, but the injured throat and the emotions swelling up inside him, prevented him from making a sound. He sat there with tears streaming down his face. They all waited for his answer. Finally his face beamed as he pointed to himself.

"You are Rabbi Boni?"

He gently moved his head up and down.

By the use of sign language, writing and an occasional word, they were able to piece most of the story together.

He left Jerusalem too late to make Jericho before nightfall. He was robbed and beaten by two men. One was large and older, the other about his age and size.

They had taken all his money, his clothes and the parchment stating that he was Rabbi Boni. They also took his letter of introduction to the synagogue in Jericho, where he was to go through a store room filled with information left by a Rabbi, who had recently passed away, had left for Rabbis that were starting their service.

He was sure that without his identifying parchment and the letter of introduction, the Rabbi at the synagogue in Jericho would never let him have any of the things he felt he so desperately needed.

Rabbi Abdon said, "I knew the Rabbi that passed away. In fact he was my mentor when I was your age. The Rabbi that is there now was in the same class I was in and he and I have kept up with each other over all these years. You rest, while Merchant, Ezra and I go the synagogue and see what you might be able to use."

The Synagogue was just a short walk from the inn. Rabbi Abdon was sure he and his two companions would be welcome to stay there while they were in Jericho. As they entered the Synagogue compound, four young rabbinical students were standing just inside the gate.

Rabbi Abdon said, "Hello, you look like you are in a deep debate about something."

"We were just talking about the Rabbi that is going to be replacing the Rabbi in Hippos."

"I'm Rabbi Abdon from Hippos and these gentlemen are my friends. Do you know Rabbi Boni?"

"We don't know him but we met him this morning and frankly there is no way he is going to be able to replace anyone."

"Don't be so critical of him. You must remember that just a few days ago he was near death, when this gentleman found him alongside the road and took him to the inn. We hope he will be well enough for us to take him to Hippos with us in a couple days."

"Rabbi, I respect your opinion, but this man will never be able to replace you. He can't even quote a single scripture."

"Young man if you had taken the beating that he took, you wouldn't be able to talk either."

"My opinion is not based on what he didn't say. It's based on some of the stupid things he did say, when we took him and the man he had with him to the room where he was to pick some of the things he was to take with him to Hippos."

"When did you take him to that room?"

"We just left him there a few minutes ago. We were told to show them the room and to help them go through all the stored materials. He told us he didn't need our help and to get out."

"Young men, please come with us to the room, we may need your help. Ask one of your friends to find a couple Roman Soldiers and bring them to the room"

Standing outside the room, they could hear the sound of papers and objects being tossed about inside the room. Ezra opened the door and stepped in. The floor was covered with materials that had taken a lifetime to accumulate. The small man in a robe was filling a bag with items of gold, silver or anything that could be sold on the street. Anything written on parchment or paper was tossed on the floor as useless trash. The large man was at the far side of the room, pulling neatly stored materials from shelves and throwing them to his partner to rummage through them. When the door swung open, the startled robbers could also see the Rabbi, Merchant and two young men in the hall.

"I think we have everything I'll need in Hippos. Come on Burris let's go." He picked up the heavily laden sack and headed for the door.

A quick and powerful left hand to the jaw and a right to his neck stopped the phony Rabbi in his tracks. Burris pulled a dagger from his belt, raised the dagger above his head and started toward Ezra. His first lunging step caused the papers on the floor to slip under his feet. A strap on his recently obtained sandals broke and the large man hit the floor. The sound of his body crashing into the floor along with the rapid release of his breath, caused a very loud noise, but you could still hear," I stabbed myself," coming from the fallen giant.

The two young men jumped on the fallen robbers while they waited for the Roman soldiers.

The temple Rabbi came running down the hall. "I told you to help the men get what they needed, not to beat them up."

"Hold on my friend. We have everything under control."

A few comments between two old friends and they were laughing and renewing old friendships.

Three Roman soldiers rushed in. Rabbi Abdon and Merchant told them what had happened.

"We have been looking for these crooks for months. We know what to do with them. Our captain will come by later to get some information from you for their trial. Where can he find you?"

"They'll be staying here with us."

Rabbi Abdon said, "I'd like the robe that one is wearing. He took it from one of our new Rabbis."

"You take off that robe and hand it to me."

The robe was removed and as he was handing it to the soldier he whispered, "There is something I need in one of the pockets that belongs to me." The soldier held the robe while the robber reached into a pocket and brought out a small pouch.

The Temple Rabbi said, "Wait a minute that is the pouch our dear friend asked me to send to Jerusalem." He opened the pouch and sure enough, there was the money that had been given to Rabbi Boni.

"Come on. I know where you will spend the night. Stop complaining about that little cut on your side. You should be more like your friend; he's not yelling about his wounds."

Rabbi Abdon and his old classmate were able to straighten up the room that has been trashed by the crooks and selected what they thought Rabbi Boni could use in Hippos.

One of the members of the Synagogue in Jericho offered to let Rabbi Abdon use a wagon large enough to carry a bed for Rabbi Boni to rest on during the trip to Hippos. There was also room for all the materials they had selected and two additional men.

Merchant's wagon was no longer needed to carry everyone back to Hippos so he picked up a load to be delivered there. One of the young men that helped hold down the crooks until the Roman soldiers came went with Merchant. The plan was to have the young man stay in Hippos a while and then bring the wagon back to Jericho.

Each day brought more healing to the young Rabbi. In the evening of the second day since Rabbi Abdon, Ezra and Merchant had arrived in Jericho, Rabbi Boni said he felt well enough to travel to Hippos. The next morning he was helped into the wagon and with a wave to all the friends he had made in Jericho, they were headed to Hippos.

The trip to Hippos took two days. By the time they came to the Roman gate, they had rushed through about a week ago, the whole village was there to greet them. Rabbi Abdon and Ezra got off the wagon to greet their family and friends. After about ten minutes Mrs. Ruby climbed on the wagon and said, "Clear the way. need to get this young man to his new home so I can get him well."

Chapter 6
The Sabbath

This had been an unusual week. The storm had affected everyone in the village. Carpenters were putting the final planks on the pier. The marketplace was again the center of activity. A few fishermen had managed to bring in fish. There were still several merchants' carts waiting at the pier.

Delaeh, although he was not well, was at his post planning, scheduling and coordinating what the villagers needed the merchants to bring back on their return trip.

"We need materials for new sails, rope and fish netting." The list kept growing. Delaeh knew just which merchant could get each needed item and how long it should take for the merchant to return with the items.

"We have enough fish coming in to load three more carts. If you promise to return quickly with canvas and ropes, we will load you first, now move those two carts over here and you will be the next ones loaded."

Sam and her cousin Cara liked to visit Delaeh at the pier. At first they liked to just watch all the activities that went on there. They knew most of the fishermen, the merchants and the Roman guards. They particularly enjoyed talking to the people and hearing their amazing stories. In the last couple of months, there was less time for talking and visiting. They were now helping Delaeh with some of the things he could no longer do.

"Cara, whose boat is that out there? Sam, ask around to see if anyone knows about the shipments from Damascus." Each girl eagerly responded to Delaeh's requests, but their concerns for Delaeh's health grew as the requests increased.

Delaeh and the other Jewish men were hurrying to get ready for their Sabbath. Cara and Sam were there to first carry home the charts and schedules, and then they would quickly return to help Delaeh. His weakness far exceeded their strength and determination.

Devas and Uncle Ezra had been watching Delaeh for some time and realized they had to help the girls with Delaeh. Earlier that day they made a stretcher from some branches, rope and part of the old sail that was not lost in the storm. What a sad scene. Father was in front, Uncle Ezra was in back, carrying Delaeh on the stretcher, and the girls were walking along each side holding Delaeh's hands.

Mother and the other children were busy finishing all their chores in preparation for the Sabbath. The house was cleaned, food was simmering over a low fire and the table was set. There was no reason for Mother to be surprised when she saw Delaeh being carried home. She had taken water and food to him several times that day and each trip found him growing weaker. She asked him to come home but each time he would say. "I'm all right and I need to complete my work."

Mother opened the door to let them in. Sam went straight to the back room at the base of the ladder and held the curtain back. Uncle Ezra and Father put the stretcher down beside the bed and carefully lifted Delaeh into his bed. Father knew the stretcher would be needed again, so he quietly slid it under the bed. Sam picked up the crutches Delaeh had been using and carefully stood them in the corner.

Sabbath is a day set aside to celebrate God's creations and his people's deliverance from slavery. Children are encouraged to ask, "Why do we celebrate this day?"

The head of the house will answer; "Because God has chosen us as a nation set aside to bless all nations. Sabbath is a day of the week for giving thanks and remembering that in six days God made the heavens and the earth, the seas and all that is in them and on the seventh day, He rested. God blessed the Sabbath day and sanctified it. We follow God's example by not working on the seventh day. If God can set aside one day for rest each week, how can we believe that our own work is too important to be set aside for one day a week?"

Mother, Father and the children always looked forward to this day each week when they would sit around the table that Mother so tenderly prepared, sharing their family heritage and spending time with their family as they enjoyed their meal. Mother would light two candles and say a prayer. Talk is usually about the events of the week, studies, fishing and village matters; also there is time for playing games and laughter. This Sabbath there were two empty chairs at the table. Sam was at the side of her brother, Delaeh's bed.

Devas went to Delaeh's room, felt his forehead and said, "Come, Sam, Mother will stay with Delaeh while you and the other children and I go to the synagogue for evening services."

Uncle Ezra, Aunt Ruth, Joshua and Cara lived down a path from Devas' home. There were several other Jewish families that lived in this area and most made their living fishing. There were two other areas that were predominately Jewish. One was on the other side of the marketplace where the families were involved in marketing. The other area was near the synagogue where about half of the families made their living farming and the other half were tradesman. None of these areas were either all Jewish or all Gentile and many Jewish families lived in parts of the village that were mostly Gentile and for the most part, they all lived in harmony. This had not always been the case, for there was a time when Jews and Gentiles in our little village would have nothing to do with each other. There was constant bickering and more than a few outright fights. The fishing pier was a good example of how things used to be. The Gentile and Jewish fishermen would race for the pier with their catch. Boats were battered and the pier trembled each time more than two boats came racing in under full sail at the same time. Many a fisherman felt a well-aimed fish upside his head. The altercations would get worse as the Jewish and Gentile merchants jockeyed their carts for the best position to get loaded with fish. Biting and kicking became the order of the day and even some of the animals occasionally would bite and kick each other. Eventually common sense calmed some of this rivalry down, but is wasn't until Delaeh began to provide guidance that activity at the pier began to run smoothly. Everyone knew what Delaeh had done for their village and all showed their appreciation for what he was doing and they were concerned for his failing health.

The first out of their home, dressed in his finest apparel, was Devas. He was followed by Sam and Lydia. Down the path they were joined by Uncle Ezra, Aunt Ruth, Joshua and Cara. By the time they had walked to the road leading to the pier, several other Jewish families joined the procession to the synagogue. The road turned slightly to the left, ran along the eastern side of the marketplace and continued out of town. About midway through the marketplace, a small connecting lane led to the synagogue, the community building and the home for the Rabbi. By now most of the Jewish families had joined for the short walk to where they would attend the evening service, called the Ma'ariv.

Rabbi Boni knew each worshiper by name and he personally greeted them as they came onto the synagogue property. Over the past two years he had become a big part of their lives and the whole village loved him.

"Be careful now. Stay on the stone path around the mud. The synagogue needs a lot more repairs, so we're meeting in the community building tonight. Now watch your step."

After being greeted by Rabbi Boni, Ezra and Ruth walked a little way down the path. They stopped, stepped off the path and just watched as Rabbi B continued to greet the arriving parishioners.

"What a difference two years make," Ruth said.

"Oh yes. I remember how concerned everyone was when they found out how young and inexperienced he was. How Rabbi Abdon kept telling us that he would grow into the job and to just give him a chance"

Ezra and Ruth were with Rabbi Abdon two years ago when he received the message, telling him that he was being called to Jerusalem. They remember how saddened he was at the thought of leaving Hippos and the people he cared so much about. The rest of the message was a brief resume of the young Rabbi that would be replacing him. He had done well in his studies and came highly acclaimed by his professors, but he was so young. The message concluded with, "Rabbi Boni left Jerusalem this morning and should arrive in Hippos in three days. You are to stay in Hippos to help Rabbi Boni get started in his new position. You are to report for your new assignment in forty days from the date you receive this message."

Ezra said, "I remember that day very well. When he didn't show up when he was expected we thought he decided not to come to Hippos." Ruth and Ezra watched a little longer and then headed for the community building.

"So much has happened in the last two years and I'm glad that we have had a part in it."

"I'm proud of that young man and I will never forget the first time he spoke to the congregation and explained what had happened to him when he left Jerusalem headed to Hippos to be the new Rabbi. Really, it would have been difficult for anyone to replace Rabbi Abdon. He was sent here when this tiny village was little more than a mixture of Greek farmers and fishermen that stayed after the Roman Empire defeated the Greeks and captured this territory over a hundred years ago. The Jewish population in Hippos started to increase when many of the families began returning from the lands they had been carried off to by the foreign invaders."

The leaders of the Temple in Jerusalem sent a few Rabbis over the years but few of them lasted more than a couple of months. Rabbi Abdon was sent here eighteen years ago. He arrived on the very day that Delaeh was born. He always said, "Delaeh was his welcoming gift." Rabbi Abdon organized the Jewish community, obtained the property for the synagogue compound and the Rabbi's residence. He cared for his Jewish families, but more importantly he cared for all the people with whom he came in contact.

Devas' family remembered how he was there when Delaeh became ill when he was four years old. Rabbi Abdon was there to comfort the family and he found the best medical help available for Delaeh. Rabbi Abdon was trained in Jewish law, history and church administration, but his love for people was natural. When it became difficult for Delaeh to get around, Rabbi Abdon came to his home to see that Delaeh kept up with the children his age, but he also explained mapping, navigation by the stars, scheduling and above all to have faith in his own abilities. It was Rabbi Abdon that first suggested to Devas that his son could one day run the fishing pier.

After the service that night, Rabbi Boni listed several things that needed to be done at the synagogue and community building, but added these items would wait until the repairs to their homes were completed. He announced that the programs for the children would not be held for the next week and that the community building would be available to anyone that needed shelter or a warm meal. Rabbi Boni closed the meeting with a prayer for Delaeh and his family.

On their way home after the service, when they were passing the marketplace, they could hear the sound of the busy marketplace, the carts rushing down the streets, the sound of builder's tools and the farmers harvesting wheat. The housewives were busy with their labors and in the courtroom you could hear the debates. All of Hippos was busy, except for the Jewish community, which was honoring the Sabbath. It is said," More than Jewish people keeping the Sabbath, the Sabbath has kept the Jewish people."

    The village seems to have taken on a feeling of quiet excitement. More people were in the marketplace and you could sense something was about to happen. Devas had observed the Sabbath for so many years that he was able to almost close his mind to the sounds of the outside world on the Sabbath Day. Sam's mind was fixed on getting home to Delaeh. When they reached the turn in the road, at the center of the marketplace, Sam and Joshua saw a large crowd. Their eyes focused on the man in the center of the marketplace. Seeing those eyes, that smile, they immediately recognized Jesus. The other children in the group paused for just a moment. Devas whispered, "Come on children, this is the Lord's Day. What is going on in the marketplace is none of our concern."

Chapter 7
Sailing to Capernaum

Most of the storm damage had been repaired. The remaining repairs would have to wait until the needed materials arrived. Delaeh was still at home; his condition had not improved and if anything he was growing weaker. He had not been out of bed for five days and his arms lay motionless at his side. His father and uncle were trying to do their work and to help with the many details at the pier.

Cara was up early, grabbed a bite to eat and headed for the pier.

"Where are you going so early in the morning?" her father asked.

"I finished my chores and I want to help at the pier."

"What do you have in your hands?"

"I stayed up last night and prepared schedules and charts just as Delaeh taught me. I know that I can do what is necessary to run the pier until he gets better."

"I know you will do a great job. I'm proud of you."

The cart, carrying the canvas needed for Devas' and Ezra's boat, was due in later today. In the meantime, there was plenty to do that kept them near home and the pier in case they were needed.

Ezra suggested Devas go into town and see if any of the merchants knew anything about their canvas. Devas knew Ezra just wanted him to get his mind off Delaeh for a little while.

"I'll be back soon," he said, as he started walking toward the marketplace.

Mother, like her brother-in-law, Ezra, felt Sam needed a break also. "Run along now Sam, Delaeh is sleeping and you need a break. Go into town and see if some of your friends are there."

The breeze felt good on Sam's face as she walked down the path to the road that led to the pier. Looking to her right, as if to check on how Delaeh was doing, she saw her father slowly walking up the road. Soon they were walking, hand in hand toward the marketplace. There was more than a gentle breeze in the air that seemed to quicken their pace. There was an excitement, a feeling that something unusual was happening in the main square. Almost at the same time they began to hum.

*"Shine the light for Father to see.
Bring him home for Mother and me."*

The marketplace had never been as full of strangers as it was today. Many wore the robe and headdress of the Pharisees and Scribes from Jerusalem. There were many people that Sam and Devas had never seen before. Some were walking on crutches, some were being carried on stretchers and some were leading people that were blind. Most of the activity seemed to be in the center of the marketplace.

"I see Peter and James and that fellow we saw in the storm," Devas said.

"Let me see! Let me see!" Sam shouted

Devas' big strong hands reached down and gently placed Sam on his broad shoulders.

"That's Jesus," Sam shouted. "Get closer, get closer," Sam kept repeating.

Finally both Devas and Sam could hear and see what was going on. There were Peter, James and John. Devas grew up with these men and he knew they were good honest and hard-working fishermen. Devas would always be grateful to them for following their boat in the storm. If you are ever in troubled waters, you want men like them around to lend a helping hand.

The Pharisees were shouting questions to Jesus. Jesus responded in such a way as to show that he understood what they were saying and that He also understood their thoughts and motives. His answers were more refreshing than the gentle breeze Sam had felt as she walked into her yard. Devas and Sam watched and listened as Jesus healed the sick, made the blind see and the lame walk.

A teacher brought several children to see Jesus. The crowd of religious leaders in front said, "Get those children back, can't you see this is no place for children." Jesus answered the crowd by saying, "Let the little children come to me and do not forbid them; for such is the Kingdom of Heaven."

When Sam saw what was happening she said," Father, let's go get Delaeh."

Devas wanted to act with a little restraint, but what he had seen gave him the assurance that Jesus could heal Delaeh. He quickly worked his way out of the crowd and was running for home before he realized Sam was still on his shoulders.

"Put me down! Put me down!" Sam kept shouting.

When they came to the turn in the road, Sam was holding on for dear life. As they were turning into the path that led to their home, a man with a donkey shouted, "Devas! Devas! I have your new sail, just as I promised Delaeh I would."

"Take it to Ezra at the boat," Devas shouted.

Devas continued to run like a hungry horse headed for the barn and Sam was grabbing hair, nose, ears and anything else to keep from falling off this wild horse. They charged through the gate to their yard. Devas stopped only long enough for Sam to be placed back on the ground. Sam stood there, her body still bouncing, her brain rattling in her head and her eyes trying to focus on something stable. She quickly recovered just in time to hear her father say, "Sam, your mother is not going to like this. I can almost hear her saying, "NOW CALM DOWN. WE ARE NOT GOING TO TAKE THAT SICK BOY OUT TO SOME STRANGER IN THE MIDDLE OF TOWN, TO SEE IF HE CAN HEAL HIM. WHAT HAS GOTTEN INTO YOU TWO?"

"Oh, I wish I had thought this before we got to our door."

"Open the door, father. We need to tell her what we saw Jesus do for those sick people in the marketplace."

Mother had been sitting with Delaeh. When the ruckus caused by the charging horse and its screaming rider reached Mother's ears, she jumped to her feet and was waiting just inside the door, when Devas and Sam came running in. With her hands on her hips and her feet firmly planted on the floor, she presented a picture that only a mother can. You couldn't get through her, around her or over her if you were a whole herd of wild horses.

She didn't say a word, but everyone in that house or yard knew it was time to do some explaining and it had better be good. This big brawny man who had just been the wild horse of Hippos was reduced to a little boy who had just been caught with his hand in the cookie basket. First one foot shuffled and then the other. His hands moved, his head made motions, his mouth moved, but no words came from his mouth. Mother stood her ground and never moved a muscle. Her eyes were staring straight at Devas.

Finally, a small voice said, "We saw Jesus today."

Then in rapid succession, Sam recounted how Jesus had healed the blind, the sick, and the lame. All Devas could do was shake his head in agreement.

"Mother, I know He can heal Delaeh too."

Mother's first thought was, we are not going to take Delaeh, to be healed by some stranger, in the middle of the marketplace. Before she began to speak her thought, she hesitated, for only a moment and then began to bark out orders like a Roman Centurion. "Sam, take Lydia over to Aunt Ruth's house. Then come back here so you can go with us. I need someone," Mother was looking straight at Devas, "that can tell me or show me where to go. Devas, you get Ezra and that merchant headed for the pier. We need one other to help carry the stretcher. Get Bird; he is repairing our roof. Now hurry back."

Mother slid the stretcher out from under Delaeh's bed and grabbed two blankets. She bent down and explained to Delaeh what was going on, even though she knew he could not hear her.

When Mother was sure Delaeh was secure on the stretcher she said, "Follow me," and she led her group up the same road Sam and her mount had so wildly cascaded down moments ago. Mother was marching in front, followed by the four stretcher carriers, two of whom had no idea what was going on, but when they saw Mother, they weren't about to ask. Sam was walking alongside the stretcher holding Delaeh's hand and making sure the blankets stayed on him.

"He's in the middle of the marketplace," Sam said.

This time something was different. The crowds were still there, but they were less focused. Everyone seemed to be talking at the same time, where before all eyes and ears, were straining to hear and see what Jesus was doing and saying. Now groups of people were talking to each other about what Jesus had done and someone was going through the marketplace saying, "Jesus kilt all my pigs."

"Where is He?" Mother inquired of the first group of people she saw. Well really, she loudly demanded to know where Jesus was.

"He's gone. He and his followers have gone to Capernaum."

"How long ago did He leave and which road did He take?"

"They left a little while ago. They went down the road headed for the pier."

"Quick, turn around and head for the pier", she shouted to her stretcher bearers.

No one dared to ask Mother what she planned to do. As a matter of fact, the four stretcher bearers had visions of them carrying Delaeh all the way to Capernaum and they would have if Mother had told them to. The possibility of catching Jesus and his followers at the pier came as a welcome relief.

"Don't go down the main road, the back road is quicker," Mother shouted. Just as they got to the path that turns to their home, Mother could see the pier. A boat had just left and was headed in the direction of Capernaum.

When they reached the pier, Mother said, "Put Delaeh down here. You men get our boat, rig that new sail and bring it to the end of the pier."

Merchant ran to his cart and brought his cart and donkey to the pier. Bird helped Merchant carry the new sail to the boat. While the sail was being rigged, Ezra and Devas thanked them for their help. Once Delaeh is on the boat, he and Devas would sail to Capernaum and find someone there to help carry the stretcher.

"What about Mother and Sam, aren't they going?"

"Sam may go, but there is no way Mother will get on a boat. She likes water slightly less than a house cat does. She gets seasick standing on a pier and the last time she was on a boat was when she was four years old and anyone still living remembers that day."

Merchant said, "I remember now. Some of her friends still tease her about her fear of water. They say she gets so mad, when she is teased about her fear of water, her eyes almost pop out of her head. "Some people call her, "the bulging eye sailor woman".

"You had better not let her hear you call her that."

Devas and Ezra brought the boat to the end of the pier and Merchant and Bird joined them there.

"Gently now! Gently! Put Delaeh on the boat. Ezra, tighten that sail. Man the rudder, Devas." Bird and Merchant, you untie the lines and give us a big shove. Now jump in the boat." Bird and Merchant had thought their part in this rescue mission was over but when Mother said, "Jump, so they jumped into the boat. "Pull that rope, Ezra, I want a full set of sails. Watch the end of the pier. That's it, now bring this tub around that sand bar, and stay in the channel. Now work with me, you sailors. We have a boat to catch."

"Pull, Ezra, pull. Don't just sit there Bird, Give Ezra a hand. Devas, don't just follow them; take a course ten degrees off their stern. We can tack back on their wake and pick up 200 yards." They began gaining slightly, but with all this weight their boat could not overtake the boat Jesus was in.

Mother continued to bark out orders. "Pull that rope, steer this course, prepare to come about." Each order was executed with the precision and obedience of seasoned sailors. When Mother announced the reason they couldn't catch up was because there was too much weight in the boat. Every man on the boat was sure they were about to be tossed overboard. I'm pretty sure the thought crossed her mind. After thinking through her options, Mother announced, "We'll catch them if we have to follow them to Capernaum." That is exactly what they did.

Once they had tied up behind the boat that had carried Jesus and his followers, Mother began organizing her crew. Bird and Merchant were still trying to figure out how they had become members of this crew.

"Sam, ask those men where the crew of that boat went. Devas, Ezra, Bird and Merchant, each of you take a corner of the stretcher. Be careful now. Well, where did He go?"

"They said they went to the center of town."

That was all Mother needed to know. The walk to the center of town was short, but the closer they got, the larger the crowd grew. "Sam, stay with me. Men keep up; we are headed for that door over there."

"Slow down, Mother. We can't keep up." Try as they could, they could not get through the door.

Bird, who was also as meek as a bird, seldom said anything (and especially not to Mother in her present mood) said, "I know how we can get in; come on men, follow me," and they began to back out of the crowd.

Bird led them around to the side of the building. "Put Delaeh down here. Ezra, run to the boat and bring back all the ropes you can carry."

Bird began to re-earn his name. With little effort, he climbed to the roof. Whatever Bird had must have been contagious, for soon Devas and Merchant followed him. With the skills of a surgeon, Bird began to remove part of the roof.

Ezra returned with the rope Bird had requested. "Mother, help Ezra tie one rope to each corner of the stretcher. Ezra, get up here and help us pull Delaeh up," Bird shouted.

Soon all four men were pulling for all they were worth. The stretcher with Delaeh's weak body inched its way to the roof. Sam and Mother tried to climb to the roof, but Sam was too small and Mama - well, let us just say she was not built for climbing. Bird completed removing the roof. His work was so neat, no one in the building even noticed he had opened a hole in the roof large enough to lower a stretcher.

Sam and Mother wanted to see what was happening. They wanted to work their way as close to Jesus as they could. Sam was able to squeeze her small body through places Mother couldn't go. Now Sam was close enough to see Jesus and the hole in the roof. She looked for Mother, but she was nowhere in sight. Soon Delaeh's stretcher began to be lowered from the roof. People in the room were pointing at the stretcher. Then the ropes slacked as Delaeh's stretcher touched the floor.

Sam knew something wonderful was about to happen. Oh, how Sam wished her mother could see what she was seeing. Jesus looked first at Sam and then he looked up to see four...no....five smiling faces looking down from the hole in the roof. Sam could not believe her eyes. How did Mother get up there?

When Jesus saw their faith, He said to the paralytic boy, "Son, your sins are forgiven." Some of the scribes were sitting there and reasoning in their hearts, why does this Man speak blasphemies like this? Who can forgive sins but God alone?

And immediately, when Jesus perceived in His spirit that they reasoned thus within themselves, He said to them, "Why do you reason about these things in your hearts? Which is easier, to say to the paralytic, your sins are forgiven; or to say; arise, take up your bed and walk? But that you may know that the Son of Man has power on earth to forgive sins"--- He said to the paralytic,

"I say to you, arise, take up your bed, and go your way to your house."

And immediately he arose, took up the bed, and went out in the presence of them all, so that all were amazed and glorified God, saying, "We never saw anything like this!"

Chapter 8
Not the End,
The Beginning of Other Stories

We could end our story here; however, we still have a few loose ends to clean up. Merchant needs to get back to his donkey and wagon. Ezra and the boat need to get home. The hole in the roof has to be fixed and Mother has to be gotten off the roof. Then we need to get Mother, Devas, Sam and Delaeh home.

Bird took charge of repairing the roof. "The first thing we need to repair this roof are some strong sticks," Bird said. "See if someone can find two sticks about four feet long, and two sticks about six feet long and four sticks two feet long."

Delaeh was standing on the roof and said, "See if you can use these. I won't need them any longer." They all looked up to see Delaeh standing on the roof carrying his old crutches and stretcher. With the materials Delaeh provided and some material Bird had saved from the old roof, Bird was able to repair the opening he had made in the roof to lower Delaeh down.

I want to bring this part of our story to a pleasant end, so I'll not describe how Mother got off the roof.

Mother was now back to her normal self and there was no way she would get back on that sail boat. Mother said, "I'm going to walk home."

Devas, Sam and Delaeh said, "We'll walk with you."

Bird did such a good job repairing the roof that several people asked him to stay and work on their roof.

We all knew Ezra would go back with the boat, but he needed someone to help with the sails. Merchant liked the sea about as well as Mother did, but reluctantly he agreed to sail with Ezra.

There are two more details that need attention before we complete this part of our story. Devas saw Jesus feed the 5,000, walk on water, calm the stormy sea, heal the sick and the lame and Jesus has also healed his son. All these wonderful acts convinced Devas that Jesus was special, but when his friend, Peter, told Devas the plan of salvation, he accepted Jesus as his Lord and Savior. Once Devas accepted Jesus, his life was turned around. (What happens when you turn Devas' name around? Also turn Delaeh's name around.)

The other detail is this. I could not end this part of our story without watching Devas, Mother, Delaeh and Sam as they walked home. Devas and Mother, holding hands talking and laughing about how Mother had taken charge of the rescue mission. Sam and Delaeh ran a little way ahead and walked back to be with their parents. Just as they are about to walk over a hill, we can hear them singing;

> Shine the light for Father to see.
> Bring him home for Mother and me.
> Keep him safe while he's away.
> In his arms I want to stay

The sun was beginning to set and it was time for Mother, Devas, Sam and Delaeh to find a place to spend the night. They had walked a good way but now they needed some rest. A peaceful, starlit night was approaching and it was time to find a safe spot to spend the night. Devas called to Delaeh and Sam, "We'll be stopping soon to spend the night, so start collecting some sticks so we can have a camp fire tonight."

The sun had almost set and a cool, refreshing breeze began to stir. Devas knew Mother was concerned about where they would spend the night, so he said; "There is a perfect place to spend the night at the top of this hill. Ezra, our father and I would pull our boat to shore down there and climb to the top of this hill and spend the night while our nets were tied just off shore. We would spend the night and Father would tell us the most wonderful stories about what life was like when his family moved here. This is also the place Merchant marked on the map; he drew for us, indicating this was a good safe place for us to spend the night. Let's start a fire while we still have enough daylight."

The small clearing was just far enough off the road to be hidden by some trees. In the middle of the clearing was a pit where campers and fishermen could sit around the fire. Around the fire pit were four large boulders, just the right distance from the fire pit to be perfect for sitting on the ground, resting your back against a boulder while you enjoyed the fire. A stream with pure cold water ran nearby. The trees were far enough apart to give a clear view of the stars and the hill overlooked the sea. Devas started a fire.

Delaeh and Sam raced to the stream to get water for everyone. Sam picked a rock that was just the right size for her. What a beautiful way to end a day that had been so packed full of adventures.

"Now if we only had something to eat," Father said. Food had been the last thing on their minds even though they had not eaten since this morning.

Mother had a busy day. She fed the family breakfast this morning, prepared Delaeh for his trip, gathered a crew to carry Delaeh to town, marched the crew to the boat, barked out orders to the sailing crew, chased a boat across the Sea of Galilee, marched her rescue crew through town, directed an airlift to get Delaeh to the roof of the building Jesus was in, climbed to the roof herself, watched her son healed, gotten down from the roof (no small accomplishment) and had just completed a long walk to this lovely spot.

I don't know about you, but I would have thought Mother would be sound asleep with her head on one of the rocks.

"Oh! My goodness," Mother shouted, "I completely forgot. I have three loaves of bread that I baked last night. Didn't you see me wrap them in this cloth and tie them over my shoulder this morning? I've been carrying them all day long."

"Mother, you're almost like Jesus when he fed the five thousand, except you don't have any fish to go with the bread." Devas began to laugh (LOL for you that text) as he took two small hooks and some string from his robe. Give me two small pieces of that bread for bait and Delaeh and I will catch the fish."

If I were to write a thousand stories, none would be more beautiful than the story I am about to tell you now:

We have a fire, trees, sky, stars, stream of water, homemade bread, a cool breeze, Mother, Father, Sister, Brother, family waiting

back home and a story that has carried us to this point in our journey. The streams of life have all met at this moment.
Now let me continue with our story.

Devas began to roll a small piece of bread between his thumb and fingers. The bread became an almost dough consistency. Fisherman call this a dough ball, fish call it dessert. Delaeh was busy tying a hook on a string and making two throw lines. Devas and Delaeh started climbing down the hill to the bank below. Father was in front. He felt the need to be available, should he be needed, in case the climb was too challenging for Delaeh.

Sam started to follow, but Mother said, "Sam, please stay and watch with me."

Devas glanced back to see Mother and Sam standing next to each other. The hill, the trees, the sky and stars provided a beautiful back drop along with the fire, showing the radiance on their faces. Devas' mind quickly flashed back to when Delaeh was four years old and he had taken him to the shore to catch his first fish. Delaeh was so excited each time he caught a fish that all he could do was jump up and down yelling, "Let's do it again." Devas had kept that image of Delaeh imprinted in his mind for almost fourteen years. It was shortly after that Delaeh's health began to fail.

"I've got one", Delaeh shouted. "Oops, I hope I didn't scare them away."

"Not tonight, tonight is our night" and with that comment Devas pulled in a fish also. "Let's get these fish ready for cooking." Once the fish were cleaned, Devas and Delaeh started climbing back up the hill to the camp site. This time it was Delaeh behind Devas helping him up the hill. "You are not as young as you use to be are you, Father?"

Thanks for allowing me to tell you my version of this part of our story. I'll leave it up to you to make up, in your own mind, what happened the rest of this night. Don't go now, until you see the fish cooked, eaten and the bread warmed. What stories were told around the camp fire and who went to sleep first?

Devas walked around the camp making sure the fire was safe and his sleeping companions were settled for the night. He placed another log on the fire and settled in for the night. The last thought he had before falling asleep was that Ezra and Merchant should be getting home about now.

Chapter 9
Ezra and Merchant Return Home

Meanwhile Ezra and Merchant were nearing the pier back home. "Father, toss me a line," Cara called to her father. "I've been watching for you and manning the signal light. I saw you a good way off and I sent Joshua to tell Mother and Lydia that you were back."

Soon there was the sound of a slamming door, running feet, opening and slamming of a gate. "Father, Father, Uncle Ezra, Uncle Ezra" the children were yelling. "Oh, we are so glad you are back."

Ruth ran up looked around and said. "Where are Devas, Esther, Sam and what has happened to Delaeh?"

"It has been a long day and I'll tell you everything that has happened, but first let the children help Merchant get his donkey and cart so that he can head home," said Ezra. "Thank you, Merchant, for all your help. Now run along children and help Merchant get his donkey hitched to his cart."

Ruth's heart dropped. Was Ezra sending the children away so he could tell her that Devas was…? No, her mind could not allow her to continue her thoughts. Seeing the fear in Ruth's eyes, Ezra said, "You're not going to believe what has happened. Delaeh is healed."

"What do you mean he's healed? Where is he? Where is Esther? Where's Sam and Devas?"

Ezra began to reveal the wonderful story in detail. Ruth's fearful and worried expression turned to amazement.

Walking home, they saw Merchant with the Roman guard at the tax gate. Many of the neighbors had gathered around Merchant's cart and he was talking fast and making jesters with his hands. He pointed up, moved his hands as if he were climbing. He bent over and acted as if he was pulling something up.

Then he pantomimed cutting and removing part of a roof, as though he were lowering something on a rope. It seemed that half of the village had gathered around Merchant and he was telling and acting out all the events of Delaeh's miraculous healing. When Merchant pretended to lie down on the seat of his cart and then stood up, his audience yelled, "Tell us more." Merchant continued acting out the amazing story, but little by little the neighbors began to leave, they could not wait to tell this story to anyone that had not heard it. Soon there was only Merchant and the Roman guard there.

The Roman gate guards raised the gate and motioned Merchant through. "Have a good trip; we'll see you on your next trip."

Ruth said, "Let's go home, I know you are tired and hungry."

Ezra said, "I'm tired, but someone left two fresh loaves of bread on the boat, I couldn't eat a thing."

Chapter 10
Continuing Walk Home
From Capernaum

Mother was the first one up. She was greeted with blue sky and a gentle breeze. She walked back to the road and found a fig tree loaded with ripe figs. She brought back an apron full and with the bread left from last night's feast, she prepared breakfast. The excitement and thrill of Delaeh's healing still filled their hearts and minds as they started to leave camp. They could hardly wait to share the good news with their family and friends back home. For a moment, there was a calm peace that seemed to indicate all was well with the world.

"Wait! Wait! Don't leave," a man in a boat quietly called, "I have a message for you. You are in danger. Wait!"

"Who are you? Why are we in danger? What are you doing with one of Peter's boats?"

"Please say no more. Come down here quickly."

"Delaeh, stay here with Mother and Sam. While I see what this is all about."

"Please hurry, we have so little time."

"What are you doing with Peter's boat?"

"Please don't use names," he whispered. "Peter sent me. He told me that I would find you here. The man you call Merchant has been taken prisoner by the Roman guards."

"Why?"

"Listen to me. We don't have time. I was sent to tell you not to walk on the road. The entire Roman garrison is under orders to capture all four of you. They are looking for a man and woman with a young adult male and a young girl walking from Capernaum to Hippos. We have arranged this boat so you and your wife can hide under a cover in the front of the boat. There are two fishermen's cloaks for your children. Stay along the coast and travel only at night. Hide under trees along the shore during the day. Do not go to your home until you are given a signal that it is safe to return."

"How will we know when it is safe to go home?"

"You'll know, but until then you and your wife must stay hidden in the boat and your children must pretend to be fishing and stay away from other fishermen. There is food for a few days. I must leave now. God bless."

Devas heard the thundering of horse hoofs rushing through the woods toward where Mother and the children were standing. A rider on horseback rushed into the camp, leading a horse ready to whisk the deliverer of the boat to some unknown location.

The man that had been talking to Devas rushed up the hill to the anxiously waiting rider. He slowed only to say, "All will be ok, just do as I have told Devas." Then the anxious riders were off.

"Quick, make sure that we have left nothing to indicate we have been here. Get in the boat. Mother go up front and get under the cover. Quick children, put these cloaks on over your clothes. Sam, you handle the sails, Delaeh, steer close to the shore. We need to get away from here now. I'll explain later, quickly, we must get away from here now."

Devas knew if they made a run for the open sea, they could be seen for miles from the hill at their camp site. "Stay as close to the shore as you can," Devas said peeking from under the cover that he and Mother were hiding under. Devas looked for a good hiding place for the boat and its frightened crew. He also kept looking back to their camp.

There seemed to be two worlds. There was the world that Mother, Delaeh, Sam and he were in and the one the rest of the world was in. The line that divided these worlds ran straight through the camp site they had just left. At first the outward appearance of these worlds didn't seem as though they were different, but they were.

Devas saw a mother duck and her brood of ducklings paddling from shore, also a few birds taking flight beyond the camp. There was no increase in the sounds that surrounded them, but there was less silence. Then beyond the camp, the birds filled the sky and then as a wave moving toward the campsite the birds were taking flight and fleeing.

Devas spotted a small cove with fallen trees jetting out. He jumped from the cover, crawled to the bow of the boat, grabbed the first fallen tree and began to guide the boat into the cove. Sam quickly lowered the sail and Delaeh grabbed branches and helped pull the boat to a hiding place. The children joined Mother under the cover, while Devas crawled to the back of the boat so he could peer through the branches.

There were at least ten Roman soldiers on horseback. Some were on the shore and some on the top of the hill. The leader ordered the horsemen on the shore to separate, some going away from them and some toward them. One of the horsemen stopped, got off his horse, kicked the ground and yelled up to his captain, "Someone has been here. They cleaned fish here and the remains are fresh."

"Do you see anything else?"

"There are some tracks that indicate a boat has been pulled ashore here."

"Get your men. Our spies tell us the people we want are walking. Some fisherman must have come ashore last night to cook their dinner. While we're here, give your horses some water and rest a few minutes. We'll catch up with them soon; they can't have walked very far."

The frightened, hiding crew could hear part of what the resting solders were saying.

"Boy, it's about time we take a rest. My bottom feels like I have been riding for days. I don't understand why we need so many soldiers to capture four Jews. You know the longer I'm stationed here the less I understand what all the fuss is about the Jews. They have always treated me well. I'm told they pay their taxes and if you let them worship as they choose, they seem to be happy. If I were in charge, I'd simply tell one of our couriers, if you see two adults and two young people walking from Capernaum to Hippos, tell them to hurry home. The High Priest wants to talk to them about some healing of their son."

"You had better hope the captain does not hear you say anything like that. I agree the Jews in general are good workers and cause few problems, but there are a few trouble makers among them."

"Now that's another thing, I've been assigned to crowd control at some of Jesus' meetings. He said many things that made sense to me. The only problems that I've seen was caused by their leaders. Tell me why the Roman leaders are worried about that half-dressed nut they call John the Baptist. He seldom goes into a city. Oh, things would be different if I were in charge."

"If you keep talking that way, someone is going to hear you and you and that John fellow you spoke of will be walking around half naked in the wilderness eating bugs dipped in honey."

"Mount up! Follow me," and with that the horsemen were gone.

No sound came from the hidden boat for several minutes… Then…. "Have I caused all this trouble? What have I done?"

"The man Peter sent to bring us the boat gave me a letter and said to read it after we got away, but if we were captured to destroy it. The letter also said that after we finished reading it to destroy it."

Chapter 11
Back in Hippos
At the Tax Gate Near the Pier

As Merchant's donkey began to move though the tax gate there was a shout.

"Stop that man! Stop that man!" The watch sergeant shouted as he ran from the guard house. "This man is charged with spreading false rumors and inciting a riot. Come with me. Pull that cart over to that building."

"What have I done? I never cited nobody in my whole life."

"Shut up and give me the reins." He swatted the mule and headed for the Roman compound.

When they got there, Merchant was pulled from his cart by two big Roman guards and practically dragged down a hallway. The guards stopped in front of a big wooden door with a sign that read 'interrogator'. Merchant was confused and frightened. He didn't know why he was where he was, but he did know where he was. No one in town talked openly about this building; however, everyone had heard horrible stories about what went on in it.

The guards opened the door and pushed Merchant in. The room had three chairs. One chair was located just inside the door. It was small with arms that had leather straps on them for restraining the chair's occupant. One chair sat on the opposite side of a heavy wooden table. That chair was large and was cushioned. The third chair sat at the end of the table. This chair was larger than the small chair with leather straps but smaller than the large chair. There were no windows and the only light was from two candles mounted on candle holders hanging on the wall behind the big chair. One guard stepped to the front of the small chair and loosened the leather strips. The other guard slammed Merchant into the chair and held him, while his partner tied the straps around his arms. Both guards made sure that Merchant was securely tied to the chair and left the room without saying a word.

Suddenly the door banged open. A giant of a man with heavy black beard and dark lifeless eyes, wearing a Roman gladiator's uniform, came into the room and began checking Merchant for weapons and to make sure that the arm restraints were secure. "Everything is clear", he shouted. The man stood at attention slightly to the right and behind the large chair. The only sound in the room was a weak whisper from Merchant. "What have I done? Why am I here?" The questions were repeated over and over as if repartition would bring an answer.

Sounds in the hall caused Merchant to raise his chin from his chest. Moments later a Roman Officer entered the room and stood beside the large cushioned chair. He was followed by five Roman soldiers in full uniform. One soldier stopped beside the third chair. The other four soldiers moved to the wall behind the first soldier, did a snappy about face, gave a Roman salute and snapped to parade rest. The officer removed his helmet and started to place it on the table. He sat down in the large cushioned chair and said, "Get someone in here to clean the dust off this table."

One soldier quickly left the room and returned with a rag and wiped the table. The soldier at the end of the table removed his helmet, placed it on the floor beside his chair and sat down. One of the soldiers lining the wall snapped to attention, walked to the corner of the table and placed some parchment on the table in front of the officer, snapped a Roman salute and smartly returned to his position along the wall.

The Roman officer read the parchments placed before him, thought for a while and looked at his prisoner. "Prisoner, tell me your name?"

"I am known as, Merchant."

"What is your given name?"

"My name is Philip of Gerasenes. I am a Roman citizen."

"Well, Philip of Gerasenes, you are charged with treason against the Roman Empire. How do you plead?"

Meekly Merchant replied, "I have never done nothing against The Roman Empire. I am a loyal Roman citizen."

The officer looked directly at Merchant and asked.

"Do you deny that you disrupted the flow of traffic through the tax gate near the fishing pier? Do you deny that you were a part of a plot to fool our citizens into believing that this man called Jesus has special healing powers?"

Without hesitation Merchant responded. "I admit that I told some of Delaeh's friends that Jesus had healed him. I admit that I did tell them what happened while I was at the tax gate. I'm sorry if I disrupted any flow of traffic at the gate. I had no intension of blocking traffic. I was the only traffic there. I didn't stop nobody but me from going through the gate."

Angrily the officer shouted. "Silence! Silence! I have heard enough of your lies! We know all about the scam you and your friends have tried to pull off to promote that group of rebels that claims to follow that fraud called Jesus. You took a sick, young boy, put him on a stretcher and carried him through town so that all would see the young man was this Delaeh. You even had his parents, a sister, an uncle and some friend help carry the stretcher or walk along side this sick young man. We have a statement from people that states that the young man's mother was yelling so all could hear that they were taking Delaeh to be healed by Jesus. You and a man called Bird, Delaeh's father and uncle were carrying the stretcher and his sister was making sure that covers were pulled up covering most of the young man's head, and that she bent over the stretcher so no one could say for sure that the young man was actually Delaeh. Two Roman soldiers saw the stretcher being loaded onto the boat and were pretty sure it was Delaeh, but that he looked like he was dead or about to die."

"It was Delaeh. I was there," Merchant boldly answered.

"Silence! I'll tell you more about your scam. When we were told that this fellow Jesus was coming to our town, we doubled the amount of soldiers patrolling the pier and marketplace. My guards reported that there was a large crowd of Jesus' followers at the pier when his boat left the pier. Shortly after the boat, carrying this Jesus fellow and while his followers were still on the pier, you and your scam artist came along. Some of the people on the pier helped you put the stretcher on the boat. It was at this time you removed the sick or dead boy and replaced him with a healthy look alike."

"No. No. Some people helped us put Delaeh on the boat but nothing like you said happened. "

"We believe the sick or dead boy was on the boat when it left the pier and that once you were out of sight, his clothes were taken off of him, he was weighted down and his body was tossed overboard."

The officer stopped, looked up at the underside of the roof, brushed a piece of straw from his hat and continued. "Once you got to Capernaum, the look alike put on the dead boy's clothes, got on the stretcher, was covered with the blankets and you continued the scam. We have reason to believe that you also found a look alike for Delaeh's mother. Everyone we have talked to said his mother would never do the things we have been told she did. You then marched into town with this lookalike mother barking out orders and telling everyone that the sick boy on the stretcher had not walked in fourteen years and she was taking him to Jesus to be healed. We have people that have told us this lookalike mother climbed up on the roof from where this fake boy was lowered so that Jesus could pretend to heal him. Everyone, that knows the real boy's mother, says that would never happen."

"She did. She did. I couldn't believe it neither."

"We believe you and the other deceivers have killed the boy's family and disposed of their bodies."

"No. No. No! You are wrong!" You'll see! Delaeh, his mother, father and sister are walking home. I have traveled the road from Capernaum to Hippos for years. I told them to go north keeping the Sea of Galilee on their right. I drew them a map that showed the best places to stop for the night. I saw them leave Capernaum. They should be able to leisurely walk home in three days."

"You say you drew them a map showing where they could spend the night. Are you right handed or left handed?"

"Left handed"

"Will you draw me a map like the one you claimed you drew for them?"

"Yes"

Turning to the guard behind him, the officer said, "Untie his left hand." The guard then took a new position directly behind Merchant.

The Roman solder at the end of the table slid a piece of parchment and a pen to Merchant.

"Now draw me a map like the one you claimed you drew for them. Show the route and all the places you recommended they spend the night."

Once the map was completed, the guard behind Merchant took the map and the pen. He slid the map to the officer and gave the pen to the guard at the table. He then reached over Merchant and retied his left hand. The guard quickly moved back behind the officer's chair.

The officer reviewed the map for a moment. He motioned to a solder standing near the wall. The soldier stepped forward, snapped a Roman salute. The officer stood, responded to the soldier's salute. "I want you to select twelve of your best horsemen and head for Capernaum immediately. Take this map and head for this place. It is marked "good place to spend the night." You will be looking for four people walking. One is a grown man, one is a grown woman, one is a young man and one is a young girl. When you find them place them under arrest and bring them to me as quickly as possible. Make sure no one talks to them. Tell no one where you are going."

The interrogator turned to the guard behind him and whispered, "Put this man in the dungeon. Chain him to the wall and put our special prisoner next to him. Make sure he stays alive. We may need him when we capture his partners in this hoax."

Merchant was quickly untied from the small chair and while he was being dragged out of the room, he kept saying, "Delaeh is alive and so are his mother, father and sister. Jesus did heal him. We have done nothing wrong. You can check with the boy's uncle. He is in town now. I helped him sail back from Capernaum tonight."

"Wait", shouted the Officer. "Where is this uncle now?"

"He was headed to his home with his."…. By now Merchant realized he had said too much and stopped talking or he passed out.

"Where did he go and who was this uncle with?"

"Never mind, take him to the dungeon."

The interrogator turned to the soldier seated at the table. "Complete your notes and prepare a confession for our prisoner to sign. Have your completed notes and the confession in my office in one hour. The commander wants a full report from me about this matter first thing in the morning."

"Sergeant, go into town. Get me information about this uncle and his family. Once you know who he is and where he lives, let me know. I'll send soldiers to bring him and his family in for questioning in the morning."

"Yes sir, will there be anything else?"

"Yes, send a couple of recruits in here to clean all this dust up and get that roofer in here to fix that roof now. It seems like every time I use this room something is wrong with the roof."

A young man, carrying his roofer's tools, approaches the security gate and tells the guards that he is ready to leave.

"We thought you had left long ago. What took you so long?"

"The roofs on some of these buildings are getting old and it took me a lot longer to make the repairs then I thought it would."

"OK, let him through."

Chapter 12
The Great Escape
From Hippos

The young roofer thanked the guard and started walking down the road from the Roman Outpost. Once he was out of site of the guards, he began to run toward the marketplace. When he reached the marketplace, he resumed walking to avoid drawing any attention. There were few people out this late at night, but he kept looking for someone, anyone he could trust. The only people he saw were some foreign merchants, guarding their merchandise. He walked across the marketplace to the road leading to the synagogue and then he started running as fast as he could to the Rabbi's residence. He began to tap firmly on the door and called, "Rabbi, Rabbi."

The door opened slightly and Rabbi Boni said, "How can I help you?"

"May I come in so no one will see us talking?"

Rabbi Boni did not know the young man's name, but he had seen him around the village and at the synagogue a few times.

"Come in. What is the problem?"

The young man started telling about the soldiers that had been sent to take Devas and his family as prisoners and how they planned to take Ezra and his family also. By the time the young man told about Merchant being held in prison and the scam he was charged with, Rabbi Boni was as frightened and as out of breath as the young man was.

"I must get out of the village before day breaks. I don't want anyone to see me. I can help Devas and his family but I need someone to go to Ezra's home and tell them what has happened and to hide them until it is safe for them to come out of hiding. There is a caravan of Chinese merchants on the other side of the marketplace that will be leaving early in the morning. I know one of the leaders of the caravan. We have done some business with him before.

I'll stop on my way out of the village and make arrangements for them to conceal Ezra and his family in their caravan until they are safely out of Hippos. Tell Ezra to stay with the caravan until someone they know meets them. They will then be taken to a safe hiding place. I have to go now. Thank you Rabbi."

He left as quickly as he came, first running to the marketplace and then walking across the marketplace. This time he stopped at the Chinese caravan. Arrangements were made with the leader of the caravan to conceal Ezra and his family and take them about ten miles out of town where they would be met by someone they knew.

Rabbi Boni left his home shortly after his brief meeting with the young man. He ran down the road that led to Ezra's home. Before turning into the small path that led to Ezra's home, he saw there were more Roman guards watching the pier than usual. He quickly moved to the side of the road and crept to the path that led to Ezra's home. He softly tapped on Ezra's door. Soon he heard a voice saying, "Who is it?"

"It is Rabbi Boni. Please hurry and let me in."

"What's wrong?"

"Don't light that candle. I need to tell you what is happening and I need to tell you quickly. Please wake up Ruth and the children and tell them to get dressed and be quiet. Tell them to take only what they can wear and please hurry. I'll tell you what has happened but you most trust me for now."

Ruth and the children joined them near the door that led to the yard. Rabbi Boni said, "Be as quiet as you can and follow me. Is there another way to get back to the main road without passing the road to the pier?"

"Yes, follow me."

Ezra led them to a path the children sometime used when they played hide and seek. This time it was no game they were playing. When they came to where the hidden path met the main road, Rabbi motioned for everyone to stop. He then stepped out on the main road and walked a short distance toward the marketplace to make sure the road was clear. Hurrying back to the concealed path, he motioned for the group to come out of hiding. "I'll walk a little ahead of you. If I raise my hand as though I'm waving to someone, you take cover on the side of the road until I come back to get you."

On the short walk up the "hide and seek path", Rabbi Boni was able to tell them about Merchant, the soldiers that were looking for Devas and his family and that they were going to be leaving the village with a caravan of Chinese merchants that would conceal them until they were safely out of Hippos.

The walk on the road to the marketplace was only disturbed by a few rustles in the brush that were caused by creatures that were not use to people being there so late at night. The caravan was on the opposite side of the marketplace, but a direct path would take them near the road that led to the Roman outpost. As they approached the marketplace Rabbi Boni held his hand up indicating that everyone should stop. He walked a little closer to the road leading to the outpost.

The outpost was brightly lighted and the sounds coming from behind those tall walls indicated that something was happening inside. The large wooden gates were open and several Roman soldiers were lining both sides of the road leading to the outpost. The Rabbi was standing on the side of the road, trying to determine the safest way to the caravan. The faint sound of a horse's hoofs running at full speed caught Rabbi's ears. He motioned for Ezra and his family to get off the road and to hide in the brush beside the road. Rabbi Boni took cover behind a small sapling where he could still see down the road. He could see in the distance that the rider was a Roman soldier, rushing toward the outpost. Just as the rider came to where the Rabbi was hiding the soldier stopped. Had the soldier seen him? The soldier just stayed there on his horse. The horse was breathing so hard that any noise the Rabbi made could not have been heard and he knew he could not be seen. What was the rider doing? It seemed like he just sat there for an hour but it was really just a minute. Rabbi could see what must be a hundred Roman soldiers on horseback coming into view. The first rider, that was a couple feet from him, must have been a scout for reinforcements coming to Hippos. Soon Rabbi Boni could see the whole thundering Roman reinforcement of riders. The riders were four abreast and covered the width of the road. The lead rider's horse quickly side stepped off the road.

The quick movement brought the enormous horse directly to the sapling the Rabbi was hiding behind. The collision sent Rabbi B hurdling through the air. He landed ten feet from his original hiding spot. The impact broke the sapling and the Rabbi's body took out several other bushes. He landed with a thud and he was disoriented. He lay there motionlessly in full view of the rider, if he were to look in his direction. The noise from the horses and riders roaring by covered up the Rabbi's gasping for air. Soon the riders and the scout had passed and were nearing the outpost.

"Rabbi, are you all right?" Ezra was kneeling beside him removing the brush and sapling branches that were covering him.

"Yes. I'm fine. Where are Ruth and the children?"

"They are fine. I told them to stay hidden until I came back for them."

Rabbi Boni brushed himself off, looked around and said, "We must hurry it will be light in a little less than an hour."

"By the time we walk around the marketplace it will be light," Ezra said. "I think we should head straight for the caravan. Rabbi, when we get to the marketplace Ruth and I will go in first and head to the spice vendor's area. You and the children follow us. Walk slowly and don't stop to talk to anyone."

Some of the villagers knew the Silk Route Caravan was leaving at day break and wanted to watch the elephants, camels and the other animals as they left. The other villagers were up because they sensed something was going on and the noise from the Roman reinforcements awoke anyone else that wasn't already up.

"I can see some movement in the marketplace and the Roman guards are distracted by the arrival of the reinforcements. I think if we hurry, we can head directly across the marketplace and go through the spice vendor's booth to the Chinese caravan without being noticed."

There was so much going on around the village that the fleeing group walked through the marketplace unnoticed. As the group neared the first spice building a voice came from inside the building. "Ezra?"

"Yes."

"Meet me behind the building. "

"Please hurry, the caravan will be leaving soon. Come inside quickly. I am Chuma. My job is to get you dressed so that you look like you belong in a caravan on the silk trade route, and to place you in the caravan so that you will blend in.

Young man put these clothes on over your clothes. When you are ready, go to the pony area. Four young men are waiting for you there. They will show you what to do. Now girls, put these clothes on. You will be walking with the sheep and goats. There are girls there your age that will show you what to do."

"How do we know the children will be safe?"

"Because my job is to see that you all get out of Hippos safely. Here Ruth, put this silk garment over your clothes. You will be in a wagon with four other ladies. Ezra this clothing will make you look like a camel herdsman. You will be walking between two camels where you will be out of sight. Hurry, the caravan is ready to leave. Come with me, I'll get you to your places."

The caravan was led by four large, heavily packed elephants. They were followed by six camel herdsmen, each holding the reins of two camels. A long line of horse drawn wagons followed and were filled with merchandise, and some carried the very young children and ladies. Most were loaded with supplies for the trip to the next marketplace. The rest of the caravan consisted of about thirty young horses and over 100 sheep and goats that would be sold or traded at the next stop or eaten on the trip. The caravan leader rode on the lead elephant. Twenty horsemen constantly rode around the caravan, making sure all was going well. Chuma was in charge of these riders. He kept his eyes on every person and animal in the caravan, but on this trip he was paying special attention to his five special charges. The children all blended in with the other children and he could tell they were enjoying their new experience. He had to strain his eyes to pick out Ruth from the other ladies. Ezra was his big concern. He stood out like a sore thumb. He was eight inches taller and weighed at least seventy pounds more than any other man in the caravan. Chuma knew the caravan would come to a Roman guard gate before it was time for the caravan to stop for the night. He kept asking himself, how can I conceal this large man? Then he came up with a plan. Chuma signaled for two of his men to come to him. He told one man to take Ezra's place with the camels and the other man to bring Ezra to him. Chuma got off his horse and waited for Ezra to join him.

"What's wrong?" Ezra asked.

"We are approaching a Roman guard gate.
We have received word that the Romans are looking for an unusually tall man and his family. Your family is blending in but you are a

challenge. I could put you on a good horse and send you and one of our best horsemen to try to go around the guard gate. The Romans are aware that people try this tactic and usually have well trained archers hiding in the areas near gates. I think that would be too risky a plan."

Chuma motioned to one of his riders. Soon a rider approached on a large horse. Chuma told the rider to go to the pony pen and pick a strong pony and bring the pony back to him. When he returned, Chuma asked Ezra to sit on the pony. Chuma looked at Ezra sitting on the pony, then at the other rider, then back at Ezra. Their heads were about the same height but Ezra's feet were dragging on the ground.

"This might work. I want you two to ride together and stay as far from any guard as you can. Now, I want both of you go to the other side of the caravan. Chuma watched Ezra ride away with his feet dragging the ground and then said to himself, "It may just work." Chuma rode around the caravan, trying to pick out anything that might cause the guards at the next post to want to walk through the caravan.

One of the forward scouts rode in and went straight to Chuma. The rider reported the Romans had set up a security gate about two miles ahead. Chuma rode to the lead elephant and signaled to the caravan leader to stop the caravan. The leader and Chuma talked for a while. The leader signaled for everyone to take a brief break and to water the animals.

Roman law mandated that anyone using a road was responsible for keeping the road clean. This included cleaning up after the animals. For a caravan this size the Romans demand that no less than two oxen drawn wagons be used to carry the waste, no less than fifty feet off the road, and dump the waste there. The law further stated that each wagon should have one driver, two men shoveling and two men sweeping.

Chuma motioned for Ezra and his riding companion to meet him at the back of the caravan.

"Ezra, our plan will not work. Every time I look over the caravan all I can see is you. Our scouts tell me the Romans have what we call leaf men all around us."

"What are leaf men?"

"They are Roman soldiers that hide in the bushes near security gates to catch anyone trying to go around the gate. Their orders are to shoot to kill. You may not like it but this is our new plan. You and your riding partner will be assigned to follow the cleanup crew. As we approach the security gate, all my other riders will move to the back of the caravan just ahead of the cleanup crew. The cleanup crew will stay fifty yards behind my riders. When I give a signal they will stop emptying the wagons and start filling them to over flowing. Just before my riders go through the gate, they will quickly turn around and move behind the cleanup crew and ahead of you and your partner. We do this maneuver each time we pass through a security gate. It's our way of honoring the Roman Empire for providing such good roads for us to travel on. On my signal, two of the cleanup crew will pull the dump pin on the wagons. The sudden noise and shifting load will startle the oxen and the contents of the wagons will spread all over the road and anyone standing near the gate. My riders will spring into action to stop the run away oxen. The results of twenty galloping horses running through this mess will cause more mess and unpleasant aroma then you can imagine. My riders will catch the oxen and wagons and bring them back to start cleaning up the mess. You and your partner along with ten of my men will rejoin the caravan and keep going. I will stay at the security gate to see that the mess is cleaned up and to apologize to the captain of the guards. Does everyone understand what they are to do?"

    Chuma rode to the leader of the caravan and after a brief conversation, he rode a little ahead of the caravan. Soon one of the riders, Chuma had sent out to scout the road ahead came rushing back. The rider reported that the Roman gate was just around the next turn in the road. Chuma had expected that the gate was near, so this part of the report was just business as usual. The next part of the scout's report made chills run up Chuma's back. There were the two guards manning the gate as usual but now there were twenty additional Roman soldiers, all in full dress uniforms and carrying weapons. The soldiers were stationed ten on each side of the road about ten feet apart. The scout was told to report to the caravan leader and then to join Ezra and his partner at the back of the caravan.

Chuma motioned for the caravan to follow him. By the time Chuma reached the first soldiers on the side of the road, he had slowed his horse to a walk. The front of the caravan was two hundred yards back. Chuma was very familiar with the Roman rules governing how a caravan was to approach a security gate. He had been through this gate many times and knew the guards by name and considered them as friends. Normally, he was greeted by a warm welcome, some small talk, a quick glance at the caravan permit and tax receipt and they would be waved through.

This time the senior guard stepped forward, held his hand up, and shouted, "Halt, Rider dismount and state your business."

Chuma stopped, dismounted and called back, "My name is Chuma and I represent the Han Dynasty of China. We have the honor of bearing a letter from the Roman Empire with the stamp of the Roman Emperor. The letter states:"

'Be it known to all members of the Roman Empire. The person bearing this letter and the accompanying caravan has permission to travel all roads within the territories of Palestine, Israel, Lebanon and Syria. This permission to use such roads in the territories listed is granted in exchange for one hundred select horses trained and ready to be ridden. These horses shall be delivered, by this caravan at the location along this route, when requested by the senior officer at Roman military outposts within your route.'

"Stop all that rambling and hand me those papers. I can read."

The abrupt interruption came from one of the soldiers standing near the gate. He was apparently in charge of the other soldiers standing alongside the road.

"This letter states that all materials carried must be legal and approved by the Roman Empire. Do you have anything that is not legal that you want to declare before I have my men go through everything you have?"

"We are carrying nothing that is not legal. You are welcome to look at anything you wish to check."

"Are all the people in the caravan your regular crew?"
"Yes"
"I had better not find anyone in there that does not belong."
"I can assure you that you won't find anyone in there that doesn't belong."

"Open the gate and let them start through. You bring your horse and stand by me while they go by."

"Before I signal them to start through I would like to have my papers back."

"I'll give them back to you when I am ready."

"My government has had an outstanding working relation with the Roman Empire. The rules in this matter are quite clear. I am not allowed to move through a Roman gate until all paper work is completed. The rules state that the final act of paper work is the return of the papers to the original bearer."

"I'll give them back to you when I'm ready to. Now start them through."

"No. Those papers are extremely important to me. The caravan cannot go through that gate until I have those papers."

"We'll see about that. Lieutenant, tell the men to get their horses and mount up."

"I would like to point out a couple things to you. First, you see those men on horses in the caravan. They are the men that trained the horses your men will be riding, that is, if they even make it to their horses. I don't know why you are acting this way. You either do not know the laws about caravans or you are just plain stupid. There may be one other reason you want to hold on to those papers. You think you can sell them to a black-market caravan. Now the first two reasons will get you separated from your rank. The last reason will get you separated from your head." There was a long pause as the soldier and Chuma contemplated their next move.

Finally the soldier said, "Here are your papers, now get that caravan moving."

"I'll signal the caravan through, when you move those soldiers away. I don't trust what you will do and I will not give you the opportunity to harm any of my people."

"I cannot move the soldiers away. My orders are clear. I am to station ten soldiers on each side of the road."

"That's not a problem. They can stay where they are, just have them turn around and face away from the road."

"I can't do that, we'll look like idiots."

"You have one minute to give the order and they have one minute to execute the order. I suggest you look at the caravan"

All twenty of the caravan riders were at the front of the caravan ready to strike on a moment's notice.

"All right! All right! Men! Attention! About-face! You are to look away from the road until the caravan has passed."

"You have what you wanted, now you and your caravan get out of here."

"I'll be the last one through that gate, and I'll be right here with you until the entire caravan has cleared the gate. Now join your men and look away from the road,"

"How can I be sure my men are obeying my order to look away if I can't see them?"

"I assure you that my men will let you know, if anyone of your men disobeys your order to look away."

The caravan moved through the gate with no problems. Chuma watched the last of the caravan around the next curve in the road.

"I'll be leaving now. You keep your men where they are for a couple of minutes and I'll be gone."

"What will keep us from mounting up and catching up with that slow moving caravan?"

"Common sense, and I doubt these good men will follow you any place. By the way, you did say something that I agree with."

"And what is that?"

"You all did look like idiots standing there facing away from the road."

Chuma mounted his horse and as he went through the gate, he smiled and winked at the two guards that were usually there. They returned the gestures.

Soon Chuma was back with the caravan. Ezra had been moved to his original position between the two lead camels. The children were having the time of their life, tending the animals and playing with the other children and Ruth had made some new friends.

Chuma asked one of his riders to get a horse for Ezra and have him come and ride along side of him. Soon Ezra rode up.

"I can never repay you for getting my family safely out of Hippos."

Chuma explained that the caravan would be stopping for the night and that his family was welcome to stay with them as long as they wanted.

"My instructions are to get you safely out of Hippos and someone would meet you along our route to find a safe hiding place for you. I was told that you would recognize the person that is to meet us."

Chapter 13
Back At The Sanhedrim
In Jerusalem

"The council will come to order. Order!!...Order!! We must stop all this bickering and wasting of time. How long do you think Rome will sit back while we allow some renegade Jews to talk of over throwing their government? Rome allows us...No they assist and encourage us to observe our religious traditions and customs. We are no longer the great and glorious nation of David and Solomon. Our enemies have captured our lands, stolen our goods, carried off most of our temple treasures and carried many of our families off to foreign land as slaves. The Romans have provided us good roads, good water carried by aqueducts to all of the cities and villages where we live. We trade with those who would otherwise be our enemies if it were not for Rome. Our purses and treasury are full. What do they ask from us? They ask that we live our lives in peace, obey their laws, not cause trouble and pay our taxes. The Romans expect that we, as members of the Sanhedrin, govern our people to assure they follow these rules and that no word of trouble or discontentment reaches the ears of the Emperor in Rome."

"Caiaphas, our high priest, called me to his chambers to tell me about a meeting he had with Pontius Pilate. Pilate is very worried about what is happening around Capernaum and the Jordan River. There are two main troublemakers there. One is a strange little fellow that is talking about a new king that is coming and he is telling every Jew to prepare the way for this new king. You can imagine now much this is upsetting Pilate and Herod and when they are unhappy, nobody is happy. The other fellow is called Jesus. I believe I heard him when he was here in Jerusalem when he was a twelve year old boy. I remember him because for such a young boy he taught as though he truly understood the Jewish scriptures and laws. Herod told Caiaphas that this Jesus fellow has a large following that is growing every day and he is talking about setting the Jewish people free. Caiaphas directed me to form a committee and secretly go to the area around the Sea of Galilee and figure out how to stop these troublemakers before Rome gets tired of hearing about this problem. Most of the troubles these two are causing are in the region near the Sea of Galilee and the Jordan River. I have personally told Herod Antipas that I would see that a fellow they call John the Baptist will cause him no more trouble. Now this fellow they call Jesus is a little more troublesome. He is mostly up in the northern and western region of the Sea of Galilee. He has more followers and some of the stories my committee has told me are the most amusing and unbelievable you will ever hear."

"Two years ago our appointment chairman assigned a young Rabbi to take the place of Rabbi Abdon in Hippos so that Rabbi Abdon could come to Jerusalem to continue his research of the scriptures. My committee will make its temporary headquarters in Hippos. This is a lovely, peaceful little village that not only gets along with the Romans, but also gets along with the Gentiles. I am told that ever since Rabbi Abdon has been back, he constantly talks about a wonderful young crippled boy he befriended there and what a great family he has. The whole village sings praises about his ability to organize and encourage people to get along. Maybe I should have this young handicapped boy brought to Jerusalem to get us organized and working together. When I get to Hippos, I plan to have this young man with me when I address the people in Hippos. Nothing inspires people more than seeing a young person, with a physical handicap, accomplish as much as this young man has. I will lead this team to Hippos. My team will include Rabbi Abdon because he is familiar with the area and the people. Oh! I can hardly wait to meet this young man and this Rabbi we sent there two years ago. He must be doing a magnificent job, keeping things running smoothly. We never hear of any problems there. I will set up our headquarters there because I am told that the roads are good and if I chose I can travel by boat to the regions where these two madmen are causing so much trouble. I plan to leave tonight, arrive in Hippos in two days and complete my mission in two weeks. My assistant and I are preparing an official notice to be delivered by Roman courier to the young Rabbi in Hippos.

See how easy these problems can be solved, when you understand the problem and do a little planning. Now before I tell the chief cook to refresh our wine and serve the first course. I must remind you not to tell anyone outside of this chamber about this secret trip and what I plan to accomplish. You know, I just don't see why all Jews can't be as happy as we are."

Chapter 14
Back In Capernaum

Bird was repairing his second roof in Capernaum, when he saw a man motioning to him to come down.

"What do you want?"

The man put his finger to his lips and whispered, "Please come down." There was something unusual about the look on the man's face. Once Bird was on the ground, the man walked quickly to him.

"Please follow me."

"Do I know you?"

"No, but we have communicated with each other before."

Bird flushed. He looked around to make sure no one was watching them. "How did you know?"

"Simple, my name is Hahab. I'm also known as Bird. We have a lot in common."

"What do you want me to do?"

"First, I want you to know that we are your friends and that your secret is safe with us. I suggest you complete repairing this roof. We don't want to do anything that looks suspicious. Make the job last until it is dark. I'll meet you here and take you to meet some people that need our help."

Bird returned to repairing the roof he had been working on. He slowed his efforts to make sure the remaining work would last until the sun set. His mind was racing. *How did they find me? How do they know what I've been doing? Are they really friends? Oh, I should have sailed home with Ezra and Merchant.*

Now is a good time to give you some information about Bird's secret. Bird's father and grandfather had been members of the Sanhedrin. We tend to think the Sanhedrin was a unified group of Jewish leaders doing priestly duties and governing the Jewish people. In fact over the years, they had developed into many different sub-groups. All members believed and practiced some basic aspects of their religion (Monotheism, the Law of Moses, Honoring the Sabbath, etc.), but within the Sanhedrin groups, there were disagreements with each other about many details (what was expected of the Messiah, ritual and purity laws, how to live under foreign rule.) To understand, we need to learn a little about the wide variety of different Jewish groups that existed in the first century. Josephus, the first-century Jewish historian, describes the three major groups as: Pharisees, Sadducees, and Essenes.

The Pharisees were a group of influential Jews, active in Palestine from 2nd century BCE through 1st century CE; they advocated and adhered to strict observance of the Sabbath rest, purity rituals, tithing, and food restrictions based on the Hebrew Scriptures. They also believed in the resurrection of the dead.

The Sadducees were a prominent group of Jews in Palestine from 2nd century BCE through 1st century CE; they were probably a smaller "elite" group, but even more influential than the Pharisees. They followed the laws of the Hebrew Bible (the Torah), but rejected newer traditions. The Sadducees did not believe in life after death.

The Essenes were a much smaller group that lived a communal "monastic" lifestyle from 2nd century BCE through 1st century CE. They were originally a group of priests, founded and/or led by a "Teacher of Righteousness" during the early Maccabean/Hasmonean era (166-63 BCE). They rejected the validity of the Temple worship, and thus refused to attend the festivals or support the Jerusalem Temple. They expected God to send a great prophet and two different "Messiahs" (anointed leaders), one kingly and one priestly. Some scholars think John the Baptist and his cousin, Jesus, were closely associated with the Essenes.

While Bird's father and grandfather were members of the Sanhedrin, they were in charge of raising birds to be sold to worshipers headed to the Temple to make a sacrifice. Because of the nature of their business and the birds doing their business on everything, they lived about 5 miles outside of Jerusalem in a remote valley. The valley has some large natural limestone caves where the birds built their nests and raised their young. Once the birds were ready to be sold, they were placed in small containers made from sticks, bent and tied to form a cage. These cages, each with as many as five birds were then stacked on a cart and taken to the priest at the temple where they were sold. These birds were headed for a one way trip.

Grandfather noticed that certain birds could be turned loose and they would stay in the area and return to their roost each night. He began to ask merchants to take some of the pigeons with them on their trips and turn them loose at different locations along their journey. Bird's grandfather began noticing that certain pigeons always returned quicker than other pigeons. He would separate the best pigeons from the pigeons that were to be sold. The use of homing pigeons was not something new. The Greeks sent homing pigeons to tell the large cities who had won the Olympic Games.

The Roman military used homing pigeons to keep up with the troops in the field and so that they could tell if there were any problems in their empire. Bird's grandfather realized that if several secret homing pigeon stations were established around Israel's larger populations, it would be possible to send and receive information that would be useful to the Jewish people.

There is a lot to do to make a system of homing pigeons work. First, if you turn a pigeon loose in the place it was born, it will stay there. To send a message to a city, you must have a homing pigeon with you that was born and raised in the city you want to send the message. This means that someone must bring a pigeon from the city you will be sending the messages. Then you must keep that pigeon separated from all the other pigeons and make sure the pigeon stays in its cage until you want to send a message to that city. To receive a message, you must first get your pigeon to the location from where the message will be coming, so when they wanted to send you a message, they would fasten it to the pigeon and release the pigeon.

Before leaving the roof, Bird looked around the neighborhood. The yards and streets were empty except for one man that seemed to be milling around as if he were waiting for Bird to follow him. Bird gathered his tools and climbed to the ground. He could now see that this was not the same man he talked to earlier in the day. The stranger nodded to Bird and motioned for Bird to follow him. They crossed several streets and Bird began to wonder if he was following the wrong man. The man stopped and waited for Bird to catch up. "When we get to the next street I will go straight, you turn left and keep walking. Just keep walking; the people that want to talk to you are waiting."

When they reached the next street, Bird turned left. The street was darker then the streets they had been on. Bird was considering turning around and running back to the main street. He looked behind him and saw the man he had been following was standing at the cross road. Was he blocking my escape or making sure I was not being followed? Bird was about to start running when a voice from behind a fence said, "Bird, thank you for coming. Go to the gate and come in." The urge to run was strong but Bird followed the instruction.

"Bird, we are sorry we had to take so many precautions but we knew you would understand. We know who you are and the risks you and your family have taken over the years to free our people from foreign domination."

"How do you know who I am?"

"Your son sent a carrier pigeon message to us."

"I don't believe you. He would never do that."

"Here, you read the message,"

3653   Hawk   7667 7533
2087 is in 7533. Get message to 2087. Four walking home are in danger. Rome declares them to be enemy of Empire. Get them. Hide them. They are in extreme danger.   Brother, wife, 3 children safe in hiding. Merchant is in dungeon.   7533 carriers 2 R, 4N

Bird read the message. 3653 is his son's ID. 7533 is Capernaum. 7667 is Hippos. Hawk means the Roman outpost was using trained hawks to kill homing pigeons that may be carrying messages they want to stop. 2087 was Bird's ID. 2R means 7667 has 2 remaining homing pigeons from 7533. 4N means 7667 needs 4 more homing pigeons from 7533.

The news in the message made Bird's knees feel weak for only a moment. Then he looked at his new comrades and said, "My Son has done a good job, I'm proud of him."

"You have every reason to be proud of him. Remember he is from a long line of the Jewish Carrier Pigeon Service. One day we will be able to freely send our messages to the world."

"My brothers, I must get back to Hippos"

"We have already sent a message to your son. I mean to 3653 at 7667. He knows to meet you at Gerasenes at three hours after midnight. A boat is ready to take you home. The pier at your home is heavily guarded so we have arranged to take you to Gerasenes. Peter told us about a new follower of Jesus there. He and 3653 are to meet you at the Gerasenes beach and take you home through a back way. Peter said that he is one of the nicest men he ever met." When you get to the beach, just call his name."

"What is his name?"

"Oh yes, his name is Legion."

"God bless you, Bird. Hahab will take you to the boat and sail you to Gerasenes. You will find food on the boat and four pigeons from 3653. Hahab can tell you what we have done so far."

There was no conversation between Bird and Hahab on the way to the boat. Once the pier was in site Bird could see a Roman guard standing at the gate. The pier was dark but Bird could see two men bringing a boat in at the end of the pier. Hahab moved to a bush and motioned for Bird to follow. They could see the two men tied the boat near the end of the pier and began to walk toward the guard.

"What is your business in Capernaum?" The guard shouted.

"We are here to deliver a boat. We got here later than we had planned. I guess the people we were to meet here have left. We will wait, they'll come back in the morning."

"You cannot stay here. This area is closed for the night."

"We have never been in Capernaum. Can you tell us where we can stay for the night?"

"Go down this road until you come to a wide place in the road. There are three roads off the wide place in the road. Take the first road to the left and you will find a small stream about 200 yards down that road. You can spend the night there."

"Now let me see if I have this right. We go down this road for 200 yards until we come to a wide…."

"No. No. Not that road. You go down this road until you come to a wide place in the road."

"Ok. Ok I've got it. We go to the wide place in the road where a stream runs off to the"

"No. No. You go down this road until.... Oh, come on, I'll take you to the wide place in the road and start you on the right road to the stream."

"I thought you said the first road on the left."

"Never mind. Never mind. Come with me."

Chapter 15
Bird Headed To 3653

Once the guard and his directionally challenged companions were a little way down the road, Hahab motioned for Bird to follow him. They quietly walked down the pier to the boat that had just been tied to the end of the pier. "Get in Bird, I'll push us off."

When the boat had drifted away from the pier, Hahab said, "Bird, please raise the sail and pull it tight." No one spoke until the pier was out of sight.

Bird said, "We forgot to get the pigeons that 3653 requested"

"No, we didn't they are under the cover up front along with the food."

Bird's eyes grew large and his head cocked slightly and he had a puzzled look on his face. "You mean."

Hahab laughed. "You have been around pigeons too long. You looked just like one when they are confused. Yes, those two buffoons were part of our plan to distract the guard so we could get you out of Capernaum without being seen."

Hahab began telling Bird about Peter sending the boat to Devas and his family just in time for them to escape certain capture. "If your son had not sent that message, they would have been captured. He also notified Rabbi Boni that the captain of the guards at the Roman outpost in Hippos was planning to take Ezra, Ruth, Joshua, Cara and Lydia into custody for questioning and keep them until this matter was settled. Your son and Rabbi Boni came up with a plan to get them safely out of Hippos. Your son made arrangements with a Chinese caravan to hide them in the caravan until they were safely out of Hippos and then he headed back to your hidden valley farm. Rabbi Boni was to get Ezra and his family to the caravan. The last report, I received, was that they were all intermingled throughout the caravan and that the caravan was headed north."

"You and my son have done a wonderful service for the Jewish People. When our young people dedicate their lives to driving the foreign oppressors from our land, we will live in peace. I wish you and my son could have met before now."

"We did. I hope what I'm about to tell you won't get your son in trouble. When I was just a little boy, my father started bringing me with him when he picked up and delivered pigeons to 3653. Your father would take the birds at the gate, but would not let my father go beyond the gate. He always said," There's no need for you to see anything or anyone here. The less we know about each other, the better we can do our job. If I'm caught, they can't make me identify you and you can't identify us or tell anything about our business."

"I know, I have never had many friends over the years. I know how difficult it is for young folks, in this business, to understand our need for secrecy."

"Oh, I understand but on my first visit to 3653, your son sneaked me through the fence and we played in the caves. The same thing happened when you brought your son to Capernaum. I mean 3653. We have been close friends for years."

While Bird was pondering what he had just learned, he began to smile. "Why you two rascals, I guess that is where you learned to be so sneaky."

They continued to talk as they sailed on toward their destination.

Back at the pier in Capernaum the guard was back at his post. When the captain of the guards came by, the guard snapped to attention, gave a Roman salute and reported that all was secure. As the captain was leaving the guard said, "You should have seen the two clowns that brought a boat in just after I had secured the pier for the night. When I asked them what they were doing, they said they were bringing the boat in for some people that were coming to pick it up in the morning."

"Why didn't you report that to me when I asked if you had anything to report? Where are these men now? Do you have their names?"

"They brought a boat for some people that are coming to pick it up in the morning. I sent them to stay by the stream down the road. Captain, them men were too stupid to cause any problems.

They also don't know nothing about tying up a boat, cause when I got back the boat had drifted away."

Back on the boat Bird and Hahab were nearing their destination.

Hahab said, "We should see a light signal on the beach soon. Bird, keep a close watch, I was told that you would recognize the signal."

Bird moved to the bow to get a better view of the beach. He began to smell something that wasn't pleasant and the smell kept getting worse. All of a sudden the boat hit something floating in the water. Before Bird could see what the boat had hit, there was another bump. Each bump came with a sickening increase in the terrible smell. It didn't take long to determine that the water was full of dead, bloated, smelly pigs.

A flash of light. A pause. Then a flash of light. A pause. Then the rhythmic cadence Bird knew so well. "I see the light over there," Bird whispered.

Finally after many more encounters with dead smelly pigs, they were met on the beach by a man that Bird did not recognize and Bird's son. Hahab and Bird's son gave each other a quick friendly greeting and exchanged pigeon cages. Bird and his son helped turned Hahab's boat around and Hahab headed back to 7533 (Capernaum.) Bird's son and the other man picked up the pigeon cages and headed for a tall cliff.

"Father, follow us. We must get off the beach before we are spotted and I want to get away from the smell on the beach."

"How are we going to get up that cliff?"

"Father, just follow us. I'll tell you what is going on after we get where we can't be seen."

Bird did not recognize the man with his son. The man did seem to know his way around this area and he was very friendly and helpful.

The first part of the cliff was steep, difficult to climb and they could have been spotted by anyone on the beach.

"OK, no one can see us here. Let's stop, get our breath, eat a bite and watch to make sure we are not being followed. I have hidden some food for us behind that rock. A Roman patrol on horseback should come by within an hour, so we need to wait until they have passed before we climb the rest of the way up this cliff."

"I have been asked to guide you back to your home from here. It's going to be a rough walk but it will be safe."

"How does a man of your stature and obviously well-educated know this desolate area. Most people are afraid to even come near here. I've been here only a couple times, when I was young, and each time I was chased away by a madman that cursed and threw large stones at us. He is possessed by many demons and stays in the cemetery on the top of this cliff. I sure hope we don't run into him tonight."

"You already have run into him. My name is Legion and I was that mad man."

"How can that be? Legion is a wild man living among the graves and he has been frightening everyone away from here for years."

"Jesus was here three days ago and He drove the legions of unclean spirits out of me. He sent the unclean spirits into a herd of swine and then they ran off this cliff into the sea. I implored Jesus to take me with Him, but He instructed me to go home to my people and report to them what great things the Lord had done for me and how He had mercy on me."

"Where is your home?"

"My home for the last thirty-five years has been here, living among the tombs."

"We had better eat a little and rest for we have a long walk to get you back to your home. I'll tell you more later."

Bird said, "Now that we have some time, I want to tell my son that I'm proud of him. You did a great job getting that message to Capernaum. In this business you need to be sneaky and it appears that you're a natural."

Hahab cleared the bloated pigs and the terrible smell. The moon and stars were bright, the sea was calm and the winds were just right for a smooth sail back to Capernaum. He set the sails, secured the line, hitched the rudder to the gunnels and leaned back thinking about a restful trip home. His mind began to have thoughts of a good home cooked meal. He could almost smell the fish roasting over a bed of charcoal. Suddenly he said to himself, "Boy, it's going to be good to get home, I can almost…… Wait a minute; I can smell fish roasting over a charcoal fire."

Leaving the sails and rudder secured, Hahab stood up and tried to locate where the wonderful aroma was coming from. A silhouette of a boat appeared off his bow. Hahab quickly resumed control of the sails and rudder and steered toward the boat he had spotted. As he approached the other boat, he could see two people on board. He saw the sails billow with air and the boat turned away. Their efforts to run from Hahab were in vain. His boat was lighter and he was already traveling faster than the other boat. As Hahab came closer, he recognized the boat belonged to Peter. "Wait," he called, "I am Hahab, I know who you are. I delivered Peter's boat to you at the campsite. We have been looking for you."

Peter's boat began to slow. Devas raised his head from under the cover he and Mother had been hiding under and called out, "We have followed the instructions that Peter wrote in his letter. We hid near the shore during the day and sailed out at night looking for a signal."

"Quick, catch this line and help me come on board your boat. I know you have a lot of questions, but right now I need you to tie my boat to your boat so that it will follow us. Devas, pull the sails as tight as you can and let me steer. I need the rest of you to start fanning those charcoals and get a flame started. We may have time to signal Bird and his son to wait for you."

"Bird is in Capernaum repairing roofs. We don't need to go to Capernaum; we need to go to our home in Hippos."

"No, I just took him ashore at Greasiness. I promise that I will fill you in as soon as I can. Right now I need a fair size flame in that fire basket. Delaeh, you and Sam take this canvas cover you have been using to hide under and get in my boat. When I tell you to, I want you to pull my boat between this boat and the beach and start flashing your family's signal toward the beach. Devas, hand me the line for the sails. I can manage the boat if you will help Delaeh and Sam get into my boat and then help Esther get the flame as high as you can safely."

Hahab turned the boat to parallel the beach. Delaeh pulled Hahab's boat where he and Sam could use the cover they had used to hide under to control when the light from the fire could and could not be seen on shore.

They began with one three-second light....wait five seconds....one three-second light....wait five seconds and then one minute of light. The cadence then changed to a rhythm that beat out the words to their family song.

> Shine the light for father to see.
> Bring him home for mother and me.
> Keep him safe while he's away.
> In his strong arms I want to stay.

Meanwhile back on the cliff, we find Legion seated on the ground just looking toward the sea below. There were few things that had brought peace to his troubled soul during the many years he has spent in this lonely place and this was what he enjoyed the most. The one time of the day when his mind seemed to forget the realities of his life and gave him a little time to remember the good life he once had. Thoughts of his mother and sister and his home remained vivid, but the many struggling years had faded most of the other memories, both good and bad memories. The thought that this was probably going to be his last time to sit here and think of the past brought a twinge of sadness to him. Then he said," The past is the past. I now have a bright new future." Hearing his own voice startled him. He realized he was no longer alone and his waking companions could hear him.

Bird and his son awoke from sleep at the same time Legion realized he was not alone. "Is something wrong?"

"No, I was just thinking out loud. You'll have to excuse me. I'm not use to being with people."

Bird was the first to notice the two boats. It was not unusual for fishermen to be in this part of the sea, but since the pig incident most boats had stayed away from here. The two boats were headed toward the beach and then the lead boat turned sharply to the right, revealing a rather large fire on board. Most fishing boats have a metal container that mounts on the side of the boat and extends far enough from the boat to have a small charcoal fire for cooking a meal. The fire, they saw, was much larger than a cooking fire. As the men watched, they saw the smaller boat pulled alongside of the boat that appeared to be on fire and began to attempt to smother the flames with a blanket.

Legion said, "It looks like the people in the small boat have no idea about how to put out a fire."

"Wait," Bird said, "They are sending a signal. Let me see if I can figure out what they are trying to say."

There was a pause as Bird studied the pattern caused by the blocking and then revealing the flame.

"I have it! I know what the signal is! It's Devas' family signal. They are trying to tell us that Devas and his family are on those boats. They must want us to wait for them, so they can go with us. Quick, start a fire so we can signal them back."

Soon a small fire was started on the side of the cliff where it could be seen by the boats. Bird began to block and reveal the fire to the boaters in the same cadence that the boaters had sent. The flame on the larger boat was quickly put out and both boats headed through the smell and the bloated pigs toward the beach. The three men left the pigeons and started the climb down to the beach to meet what they hoped would be Devas and his family.

When they reached the sand and started across the beach, three riders on horseback shouted. "What are you doing here?" Had they been caught by the Roman patrol? Had this all been a trick to capture Devas' family? If that is Devas and his family, what could they do to get them to turn around and sail away?

Legion turned to Bird and his son and said, "Let me handle this. Maybe they will take me and you can get away." He stepped forward and said, "I am a Roman citizen and I have a right to be here."

"We have no reason to stop you from being here. We are simply forward scouts for a Chinese caravan that will be passing through here in about an hour. What in the world happened here that is causing this terrible smell?"

Legion started telling about Jesus coming here, the pigs running off the cliff…….

Bird's son rushed to the riders and shouted," Are you with the caravan that left Hippos this morning? Do you have a man, a woman and three children from Hippos with you?"

"I have no knowledge of that."

The lead rider turned to his companion and said, "Go and get Chuma."

The boats were near enough to the beach for those onboard to see the riders and sense that this could be a trick to lure them to shore. When one rider rushed off, they were sure that he was going to get more soldiers to take them captive.

Hahab shouted, "Turn the boats around. It's a trick."

Bird and his son ran to the water's edge, shouting and waving their arms. "Come back. Come back."

"Stay here Father," Bird's son shouted as he ran into the water and began to swim for the boats.

The boats turned away from the beach but there was almost no wind to fill the sails. They could see the person in the water swimming toward them and could hear that he was yelling something at them.

Delaeh said, "Wait, and let the swimmer get closer. He can do us no harm and he can't get onboard unless we let him. Let's hear what he is trying to tell us."

The swimmer got within twenty feet of the small boat and began to tread water. He was out of breath but was able to call Devas' name. The stench in the water and the air and trying to dodge the dead pigs had sapped most of the swimmer's strength. Delaeh, forgetting that he had not swam in over fourteen years, dove into the water. He grabbed the swimmer, just as a rope was thrown to him, and between both swimmers holding on they were dragged to the larger boat.

Once they were pulled onboard, Hahab said, "We meet twice in the same day."

The boats turned around and headed for shore.

On shore they were met by Legion, Bird and the caravan scout. After some greetings and hugs the group moved toward the cliff where they were less likely to be seen if a Roman patrol came by.

The thundering beat of horses running in their direction startled the new arrivals. "Don't worry, that is the leader of our caravan security force and my fellow scout."

Chuma and another scout brought their horses to an abrupt stop and dismounted. "Who are these people and why are they asking questions about our caravan?"

"Chuma, it's me Bird. I told you that Ezra would recognize the person that would meet them and lead them to a safe hiding place. I didn't know I would be the person you would recognize."

"My brother, your word is enough for me. The caravan is about an hour from here. I'll leave you with my two scouts while I go back and tell Ezra and his family the good news.

They will be ready to join you as soon as the caravan gets here or I could go back, stop the caravan for the night before they reach this terrible smelly place and you could join us there for the night and leave for where you are headed from there in the morning."

Legion thought for a moment and said," If everyone agrees, that sounds like a good plan, Our walk to where you will be safe is going to be difficult and it would be better if we get a good night's sleep and start our walk in the morning."

Chuma mounted his horse and rushed back to the caravan. Hahab tied the smaller boat to Peter's boat and with the help of the two scouts Hahab was once again headed back to sea and home.

Legion, Bird and his son climbed up the cliff and picked up the pigeons while Devas, Mother, Delaeh and Sam began walking to meet the caravan.

Soon the two scouts trotted up to the walking group. One of the riders dismounted, walked up to Mother and asked if she would like to ride his horse instead of walking? Devas, Delaeh and Sam stopped in their tracks, turned in the direction of Mother and the scout and waited for Mother's response.

I hope you will bear with me if I pulse my story for a moment to review the events of the last several days. Having read this far in our story, you have a pretty good picture of Mother's personality. You also know that for her ill son she got on a boat for the first time in many years. Given the opportunity to leisurely sail back home, she chose to walk for several days to get home. She was then forced to get on a boat and hide under a cover that had been used to keep fish out of the sun. For the last several days she has hidden along the shore during the day and stayed at sea during the night looking for a signal that would show them where they could find a safe place to hide. She was chased down by what she thought was a Roman soldier that for some unknown reason was trying to take her and her family prisoner. She and her family were almost lost at sea when the boat nearly caught on fire. Sailing through smelly dead pigs, wading ashore, pushing dead bloated pigs out of the way, she struggled through waist deep water. I think you get the idea so let's get back to our story.

Mother turns to the scout, took her familiar stance with her feet firmly planted in the sand, her hands on her hips. All her family could think was......Ah...Ah and Wait for the explosion.

Mother raised her right hand, placed it on the horse's neck and with her left hand she took the hand of the scout. She began to gently pat the horse's neck, looked into the scout's eyes and said,

"That's a very kind offer and your horse is a beautiful animal. It would be an honor to ride such a well-trained Arabian horse but I would rather walk along with you while you tell me about you and your family." Mother took the reins from the scout and the whole group started walking again.

Delaeh turned to Sam and said, "Are you sure that is our real mother?"

Devas said, "I think it's your mother but now I'm not sure. Your mother is a very gracious lady. She also never forgets a thing. You know that list we all thought we were about to hear. I assure you she has that list stored away and someday we'll hear all about it."

Chapter 16
At the Caravan

Chuma arriving back at the caravan, went straight to the caravan leader and brought him up to date about finding the people that would be taking their guest to a safe place. He then told the leader about the terrible smell a little way down the beach. They decided to spend the night where they were. The leader gave the signal to prepare to set up camp.

Chuma rounded up his men, instructing them to ride through the area to make sure this would be a safe place to camp. Setting up a camp along their route, is something the caravan's members are accustom to doing. Chuma brought four young men and instructed them where to set up the central camp fire.

Ezra offered to help set up the camp fire but was told the best thing he could do was to keep his family near where the camp fire, was being set up and to stay there so that he would know where to find them, when their family arrived.

The overnight site was almost set up by the time our beach walkers were sighted by Chuma's security guards. Chuma walked to the camp fire where he had asked Ezra and his family to wait until the rest of their family arrived. "Your family will be here in a few minutes. I'll meet them because no one is allowed into the camp unless I escort them."

"May I go with you?" Lydia asked.

"Sure. Come on let's go meet your parents, brother and sister, I know you have not seen them for several days."

"Oh. I miss them, but I can't wait to see my brother walking. I have never seen him walking before."

Hand in hand the two headed to the edge of the camp. There was no conversation between the two of them. Chuma used his free hand to wipe the tears from his eyes.

"There they are! There they are! He's walking! He's walking!" Lydia let loose of Chuma's hand and started to run toward her brother. A guard stepped out to stop her. Chuma motioned the guard to let her through.

"But your instruction are…"

"I know. I know. This is a special occasion." Chuma was careful not to let the guard see his eyes.

Lydia ran to meet her family and after a short greeting they continued to walk toward Chuma.

Chapter 17
Family Reunion at Caravan Camp

Soon there was another larger family reunion at the camp fire. After greeting each other, they all sat down around the camp fire and Ruth said, "Bird, we have known you for years and I had no idea that you were so involved in the Jewish movement. We have known you as a friend and the best roofer in our village but how did you keep so much hidden from us. We didn't even know that you had a son and a family."

"Ruth, I wanted to tell you all many times but secrecy is the most important part of this business. My Grandfather was brought into the Sanhedrin because he was the best bird supplier in Israel. At first he was to bring only the best birds to the temple to be sold to the worshipers to be sacrificed. When the Romans conquered our land they forced the temple to pay higher and higher taxes. Because the temple needed more and more money, the leader of the Sanhedrin insisted that we first send the birds that were less than perfect to the temple and sell the perfect birds to the public. My grandfather was devoted to the Jewish nation and religion. He started communication with other Jews that felt as he did. Their goal was to overthrow the foreign governments and regain their land. The best way to communicate was with homing pigeons. He set up the way this Jewish carrier pigeon system was to work. The key was secrecy. He found land that was away from the main cities of Jerusalem, Capernaum, Tiberius and using his connections through the Jewish communities, he was able to set up carrier pigeon stations and teach them how to raise and train the pigeons. He became the most famous person that no one knew in the Jewish underground. Once we had the information, we had no trouble getting the information out. The problem was getting the most important information in a timely manner. My father would never admit it, but he found the best way to get the latest and most important information was to keep your ear to the roof. He studied how to repair roofs and because of his good reputation he was asked to repair the roofs of the finest homes and the most important buildings in the area. Some of these homes belonged to Roman and Jewish leaders and government buildings, such as the military complex on the hill. Most of the information we gather is by being at the right place at the right time, but there are times when we have inside helpers that will cause a roof to need repairs at just the right time and place. By the way, son, how did you get the information about Merchant being taken prisoner?"

"I think you have a pretty good idea of how I got it. Let's just say that it was a long night and I'm glad no one in the Interrogation Room heard the pigeons fly off."

While they were talking, several ladies brought food and water to them.

After a good meal and more talk, they were shown where they could sleep. Morning came early. Caravan life starts early and with a good meal. There would be little time for eating along the trail.

Devas' and Ezra's family said their goodbyes and Chuma led his new friends to the edge of the camp.

Chapter 18
Bird's Hidden Valley

The walk back, to the hidden valley home of Bird and his family took fourteen hours of tough walking. By the time they arrived it was late at night. Bird had expected everyone that lived and worked there would be asleep, but they found everyone busy receiving pigeons, reading messages, writing messages and sending pigeons out. The returning son and grandson had expected a warm welcome and some questions about their journeys but all they got was; "Who are the strangers with you? Why did you bring them back to our working area? Did you bring the pigeons from 3653?"

Bird turned to his son and asked him to take the guests to the front of the farm, while he helped his father with all the messages coming and going.

Soon all the guests were fed and provided a place to sleep and now they were all gathered around a small camp fire. Cara, Joshua and Lydia talked about how Rabbi Boni was almost run over by the Roman Soldiers headed to the outpost and how they were taken out of Hippos in the Chinese caravan. Ruth talked about the wonderful friends she had made with some of the families in the caravan. Ezra said that if it were not for Chuma's hard work, they would have been captured by the Roman guards at the first Roman gate.

Devas told how Hahab brought Peter's boat and instructions just in time for Mother, Sam, Delaeh and him to get away from their first night camp site before the Roman soldiers got there.

Mother said, "The best thing that has happened is Jesus healed Delaeh."

Everyone agreed.

Bird walked into the camp fire area just as Mother was telling about Jesus healing Delaeh "We have someone else with us that Jesus healed."

"That's right," they all shouted

Devas jumped up, walked over to Legion, put his arm around Legion and said, "Our new dear friend, we don't want to pry but please tell us your story." Devas sat down leaving Legion standing where he could be seen and heard by all gathered around the fire.

Legion hesitated a moment. It has been a long time since anyone wanted to know anything about him except where he was and how to avoid him. For the last thirty five years he was only known as the crazy man that lived among the tombs and chased everyone away. "I don't know where to start. I remember living in a big house in Bethsaida with my mother, father and younger sister. My father headed a crew of surveyors and road builders that built the roads between Capernaum and Bethsaida. My mother took care of my sister and me and she had a garden. Everything was normal and happy until I was six years old. Then with no warning I began to yell strange words and throw things. By the time I was seven none of the parents would let their children play with me. My mother and father tried everything they could to help me control my outbursts but nothing seemed to work. The only thing that calmed me was going to the woods, where I could be alone and mother found that I did better when I avoiding eating anything other than vegetables. Every day my mother packed some vegetables and we walked a little way down a path from our home to a wooded area that overlooked the sea. My mother and I would sit on some stones surrounding a fire pit in a little clearing where we could see the sea and she taught me how to read and write.

Sam said, "Mother, that sounds just like where we stayed the first night after leaving Capernaum."

"Yes it does, Sam."

"One day Mother and I were at my favorite site when four mothers and their children ran into the site where we were and I went into one of my fits and beat several children. I don't remember hurting the children but that night several town elders came to our home and told my mother to lock me up or move away from Bethsaida. My parents would not lock me up so they decided to move away from Bethsaida. My father was a surveyor in the Roman Army and had been surveying land for a road between Bethsaida and a little fishing village at the south east corner of the Sea of

Galilee. He and mother packed what they could and we left Bethsaida late at night to avoid the angry town people. The first place we stopped was where you found me. The site had everything my parents were looking for. There were woods, a cliff overlooking the sea and no one else was living within miles. This looked like an ideal place until mother found the graves and tombs. Mother told my father that they would not live next to the tombs. She wanted to look at some other places he had found that were not next to a lot of tombs. We stopped at several places my father had noticed, while surveying for the new road. Mother had reasons why the sites would not be the right place for us to live. There are no woods, can't see the sea, too close to people. Finally we came to a small farm that was surrounded by trees, a hill overlooking the sea, a cleared area for a home, a garden and very few people lived near there. Father went to a small pier he had seen on one of his surveying trips. He asked each man that came in, if they knew who owned the small farm up the road. Finally a fisherman and two small boys tied up to the pier. My father asked the fisherman if he knew who owned the farm and if it was for sale. He told my father that all that land was his and that part of it was for sale to the right family. Father and the nice man talked for quite a while before he agreed to sell us enough land to build a home and have a garden. We now had a place to live. The fisherman helped us build a house, plant a garden and he and his sons brought us all the fish we could eat until we could get settled in our home. Our families became close friends. The fisherman explained that he was saving the rest of the open field to someday build a meeting place for the Jewish families that lived in and around the village. He even had plans to someday build a real Synagogue and a meeting building. The fisherman explained that none of the trees in the forest were ever to be cut down and someday he wanted to replace the old split rail fence around the forest with a nice strong stone wall.

My mother said, "Do you mean that no one can go into the forest?"

The fisherman said, "No, no. We want people to enjoy the forest. We just don't want anyone in the forest that will damage the trees or cut any of them down." While the fisherman and my father built our house, we lived in the forest on top of the hill overlooking the sea. The next three years were the happiest I can remember. My father finished building the road from Bethsaida to the little fishing village we were living in and was now working on the aqueduct to carry fresh water from the hills to the village. One day a Roman soldier came to our farm and told my mother that my father was dead. My father was working on the aqueduct when he saw some rocks at the top of a hill start to move. There were ten men working in a valley below the rocks. He tried to yell at the men to get out but they could not hear him. He ran down to the valley, warned the men and was helping them climb to safety. He got all the men out but the rock slide got him just as he got the last man out. The Roman army gave my father a hero's funeral, my mother got a small pension and they named the water fountain in the marketplace after him."

Before Legion could say another word, Devas and Ezra both jumped to their feet and shouted, "What is your mother's name?"

Legion looked shocked. He thought he had said something wrong. "My mother's name is Ruby. Why do you ask?"

"Because your name is not Legion, your name is Palti."

"How do you know my name? My mother and sister are the only ones that called me Palti."

"We are the two boys that were with the fisherman that sold your father the land and helped your father build your house."

Now Ruth and Esther jumped up and joined Devas and Ezra around Palti, sharing memories and firing questions about his sister. Where he had been, did he remember this and that?

Ezra, all six foot three inches of him, raised his arms and said, "Wait a minute, give the man a chance to get his breath. I'm sure our old friend will try to answer all our questions. Esther you can start the questioning."

"Where does your sister live now?"

"She moved back to our grandparent's home in Bethsaida to help them before they died. She, her husband and two children still live in the old home."

"OK, it's my turn to ask Palti a question."

"I remember how much fun our families had together. You were about three years older than my brother and your sister was my age. We spent a lot of time playing together. I remember we would fish and swim at the pier and play hide and seek on the trail near your home. Our fathers were constantly planning, where the new meeting building, the future Synagogue and the Rabbi's house should be built. They knew the old wood fence around the forest needed to be replaced. They wanted to replace the fence with a stone fence but were not sure, if they could find the necessary stones. They would walk around putting markers on the ground and when they had everything just the way they wanted them, they would call our mothers over to ask what they thought about the arrangement.

This usually ended in a heated debate with your mother saying, I don't care where you build everything else as long as my clothes line stays where it is. My father would say," Ruby you know the lane that will lead into our Synagogue compound when it is completed will be right next to your clothes line. The first thing anyone will see is what you have hanging out to dry."

Your mother always said, "I don't care if the first thing people see is our underwear drying on the line. Remember cleanliness is next to Godliness." This exchange always brought a big laugh from everyone. We would then eat together and talked well into the night. My question is this: What happened that caused you to run away?"

"A few months before my father died I began to hear strange voices again. Then a few weeks later all the problems I had in Bethsaida started to return. Without warning I would scream and throw things and then I would return to being normal. My mother asked father to build a gate in the fence behind our home. I was told, when I heard voices or felt like screaming to run through the gate and go to the cliff overlooking the sea. Mother would come to the cliff when she saw me run through the gate and we would talk and eat some vegetables together. After my father died the fits of anger and screaming came so often that I stayed up on the cliff overlooking the sea. Mother and my sister would bring me food every day and clean clothes once a week. I was always afraid that I would harm someone if they came into the forest so I asked mother to have a signs made that said, "MADMAN DO NOT ENTER," and put them on the two gates in the fence around the forest."

"Palti, we never thought of you as a madman. We always considered you to be a good friend that had a problem sometimes. We looked forward to coming to the fence and listen to you teach us how to navigate, using the stars, the history of our village, Bible stories and so much more.

I remember on Thursdays the boys and girls would bring a large pile of rocks near the old wood fence and leave them there. When we came back on Tuesday, we found you had built an additional section of the stone fence, and for a boy, you built a pretty good fence."

"Thank you Esther. I don't know how I could have stayed in those woods, by myself, if I did not have such a good family and so many friends."

I don't know exactly what happened the night I ran away. We had rain that day and I had stayed in my lean-to reading a book Rabbi Abdon gave mother to bring to me. Just after dark the rain stopped so I took a walk through the woods to get some exercise before I went to sleep. As I approached the road between the marketplace and the forest, four young men walking down the road saw me. I heard one man yell, "Let's get the crazy man."

I tried to hide but they found me and started chasing me. One man grabbed my arm. I don't remember what happened after that except when I regained my composure I had one man by his neck and two of his buddies were on the ground bleeding. The fourth man was clearing the fence yelling, "Help! Help! The crazy man is killing my friends." The man I was holding by his neck kept saying, "Please don't kill me." I turned the man loose and told him that I didn't want to hurt anyone. He started to run and I yelled wait, wait help me with your friends. He stopped, turned around more shocked by my offer to help his friends than he had been shocked by the beating they had received. The two men were badly beaten but they were able to stand and with help from their friend we were able to get them to the fence. I told the young men I was sorry and then ran to the gate behind my home. When I got to the gate, mother was there. I told her what had happened and that I had to find a safe place to hide. She gave me a hug and said she would be watching for me to return, when I was well. I ran through the forest and after running at night and hiding during the day, I found my way back to where my family and I had first stopped, when we started looking for a place to live after we were told to leave town. I lived among the tombs for thirty five years and that is where you found me three days after Jesus drove all the demons out of me

Chapter 19
Back at the Roman Outpost In Hippos

A Roman courier rushed into the outpost. He brought his horse to an abrupt stop in front of the administration building, dismounted, and rushed past the guards and headed straight to the Commander's office. There were no greetings. Just a simple, "Here, I need your response in six hours."

The courier walked out of the building, took the reins from the stunned guard and led his horse to the stable. He gave the stableman instructions and told him that he would be sleeping in the stall with his horse.

The Commander read the message carefully, thought for a moment and called three of his top aides that he knew he could trust.

To one aide he said, "I want you to call for a full uniform inspection in two hours of all the soldiers under my command. Here is a sketch, showing how I want the soldiers to be lined up. I will personally perform the inspection." To another aide he said, "I want you to have the two captains that have been conducting the search for the missing boy and his family in my office within the hour." To the third aide he said, "Go to the dungeon and take the prisoner known as Merchant to the base infirmary. Have him checked out and clean him up. Have the special prisoner we have chained next to him in my office within thirty minutes."

As soon as the aides were gone, the Commander walked to the stable. He found the courier sleeping on some fresh hay. "All right my friend, what's going on that made them send an old goat like you to bring me this message."

"Hi, I was wondering how long it would take you to find me. Let's go for a walk so we can talk"

"I sent everyone away from the stables so it is safe to talk here. So tell me what is going on that they didn't trust a younger courier?" "I assume you read the message you brought to me."

"I didn't have to read it, I helped write it."

"How would you handle this?"

"Very carefully. If you are successful doing what they want you to do, you will be a hero. If you fail, you will be a has-been old goat, like me. If you're lucky."

"You and I came from a different time. A time when the Roman military won the land and then the Roman Empire won the people by building great roads, harbors, brought fresh clean water to regions that had none and we brought a good form of government. We built alliances with those that otherwise would have been our enemy. Our leaders demanded loyalty, dedication and honesty of all who swore allegiance to the Roman Empire and in turn we could depend on the same from them. Now Emperor Tiberius has left Rome and is living a life of luxury on the Isle of Capreae, while our senators squander their time in self-promotion and the intrigue of politics, instead of handling the problems that could cause our downfall. I volunteered to bring that message to you because I wanted to make sure you were the only person that would know what you were being asked to do. I know you will make the right choice in this matter."

"Rome is putting pressure on Herod Antipas and Pontius Pilate to get the Jews under control in Judea. They are blaming the Sanhedrin for not controlling the Jews. All the fuss is mainly about two characters in your territory."

"You mean the fellow named Jesus."

"That's him. Now this last story about him healing some young boy from Hippos is really stirring things up. His followers are increasing each day. Rome is talking about sending thousands of troops to stop all this talk about freedom and a new king. The Sanhedrin has sent a committee to try to stop this Jesus and a fellow called John the Baptist. I passed that committee on the road here and they look like a circus on wheels. When I caught up to them they were stopped beside the road, trying to repair one of their wagons. I stopped and helped them put one wheel on the wagon and showed them how to fix the other wheels that were giving them trouble.

The chairman of the committee thanked me and we talked for a few minutes. When you get through all the robes, the fancy hat and the priestly airs, he is a good man. At the rate they are traveling, I would not plan on them getting here for several more days. You might want to send them some help if you can spare the men. When the chairman gets here, you should try to meet with him. I'm sure he would like to hear about what you have been doing to accommodate the Jewish soldiers."

"I'll be glad to meet with him. Maybe I'll ask if the wheel you fixed stayed on for the rest of their trip. Get some rest old friend you have a long ride tonight and I have to answer that message so you can get back to Jerusalem."

On his way back to his office, he saw three guards leading a small scrubby prisoner in chains toward the administration building. When the commander arrived at the entrance to his building, the two guards snapped to attention and saluted.

"I want both of you to go through this building and tell everyone to leave except my two personal aides. When you are sure everyone except my two aides and I are out of the building, I want you to get six additional guards and station them ten feet from the building to make sure no one gets within fifteen feet of this building. I want two additional guards, one on top of that tall building and one at the top of that barricade, to make sure no one is on the roof of this building." The Commander went to his office and told one aide to stand inside of the building entrance and see that the guards let no one in unless they were on this list or my personal aide tells you to let someone in.

To his other aide he said, "Come into my office and close the door."

With the door closed and the building emptied, the Commander told his aide to have a seat.

The Commander said, "You have proven your loyalty to me in the two years you have been my aide. What you are about to hear and see might cause you to question the wisdom of your loyalty. I want you to know that what I have been asked to do, by my superiors, is testing my loyalty, but I am going to do it. Can I count on your total loyalty and confidence?"

"Sir, you can count on me. I have been with you for two years and know what a good man you are."

"Good, let's get started. Go to the guard at the door and tell him to let one guard and the prisoner in."

The aide returned with one big gruff guard, pulling a weak dirty prisoner.

"What ya want me to do with him?"

"Just leave him here."

"Can I sit in one of those fancy chairs, while I waits to taken em back to the dungeon?"

"No, my aide will escort you out of the building. I will send for you when it's time to take the prisoner back."

The aide closed the door as he led the guard out.

As soon as they were alone, the Commander walked to the prisoner, loosened the chains and helped him to one of the fancy chairs the guard wanted to try out.

"Here, Julius have some water. I'll make sure you get all the food you want before you are taken back to the dungeon. Now, tell me about the prisoner called Merchant. Is he part of a scheme or has he been telling the truth?"

"I have been chained next to many prisoners and I can tell if someone is lying or I can extract information from them about their involvement in a crime in less than half a day. I have been chained next to this prisoner for three days and I can tell you for certain this man is telling the truth. He is not involved in any scheme about Jesus healing that boy. He never left the side of the boy, when he was carried to the marketplace, when he was placed on the sail boat, while they followed the boat to Capernaum, when the boy was raised to the roof, when he was lowered to the feet of Jesus and when Jesus made him walk. He saw the young boy, his sister, his mother and father leave Capernaum, walking home. He sailed home with the boy's uncle. He saw the uncle's wife, children and his nephew in Hippos before he was arrested. The man is absolutely telling the truth."

"How would he do on a witness stand?"

"He would be a good witness, but I don't think he will last more than another day in the dungeon."

The aide knocked on the door.

"Come in."

The aide was shocked when he saw the Commander seated next to the man he thought was a hardened criminal.

The chains were lying on the floor; he was drinking water and talking to the Commander as if they were old friends.

"I want you to take this gentleman in the next room, write down his statement word for word. When you are through, see that he is fed, place the chains around him and bring the guard in to take him back to the dungeon. When you have taken care of that, go to the front door and tell the guards to let the two Calvary captains in. Then escort the captains to my office."

The aide returned with the two leaders of the search parties. The usual Roman greeting began but it quickly stopped when the Commander said, "Come in and have a seat. Let's get down to business."

The two captains looked more uncomfortable in the fancy cushioned chairs than they would have looked at the end of a full day on horseback.

"I have read your reports about what you did and what you found during your search for the family members and the young man named Delaeh. I want you to answer a few questions for me. I want you to answer in your own words. In your report you wrote the facts, now I want your opinions."

"Yes, Sir"

"Do you think the boy call Delaeh is dead?"

"I believe the boy and his family are alive and they are hiding."

"Why do you think the boy is alive?"

"Sir, my men and I rode as fast as any horseman could ride to the first location indicated on a map given to me. I was sure we would find the boy and his family sleeping at the camp and that they would be surprised that anyone was looking for them. We searched the area thoroughly. We found evidence that someone had spent the night there but I could not determine if the family we were looking for spent the night there. I felt someone or group of people knew we were coming and took the boy and his family away just before we got there. No one could have found out about our orders sooner than we did. No one could have left before we did and no one could have ridden faster than we did. The only way anyone could have found out we were coming to arrest them is by carrier pigeon."

"Do you have anything that makes you believe the boy and his family are not dead?"

"Sir, I continued our search all the way to Capernaum, hoping to find them on the way to the site marked on our map. I stopped at our outpost there to see if they had received any orders for us and to send word back here that we had not found the boy."

"Did you find anything in Capernaum that made you think the boy was dead?"

"No Sir. I started my military career in Capernaum and have many friends there. The story of a young boy from Hippos being healed by Jesus is being told by everyone there. The crowds following Jesus are so large there; our outpost has asked for reinforcements to help control the crowds. My first assignment there was to check on Jesus and his followers anytime a crowd gathered around Him. In those days we considered a crowd around Jesus to be twenty or thirty followers. Now I was told he has thousands of followers and the number increases every day. I was told that they had received a message about Jerusalem sending a group of priests to Hippos and maybe some of them will also sail to Capernaum from Hippos."

"So you have no information that makes you believe the boy is dead?"

"That is true. In fact I believe the boy and his family are alive."

The Commander turned to the other captain. "Do you believe the boy's uncle and family are dead?"

"Sir, as I stated in my report."

"Your report is concise and to the point and full of facts. It is a good report but I want to know what you think happened to the uncle and his family."

"Sir, I think they were told that a search party would be looking for them the next morning and that they were helped to escape to a hiding place before we started looking for them in Hippos. I questioned several people that live in Hippos to see if they had seen the fisherman, named Ezra and his family. Several saw them the night before we started looking for them at the pier along with a man they called Merchant. I asked if anyone had seen anything unusual that morning. Several people I questioned said they were awakened when the reinforcements rode in and that the Chinese caravan leaving that morning caused some excitement in the marketplace."

"Captain, I'm running out of time. Please tell me if you think they are alive or dead."

"Sir, I think they are alive and left town with the Chinese caravan and are hiding about ten miles north of here in the hill country."

"Thank you men, you have been a great help to me. My aide will escort you out. Please stay in the compound in case I need you. After you escort these gentlemen out, go to the infirmary and make sure the prisoner, called Merchant, is getting all the attention he needs."

As soon as the door to the Commander's office was opened to let the two captains out, the other aide said, "Sir, the troops are ready for inspection. The troops that are twenty years and younger are lined up on the east side of the field. There is a space of ten feet and then the troops that are between forty and fifty years old and are five foot seven inches to six foot tall are next. The troops that are between forty years old and fifty years old and are over six feet one inch tall are lined up on the west side of the field."

Turning to his aide, the Commander said, "When I point to someone, you tell them to fall in at the gate to the parade grounds and wait there for further instructions."

The Commander walked up and down the line of thirty young soldiers. Without saying a word, he pointed to just one.

The next line stretched the remaining length of the parade grounds and wrapped around the south end. Taking his time but quickly passing over many of the soldiers, the Commander paused for a longer look at twenty possible candidates. When he completed his first walk through, he turned and started back down the line with his aide hurrying to keep up. He pointed to three of his potential candidates.

There were only two forty to fifty year old soldiers that were six foot one inch tall or taller. The Commander stopped in front of one soldier and asked his name. He then asked the second soldier his name.

"Thank you, gentlemen," and he pointed to the soldier on his right.

Turning to the senior officer on the parade ground the Commander said, "You may dismiss the troops except for the five I have selected."

The five selected soldiers stood wondering what they had done and how much trouble they were in. The Commander said, "I want to talk to these three soldiers." He thanked the two remaining soldiers and asked them to return to their duties.

The Commander headed for his office with his two aides straining to keep up. Looking over his shoulder he told one aide to bring the three selected soldiers to the front of the building and to stay with them until he sent for them. When he arrived at the building, he told the other aide to come with him to his office.

Once the Commander was seated at his desk, he looked up and told his aide to shut the door and take a seat near his desk.

"I have been ordered by my superiors to do a task that I think is wrong and I believe will ultimately cause great harm and embarrassment to the Roman Empire. I have no choice but to follow my orders. You, on the other hand, are not being ordered to assist me in this matter. If you choose to assist me in this matter, I will protect you in every way I can. If you choose not to be involved, I will understand and I assure you your decision will not affect your career."

"Sir, I have been under your command for two years. I respect the position you hold but more then that I respect you as a person. I consider it a privilege to assist you in anything you tell me to do."

"The message I received three hours ago informed me that the Roman Emperor had told his representatives in Judea to get the Jews under control or he would send thousands of troops with orders to eliminate any and all trouble makers in Judea. The Emperor also said that after the Jews were taken care of, he would eliminate those whose job it was to keep them under control. The message also states the Sanhedrin had sent a committee to Hippos. They are to warn the Jews to stop spreading all these false stories about Jesus and John the Baptist. They are scheduled to arrive here by mid-day tomorrow. My orders are to provide them any assistance they request while they are in our area." The Commander paused for a moment, looked at his aide and said, "Give me a brief summary of what you have heard about Jesus healing the Hippos boy."

"I've heard that he had been ill for years. His family and some friends took him to Capernaum, where he was healed by a man named Jesus. The last time the boy, his sister, mother and father were seen was when they walked out of Capernaum. I know the boy's name is Delaeh and he has run the pier for several years. He and his family are well liked in Hippos."

"Have you heard the other story?"

"You mean that the sick boy and his family were replaced by lookalikes and the healing of the boy was faked."

"Which story do you believe?"

"I believe the boy was healed."

"Good, so do I. Now read the last page of this message."

The aide began reading the last page of the message.

Your orders are as follows:

If you have found the boy called Delaeh and his family, they are to be detained and be publically questioned by the leader of the Sanhedrim committee.

If you have not found the boy called Delaeh and his family, but have captured any of the people that were a part of a hoax to replace the sick boy with a lookalike that can walk, get a confession and then have them publically questioned by the leader of the Sanhedrim committee.

If you have not found the boy called Delaeh and his family or if you have not captured anyone that was a part of a hoax to replace the sick boy with a lookalike that can walk, you are to do the following:

Select three men from the soldiers under your command. One is to resemble the boy called Delaeh, one is to resemble his father called Devas and one is to resemble his uncle called Ezra. These three soldiers are to be kept in solitary confinement until the leader of the Sanhedrim committee arrives in Hippos.

The Sanhedrim Committee is carrying a large sum of money with them. This money is to be used to pay the soldiers you select for confessing that they and others were part of a scheme to make it look like Jesus made a lame boy walk. You are to tell the soldiers you choose, if what they are doing should come to the governor's ears, we will win him over and keep them out of trouble. Also tell them that they will be reassigned to a post closer to Rome when they have completed testifying.

You are to assign one of your most trusted aides to rehearse the three soldiers in what they are to say, when they testify.

The Sanhedrin made up the following story. Your aide is to read this story, memorize it and then go over it with the three selected soldiers until they can convincingly tell their part in the story in their own words, as if the story were true.

The story goes like this. The city of Capernaum was full of people that had come to see Jesus. My two friends and I also came to town to see Jesus. The center of town was so crowded that we could not get near to where Jesus was to speak. We heard that Jesus would be arriving by boat at the pier so we headed to the pier. On our way to the pier some of Jesus' followers came up to us and asked us if we would like to make some money? We said sure. We were told that all we had to do was carry a stretcher from the pier to where Jesus would be speaking. They said we would be told what to do with the stretcher when we got to the building. They handed each of us a coin that was worth more than we would make for a full day's work and promised that they would make sure we saw Jesus up close. We followed them to the gate leading to the pier where we were told to wait with some other people that were standing there. A small boat with an unusually large sail pulled up at the end of the pier. Two men jumped off the boat and ran down the pier, through the gate and over to where we were standing. One man pointed to me and told me to go to where his partner had stopped. Soon I was joined by my two friends, two other men carrying ropes, a woman and a young girl. The man in charge came over, thanked us for helping and told us that when we finished delivering the stretcher where they wanted, he would meet us back at the pier and give each one of us five additional coins.

While we were waiting outside the gate leading to the pier, Jesus and his followers got off a boat, walked down the pier and through the gate right in front of us. Soon another boat tied up behind the boat Jesus and his followers had been on. We saw some people taking a stretcher off the boat and then there was a large crowd that seemed to want to carry the stretcher, but the people that were on the boat acted like they didn't want anybody else to carry the stretcher. There was quite a commotion at the end of the pier. A tall slender man, carrying a stretcher and a shorter slender man, carrying a set of crutches, ran from the pier. They were followed by a man carrying blankets and some clothing. The men that took us to the pier met the three men running off the pier and brought them over to where we were standing. He told me to take off my outer robe and gave me the clothes the man had carried from the pier. I was told to put the clothes on the man carried from the pier and to put my robe on the stretcher and to lie down on the stretcher. I was covered with the blankets. My two friends and the two men that came in on the first boat picked up the stretcher and started toward the town center. The little girl grabbed my hand and kept covering my face with part of the blanket. The woman kept yelling that they were taking this sick young boy that had not walked in fourteen years to Jesus to be healed.

I was confused at first but then I realized that I was supposed to be playing the part of the boy the woman kept yelling about. The money was good so I played the part. I wanted to see what was happening but that little girl kept covering my face and the woman stopped yelling long enough to tell me to shut up and stop moving or none of us would get the five additional coins. The next thing I knew they had tied ropes to my stretcher and I was being pulled to the roof of a building. I'm scared to death of heights but nobody asked me, if I was. When they started to lower me through the roof, I almost jumped off the stretcher but one of the men on the roof told me if I didn't shut up and stop moving he would drop me on my head, so I didn't move.

I was told to lie there until Jesus told me to get up. When I stood up, everyone was applauding and yelling. I thought I was in some kind of a play so I started acting the part. I picked up the stretcher, the crutches and robe and carried them over my head and ran around the stage smiling, jumping and waving to the audience. After my astounding performance, I ran out the back door of the building where I joined my friends and headed to the pier to pick up our extra money. When we got to the pier, a man told us to go to the boat that

Jesus had sailed on earlier and we would be given our extra five coins there. I looked down the pier and there was the little girl and the woman trying to get away from the two men that had selected my friends and me to be a part of the play. I realized something was wrong so I shoved the man holding my arm, turned to my friends and yelled, "Run!"

We ran as fast as we could towards the center of town where we could get lost by mingling with the crowds. I can still see the frightened look on the faces of that little girl and woman. A few days later a fisherman found their bodies not far from the pier. My friends and I hid in Capernaum that night. The next day we went to the Roman fort and told our story to a Roman soldier. We were taken into protective custody and two days later we were taken to the Roman outpost in Hippos where we have been waiting to be publically questioned by the Sanhedrin Committee from Jerusalem.

When the aide finished reading the page of the message the Commander handed him, he looked up in disbelief.

"Do you want to change your mind about assisting me in this matter?"

"No sir. Do you need me to do anything for you before I start preparing the witnesses?"

"Yes, Go to the interrogation office and tell them I need the main room for the next three days and nights. Have them move the table over to the wall opposite the door. Move the regular chairs to the wall and place the interrogator's chair to the center of the room facing the table. Tell them to remove the chair with the restraining straps and have four cots brought to the room.

"Yes, Sir."

"Please stop at the front door and have the aide bring the three soldiers I chose to my office. Tell the aide I want him to leave the soldiers with me and then help you get the interrogation office ready."

Soon the aide arrived with the selected soldiers. They stepped into the Commander's office, snapped to attention and gave a Roman salute. The Commander stood up, returned the salute and asked the men to relax and have a seat. The men hesitated, not sure if they should be seated or not. "Please gentlemen, take a seat.

We have a few things I need to discuss with you and you need to make some decisions."

The Commander began by explaining he had picked each soldier because of their age and physical characteristics. He briefly talked about the political situation in the Roman Empire, in Hippos and the surrounding areas. During his briefing he paused frequently to ask what they thought about something he had just told them. Hearing the way they answered his questions and watching their reactions, the Commander was confident these men could be trusted and that they could be trained to play the parts he was about to ask them to play.

"I would like to take the time to tell you more about what we are asking you to do. My aide will give you additional information and assist you in learning what we are asking you to do. I can tell you that each of you will be given a considerable amount of money for doing this extra assignment. You have my word that I will make sure that you will be protected from any punishment because of anything we ask you to do. You will be doing a great service for the Roman Empire and to me personally."

The aide knocked on the door. "Sir, the room is ready."

"Thank you, gentlemen. Please go with this gentleman. He will be working with you for the next few days."

The three selected soldiers jumped to attention and started to salute when the Commander said, "Stop. No military courtesies for the next few days. Remember we are going to treat you like you are civilians and you treat us the same."

The Commander sat down at his desk, read the message he received four and a half hours earlier and pondered how he should respond. He wanted to provide his superiors the truth, but he wasn't sure what the truth was.

He began his response with the general military greetings and reference to the message to which he was responding. He then included factual statements about the searches for the young boy and his family, such as information about the one person they had in prison that was known to have been with the young boy and his family on the night they left the Hippos pier shortly after the boat carrying Jesus had left the pier. This prisoner was known to have returned to the pier in Hippos with the boy's uncle early the next morning. The Commander started to write about what the special prisoner had said and to include his official signed statement in this message. After he gave some thought to what he had written, he decided not to include what the special prisoner had told him about Merchant other than what he said about his physical condition. We stand ready to assist the committee from the Sanhedrin, when they arrive. Three soldiers have been selected that meet the age and physical qualities you requested. They will be ready to perform the task you described should their services be required. The message concluded with the traditional military closing and the Commander's signature.

Soon there was a knock on the door. "Sir, the courier is here to see you."

"Have him come in."

"You are a little early aren't you? Did you want to read my response before you leave for Jerusalem?"

"Don't need to. You told them you have not found the boy or his family. You told them the only person that was known to have been with the boy and his family when they left Hippos and was with the uncle when he returned is in prison and the one witness you have is near death. You also told them you were ready to put on their little charade. You may have used a better word than charade. You gave them facts and no opinions and you attached no reports from any of your subordinates."

"The hardest part of writing that message was not what I wrote, but not writing what I wanted to write. I left out the things I felt they should know and told them what they wanted to hear."
"You're a good man, Commander. I'll be off now. By the way, I walked through the marketplace, while I was waiting for your reply. There is another good man that you need to talk to in Hippos."

"Who's that?"

"Rabbi Boni. ...So long old friend, Till we meet again."

Chapter 20
Commander walked
Through Hippos Marketplace

The aide, the Commander had checking the condition of the prisoner named Merchant reported that his condition was not good.

"Thank you. Please continue checking on the prisoner and report any changes to me."

The Commander had his mind on so many things: The committee the Sanhedrin has sent to Hippos, what had happened to the young boy and his family, the large crowd in town that was growing larger every day; there was also the extra one hundred soldiers under his command that needed to be housed, fed and assigned to useful tasks, and preparing his selected soldiers to testify. All these things, plus his normal responsibilities, should have fully occupied his mind but there was one thought that kept ringing in his mind. What was his old friend the courier trying to tell him when he said that Rabbi Boni was a good man? He had met the Rabbi several times in the two years he had been the Commander of the Hippos outpost. All the meetings had been pleasant but nothing special.

The Commander walked through the building and headed to the interrogation office. The guard outside the door acknowledged the Commander and quietly opened the door. The Commander sat in a chair nearest the door and listened to his aide working with one of the soldiers rehearsing his part.

"No! No! Your name is not Delaeh; you were paid to play the part of Delaeh."

"I never got no pay."

"You remember in the story I read you that you were each given a coin worth more than you could make for a day's work?"

"We never got no coin neither."

"No. No. Let me read the story again. This time remember you are playing yourself playing the part of one of the three men in this story."

"The city of Capernaum was full of people that had come to see Jesus. My two friends and I also came to town to see Jesus. The center of town was so crowded that we could not get near to where Jesus would be speaking. We heard that Jesus would be arriving by boat at the pier, so we headed to the pier. On our way to the pier, some of Jesus' followers came up to us and asked us, if we would like to make some money? We said sure."

The Commander left his aide reading the story, as a teacher would read to a first grade class. He walked out the front door of the building, responded to the guard's salute and decided to walk into town. He was accustomed to walking to the marketplace a couple of times a week. He met with the town elders to hear their suggestions and complaints. The other weekly visit was unscheduled and gave him a chance to check on his soldiers and to get a general feel of what was happening in Hippos. He had convinced himself that he would walk around the marketplace, visit with the merchants as he usually did. Instead he walked directly across the marketplace, between two merchant buildings and headed up the small road that led to the synagogue compound. He kept replaying in his mind the conversation he and his friend had as he was leaving his office.

"There is another good man that you need to talk to in Hippos."

"Who's that?"

"Rabbi Boni"

Then he realized that it was not so much what he said, as the look on his face as he said it.

Everyone was busy getting ready for the committee's arrival, but as soon as he was spotted, several workers dropped what they were doing and headed for the meeting building.

The Rabbi came rushing from the building, cleaning his hands with a towel shortly after the fleeing workers sounded the alarm.

"Commander, it is nice to see you."

"Thank you. I hope I haven't stopped your workers. This is a social visit and I wanted to see if I could help you get ready for your visitors."

"Commander, you are welcome here anytime. I think we will have everything ready by the time the committee gets here."

"I was informed last night that they were having some troubles with their wagons and will be at least a day late. I sent ten men to meet them and assist them repairing the wagons."

"Commander, I was at your outpost earlier today and was told you were too busy to see anyone."

"I'm sorry, but the last several days I have been extremely busy."

"I know you are busy. As I was leaving, I met an older gentleman at the stables and he told me that you had a lot going on. We talked for a while and I told him I was concerned about a prisoner named Merchant. He suggested that I come back this evening. He also said something, as I was leaving, that I can't stop thinking about."

"What did he say?"

"He said that you were a good man and that I needed to talk to you."

The surprised Commander said, "Can you meet me at my office in an hour?"

"Yes"

The Commander headed down the lane, crossed the road running along the west side of the marketplace, walked between two merchant buildings and started to cross the marketplace, when he heard a man saying Jesus had kilt all his pigs. He could see the man and hear him demanding that four of his soldiers do something about getting him pigs to replace the ones kilt. The Commander walked over to see if the man was drunk and also to help his men calm him down. The man stopped yelling when the Commander walked up.

"What seems to be your problem?"

"That troublemaker called Jesus came to where I have a pig farm and kilt all my pigs. I'm a loyal Roman citizen and I demand you replace every one of my pigs. You are supposed to protect loyal Roman citizens and their pigs."

"Did you see this fellow Jesus actually kill your pigs?"

"No, I was at home when it happened. My workers were watching my pigs. They ran to my house like scared rabbits. Their eyes were bulging like bull frogs and they told me that Jesus mesmerized them helpless pigs and they ran off a cliff and into the sea. Them pigs are nasty things when they are living, but you ain't smelled nothen' till you smell a pig that has been dead for days and floating in the sea.

"These nice solders will get all the information from you and how we can find you if we need to get up with you."

"But I haven't told you the strangest part. My men told me that they seen Old Crazy Ben yelling at this Jesus fellow and his followers, when they came ashore. Old Crazy Ben had a big rock in each hand but he didn't throw nether one of em at nobody. Old Ben is a better thrower than most people are duckers. Now when my workers told me about Old Crazy Ben I had to go see for myself. I got where I knew Old Crazy Ben would be. Course you never know where them rocks are going to be coming from. I snuck up and saw Old Ben, just setting on that ridge that my pigs ran off from. I just hid waiting to see what would happen. Soon a man came walking out of the woods and started talking to Old Ben just like me and you are talking now. I couldn't hear all they was saying to each other, but I could tell they was waiting for someone that was coming by boat. Crazy Ben and the man from the woods met the two men on the beach. One man got in the boat and left. The other man, the man from the woods and Old Crazy Ben started climbing back up the cliff where I was hiding, so I had to move before they seen me. Before I found a new hiding place, I saw a light flashing at sea. Old Ben started a fire and soon two boats came back through my dead pigs to the shore. I moved as close as I could without being seen. I couldn't tell who got off of what boat, but one was the same man that left about an hour before. Now there were seven people on the beach, I counted em'. There was Ben, two men that was with him, the man what left earlier and came back, a grown man, a grown woman a young boy and I think a young girl. She could have been a young boy cause they kept calling her Sam."

The Commander said, "Did you hear any other names?"

"The woman they called Mother, the little girl or boy they called Sam. The man they called Devas and the young man they called Delaeh."

The Commander said, "I'd like to hear more of your story about your pigs in the morning. If you will come with me, I'll see you have a place to stay tonight."

"Sure do have a lot more to tell ya."

One of the soldiers said, "Would you like for us to take this prisoner. I mean gentleman to the outpost?"

"That won't be necessary. This gentleman and I will just walk over there and one of my aides will see that he has a place to spend the night. You men go about your duties."

The Commander and the farmer headed for the outpost.

One of the soldiers said, "I bet I know where that farmer is going to spend the night."

On their walk to the outpost the farmer continued telling his story.

"The two boats were tied together and the same man that left before sailed off with both boats. The advanced guards from the Chinese caravan came along and talked to the six people on the beach. One left and came back with Chuma. You see Chuma buys pigs from me when the caravan comes through here. I wanted to tell him all my pigs was kilt. Seems Chuma had something he wanted to show the people that came in on the boat. They didn't see me, but I followed them back to the caravan. When they got near the caravan, a young girl ran out to meet them. The caravan had already set up camp for the night. I knowed how mean them guards can be, if you get too close to the camp without permission. So I spent the night where they wouldn't see me. The next morning I saw the six people I had been following, leave camp with a tall man, a woman, two young girls and a young boy."

By this time the Commander and the farmer arrived at the outpost, he could see Rabbi Boni was not far behind them. He told the guard to take the farmer to the guest quarters and see that he was taken care of.

The guard said, "Yes, commander, I'll see that he is taken care of."

The Commander recognized the smile on the soldier's face so he moved closer to the guard and whispered. "I mean the real guest quarters, and see that he is fed. He is my personnel guest."

The Commander turned to the farmer and said, "When did you last see these people?"

"About twelve hours ago."

"Do you know where they are now?"

"Yes, they're staying at a pigeon farm in the hill country north of here."

"Make yourself comfortable, I'll see you in about two hours after I finish my next meeting. I want to hear more about the people you have been following."

"Thank you for coming, Rabbi. Let's go to my office so we can talk in private."

On the way to his office, the Commander told one of his aides to make sure the farmer was comfortable and that no one talked to him. He told the other aide to check on Merchant and come to his office as soon as he found what Merchant's condition was. The Commander also told the aide to get the two captains that had been leading the search for the missing families. Have them wait outside my office door."

"Come in, Rabbi. Please have a seat."

The Commander moved one of the chairs in front of his desk so that he and the Rabbi would be facing each other.

"I'm sorry I could not meet with you earlier. Now, you told me that you met an older gentleman at the stables, when you were here earlier, and he said that I was a good man and that you needed to talk to me. Well, he said the same thing to me about you. This is no ordinary man. He was born into a very powerful and wealthy Roman family. He attended the finest schools and could have had any position in the whole of the Roman Empire but he chose to be a Roman courier. He told me many times that real power comes from understanding the people and that important sounding titles and fancy uniforms make people tell you what they think you want to hear. I have always followed his advice and he has always been right. I would like to propose that you and I talk openly with each other and keep whatever we talk about between us."

"I agree."

"Let me start by telling you that the man named, Merchant, is still here. We have been trying to find out what happened to Devas' and Ezra's family. Merchant is the only person who was seen with them when they left and the last person seen with Ezra when he returned. We had reason to believe he had something to do with their disappearance."

"I can assure you that Merchant is the most caring and loving person in the world. He would never be a part of anything that would harm anyone."

"I know that now. He has proven he is everything you said about him. Unfortunately, he did not take the interrogation well. When I found out his condition, I had him removed from the dungeon and carried to our infirmary with instructions to give him the best medical attention we have."

"May I see him?"

"My aide is checking on him now. He should be back with a report in a few minutes."

"Commander, you told me about your friend, the courier. Let me tell you what a wonderful man Merchant is. Two years ago I left Jerusalem headed to Hippos for my first assignment as a Rabbi. I was attacked by two robbers that beat me, took everything I had and left me beside the road to die. The only person that helped me was Merchant. He wrapped my wounds and took me to an inn and paid them to take care of me and then came back to carry me to Hippos."

There was a knock on the door.

"Come in"

"Sir, I have the information you asked me to get."

"Come in. This is Rabbi Boni. Tell us what you found out about the prisoner called Merchant."

"The prisoner is conscious and eating soft food. The doctor said he is amazed how well he is doing. But he is still very sick."

The Rabbi said, "Can I see him?"

The Commander asked his aide to take the Rabbi to see Merchant and on his way out to tell the two cavalry captains to come to his office.

"Rabbi, we have a lot to talk about, so please come back after visiting Merchant."

The two captains appeared at the Commander's door. "Come in gentlemen, close the door and have a seat. There is a pig farmer, staying in our guest house. I think he knows where the two families you have been searching for are hiding."

"Shall we get our men ready to go get them?"

"No. First I want you to go to the guest house and talk to the farmer. Be friendly and encourage him to talk about his dead pigs and the people he has been spying on. Listen to him carefully and get as many details as you can, about where they are hiding. Tell him I will be there in an hour and join him for a drink of wine."

"Commander, we each have our sergeants standing by. They could have our riders and their horses ready to go as soon as you give us the order."

"No. Tell no one about this. In fact don't even talk to each other about this outside the office."

The aide returned with the Rabbi. Once they were alone they each took the chairs they had occupied before.

"How is your friend, Merchant, doing?"

"He is in bad shape but he recognized me. He smiled when I told him this time, I'll take care of you. I think there was no reason to treat a good man that way."

"Rabbi, you and I live in worlds that are separated by the lack of faith and trust in our fellow man. I agree that the interrogators went way too far with how they treated Merchant, but they were trying to get information about nine missing Hippos citizens and Merchant was the only lead we had. I assure you that we are doing everything possible to nurse him back to health."

"What do you plan to do with him after he is well?"

"He will be free to leave and our doctors will continue to see that he gets the best treatment available."

"I would like to make some preparations tonight and then take him to my home, where he took care of me."

"Rabbi, I need your trust now if we are going to get those nine family members home safely and keep them safe when they get here."

"Keep them safe when they get here? What danger will they be in once they are home?"

"Rabbi, if anyone finds out that I let you read what I'm going to show you, I will be tried for treason and hung on a cross as a warning to others. Here, read the message brought to me by my friend the Roman courier, this morning. Take your time reading. Parts of the message I had to read several times. While you are reading, I am going to change into my civilian clothes."

When the Commander came back into the room, he found the Rabbi just sitting looking off into space.

"By the look on your face I can see that you have finished reading the message. I know you are shocked."

"No. I'm not shocked. I have received many messages from my superiors, telling me to include certain stories and phrases in my sermons and conversations with my congregation. I know what they tell me is not true and for the most part my congregation also knows they are not true. I'm told to tell my people things like John, known as the Baptist, is a crazy Jew running around starting troubles with the Roman leaders and that this Jew, Jesus, heals people of unclean sprits because he is the king of the unclean spirits. Jesus has been in Hippos several times and each time that I heard him speak, he talked about peace, love your brother and feed the hungry. The last message I received told me to tell my congregation that if these fellows, Jesus and the Baptist, keep causing troubles the Roman Empire will send thousands of troops to kill us all."

"That last message may be true, but now we need to work on getting those nine citizens of Hippos home safely. We have a man here that told me he has been following a man that this Jesus fellow drove evil spirits out of and the spirits' went into his pigs and the pigs went crazy, ran off a cliff and drowned in the sea."

"Yes, he came by the meeting building shortly after you left. He said he came to the Synagogue because Jesus was Jewish and we should pay for all the pigs he kilt. I mean killed. I listened for a while and then told him I had a meeting I had to go to. I told him I would be glad to hear more of his story if he would come back tomorrow."

"Do you think he knows where our missing families are?"

"I don't know, he started telling me about Jesus healing some crazy man and Jesus kilt, I mean killed, all his pigs. I wanted to hear more but that's when I told him I had to go to meet you. Like you, I had to cut my conversation short with him, so we could meet. He talked about a man he called Old Crazy Ben. Then he said he saw a boat bringing…." The more the Commander talked the more the Rabbi wanted to hear.

"Commander from what you have told me, it sounds like this man has described Devas' family and Ezra's family. I asked him to come see me in the morning but I think we should try to find him now, before he leaves Hippos."

"Rabbi, I asked him to spend the night in our guest house. He is there now with the two captains that have been leading the searches for the two families. I instructed them to have a friendly talk with the farmer and to find out where he last saw Devas' and Ezra's family and any other information the farmer had. I would like you to go with me and help me to decide if the man is telling the truth."

"I'll do anything to help bring those wonderful folks safely home."

The Commander walked to a tall cabinet in his office, opened it and took two skins of wine and headed for the door. "Thank you Rabbi, now let's find out if the man knows what he's talking about."

When they approached the guest house two guards shouted, "Halt. This is a restricted area."

The Commander realized he had on civilian clothes and said, "Guard, please ask one of the captains to come out and identify me."

One of the captains, hearing the guard's challenge, came out of the guest house, recognized the Commander and said, "I'm sorry Commander. I instructed the guard that you were the only person to let in but he didn't recognize you in civilian clothes." The Commander thanked the young guards for their diligence and he and the Rabbi followed the captain into the guest house.

"Hi, Commander, you sure it's all right for me to stay here? I don't want to get you in no trouble."

"You are more than welcome to spend the night. Now let's finish the talk we were having in the market place."

The Commander only had to ask a few questions and after each question the farmer went into great detail of what he had seen and heard. After the Commander had the answer to his question, he had to say something like, "Thank you, now let me ask you this." The farmer would take off again with more details than were necessary. "Thank you, now where is this place you saw all these people?" Again the farmer provided more details than required. He started from the Chinese caravan camp site on the beach, walking over the dunes, through some marsh lands, up some hills, through some woods and the exact amount of time it took to reach the back of the farm. "They then moved to the front of the farm and that is the last place I seen them."

"Thank you, now are there any markers, roads, paths or anything that we could look for if we tried to find this place?"

"Nope, the paths are small and the roads leading to the front of the farm are small and they seem to try to keep them that way so very few people can find them."

How will we know when we reach this farm?"

"That's simple, just follow the pigeons. You never seen so many pigeons flying around. Them pigeons are coming and going all the time. Let me tell you how."

"That's all right. Thank you, I think we get the picture. Now one last question, how would you like to stay here for a couple days while I try to get some money for you to buy more pigs you need to replace the ones you lost? I mean kilt….killed."

"I aint got no money to buy food, but I sure would like to stay here a few days."

"Don't you worry about that, I'll put two soldiers outside your door and they will see that you get two nice meals a day and a skin of wine to go with the meals. Good night, I'll see you in a couple of days. I'm sorry I don't have time to have a wine with you, but you can keep these two skins."

The Commander walked out the door of the guest house, followed by the Rabbi and the two captains. Once outside the Commander told the captains to make sure that two guards were placed outside the guest house twenty-four hours a day. They were instructed that the farmer was not to talk to anyone and he was not to leave the guest house. The captains were asked to come to his office, after they saw that the guards were assigned to guard the guest house.

The Commander and the Rabbi did not speak until they were in the Commander's office.

"Well Rabbi, Do you think we have found all our missing people?"

"The descriptions the farmer gave surely match Devas' and Ezra's families. Yes, I'm sure these people are Devas' and Ezra's families."

"Rabbi, before the captains get back I want to tell you something. I know about the Jewish carrier pigeon network. We intercept many of their messages with our hawks, and sometimes we send out misleading information to confuse them.

I'm telling you this because I believe you know how to get a message to the people we want to get safely back to Hippos and from what the farmer told us, I believe they are hiding at one of the main terminals of the Jewish carrier pigeons system. If I send thirty Roman horsemen in to bring these families home, it will look like we are coming to capture them and they will scatter and hide deeper in the hill country. If I went with you and I stayed a short distance from the farm, you could walk in and explain why we were there. The only problem is, we are expecting the Sanhedrin committee by noon tomorrow and I must be there to meet them."

"I can send some soldiers to hold them up for a full day. The soldiers can tell the committee the road is being repaired and will take twenty four hours to complete the repairs. This should give us the time to get Devas' and Ezra's family safely here and time to get you back to meet the committee when they arrive. Will two hours give you enough time to go to your synagogue, take care of what you have to do and get back here? Remember tell no one where we are going or what we will be doing."

"Yes. I can take care of everything I need to do and be back in less than two hours."

The first thing Rabbi Boni did was tell Mrs. Ruby about Merchant. Then he explained that the committee would not be here for thirty-six hours. He started telling her that he would be gone over night but Mrs. Ruby interrupted and said, "Take me to that young man now."

"Mrs. Ruby, he is being taken care of by a military doctor and I don't think they will let you into the outpost to see him."

"We'll see if they will let me in to see that sweet young man. He doesn't need to be in that place where they almost beat him to death. He needs to be here where I can take care of him like I took care of you two years ago. Now let's get over there."

Walking back to the Roman outpost the Rabbi tried to reason with Mrs. Ruby but nothing he said changed her determination.

When they reached the gate to the outpost, two guards stepped in front of the Rabbi and said, "Halt. We have orders to let you in Rabbi but I was told you would be alone."

"Well whoever told you that was wrong. Now get out of my way I'm coming through."

"No, Mrs. Ruby. I cannot let you through."

"What are you going to do? Beat me up like you did that young man the other day."

The Rabbi said, "Would one of you get the sergeant of the guards for me?"

Soon the sergeant came to the gate and before Mrs. Ruby tore into him, the Rabbi said, "Mrs. Ruby please let me talk to the sergeant."

Rabbi Boni took the sergeant aside and explained that Mrs. Ruby just found out that a young man she and he cared very much for had been mistakenly taken as a prisoner several days ago. He was beaten badly and is in your infirmary. Mrs. Ruby is determined to see this friend of ours tonight.

"Rabbi, I know about Merchant. I also know that he saved your life and I also know Mrs. Ruby nursed you back to health after you were beaten very badly. I also know that Mrs. Ruby's bark is worse than her bite. But I cannot let her in without orders to do so."

"Sergeant, is there any way you could escort Mrs. Ruby and me to the Commander's office to get permission to let her see Merchant?"

"Rabbi, I'll be happy to go to the Commander's office with you to get permission to take Mrs. Ruby to see Merchant, but she will have to stay here with the guards until the Commander gives me the o. k."

"I don't think it is a good idea to leave her here with the guards."

"Don't worry about her, the guards will take care of her until we get back."

"I'm not worried about her; I'm worried about the guards. Sergeant, I guarantee you, that her bite can be worse than her bark."

"Mrs. Ruby, if you and the Rabbi will come with me I'll take you to the Commander's office to get permission for you to see Merchant."

On the walk to the Commander's office, the sergeant turned to Mrs. Ruby and said, "It's nice to see you Mrs. Ruby."

"It's nice to see you, Rue. You and your friends have not been to the farm in several weeks."

"I know. We have been so busy with all the troop reinforcements that arrived last week and now the committee coming from Jerusalem. I haven't had time to camp out in your woods. My friends and I really enjoy camping at the top of the hill overlooking the sea. I especially miss those great vegetables you let us pull from your garden. I'm sure sorry about Merchant. He's such a nice fellow."

"You and your friends are welcome anytime."

The Commander told the sergeant to take Mrs. Ruby to see Merchant and then have her escorted home when she was ready to leave.

Once the sergeant and Mrs. Ruby left the Commander's office, the Commander told Rabbi Boni his plans. "The two captains, in civilian clothes, should be leaving the outpost now. We are to ride out together in about fifteen minutes and join the two captains outside of Hippos. Four uniformed cavalrymen and two wagons driven by two uniformed soldiers each will leave thirty minutes after we leave. They are to head north out of town. The captains will mark the route the cavalrymen and wagons are to follow. When we get within a ten minute walk of the front of the farm, you will walk in and explain what is happening in Hippos and that we have two wagons and supplies to carry them back to Hippos."

The Commander and Rabbi B caught up with the two Captains about three miles north of Hippos on the road to Bethsaida. The next three hours they rode at a moderate rate of three miles per hour. After they had ridden about two hours one of the captains would charge out to scout the area ahead of them and when he returned the other captain would repeat the same search pattern. On the third rotation of the search pattern the captain stopped ahead of the group and waited for them to join him.

"This is the area the farmer told us the Chinese caravan spent the night with the people we are looking for."

"Are you sure?"

"Yes sir. The area is clean, but I can tell that a large group stayed here. The grass has been bent down and there are signs that several large animals have been here within the last week."

"How long do you think it will it take for us to get from here to the farm where our friends were last seen?"

"Commander, I suggest that you and Rabbi Boni wait here for the wagons while we scout the area between here and the farm. We'll get as close as we can without being seen and return before morning light."

"Thank you Captain, we'll be here when you get back."

The captains had just disappeared over the first small hill on their way to the farm and the wagons had not yet arrived. The Commander and Rabbi gathered wood for a small fire to signal the wagons where to stop. The fire was started and the two new, weary friends were alone. The stars were bright; a calm breeze blew in from the sea and there were no flies or mosquitoes.

"How can the universe seem so peaceful and yet the world you and I live in is in such chaos?"

"Rabbi, I was just thinking the same thing. My old friend the Roman courier, the one you met this morning, has a saying about that. He says, "When the sky turns dark, the winds howl, lighting flashes and people shake with fear, they stop bickering and help each other through the impending disaster. Let the common enemy go away and those same people will fight each other to the death."

"You are lucky to have the courier as a friend. The few minutes I spent with him, I felt he was looking for something. As a matter of fact when we met, I asked him if I could help him find what he was looking for. He said yes and we talked for no more than ten minutes. What he said when he left surprised me. He said, "Thanks for helping me find what I've been looking for. We didn't talk about anything particular. We just talked about our little marketplace and about some of the things going in Hippos. He didn't even tell me his name."

"Oh, he never uses his name. I told you his family is very rich and powerful and many hold high positions in the Roman Empire. My friend found out long ago that people acted differently around him when they found out who he was. I assure you he remembered your name. The last thing he told me before he left was that you were a good man and that I needed to talk to you."

"Do you know that eleven of your soldiers are Jewish?"

"Yes, I do and ten of the reinforcements that came in last week are Jewish.

My predecessors kept the Jewish soldiers in a separate unit and they were used only for traffic control and as messengers. If their duties fell on their Sabbath, they had to find someone to take their place. They were welcome to eat in the mess hall but were given no consideration for their dietary laws. When I became Commander, I did away with the special Jewish unit and blended all Jewish soldiers into regular units. We now have a section of our mess hall set aside for the Jewish soldiers that follow all the Jewish dietary laws. The duty officer will not assign a Jewish soldier duty on the Sabbath."

"That sounds wonderful. Do you have any problems with that system?"

"Yes. When the Jewish food is better than the regular mess hall food, we have a lot of soldiers trying to convert to Judaism."

"Tell me Rabbi, what do you think about this Jewish fellow, Jesus?"

"He has been to Hippos two times that I know of since I have been here. I have never met him but I have been close enough to hear him speak. He says things like; blessed are the poor in spirit, for theirs is the kingdom of heaven. Blessed are they who mourn, for they shall be comforted. Blessed are the meek, for they shall inherit the earth. Blessed are they who hunger and thirst for righteousness, for they shall be satisfied. Blessed are the merciful, for they shall obtain mercy. Blessed are the pure of heart, for they shall see God. Blessed are the peacemakers, for they shall be called children of God. Blessed are they who are persecuted for the sake of righteousness, for theirs is the kingdom of heaven. Everything he says is what we as Jews have been taught all our lives. I have seen people carried to him and they walked away after he touched them. I know some things can be faked, just like the Sanhedrim are trying to say about Delaeh….I'm sorry, you asked me a simple question and I am going on and on."

"That's all right. I have heard Him also and I agree with you. He speaks as someone that understands what he is talking about."

"I believe Jesus has a real spiritual connection to God. He is the real reason I am in Hippos as the Rabbi."

"You mean you think you were divinely called to be in Hippos."

"Nothing like that. You see I was sent to replace Rabbi Abdon when the Sanhedrim first started to hear how popular Jesus was becoming in Galilee. Rabbi Abdon is as well versed in the

Jewish scriptures as anyone. He was told he was being called to Jerusalem to search the scriptures to see what is written about the coming Messiah. They really wanted the scriptures searched to find ways to discredit Jesus' claim to be the Messiah."

"So you believe Jesus is just a good man that is trying to make the world a better place to live."

"No. I believe he is a prophet and maybe the greatest prophet that has ever lived."

"You know if our superiors heard what we have said to each other and knew what we were doing out here tonight, we would be put on adjoining crosses for all to see."

The cavalrymen and wagons showed up just as planned. The horses were fed, given water and corralled for the night. One cavalryman took the first watch and everyone else slept under the stars. The two captains returned from scouting out the best way to get to the farm. They reported to the Commander that the roads were rough but the group could reach the farm in three hours. The Commander figured three hours to the farm, one hour to get the people ready for the return trip, three hours to get back to the main road and five hours to get to Hippos. That is a total of twelve hours for travel. "We should be at the farm at 7:00AM when everyone is getting up. That means we leave here at 4:00 AM.

That will get us to Hippos by 4:00 PM. That is about the time the Sanhedrim Committee will arrive in Hippos. Have the guard on duty, wake everyone at 3:30 AM. That will give us a little less than two hours sleep."

Chapter 21
To the farm and Back to Hippos

The journey to the farm started at 4:00 AM with the two captains leading the way. The Commander and Rabbi Boni followed them and they were followed by the two wagons. The four cavalrymen in full uniform brought up the rear. The first hour's travel went well because there was only a slight upward grade and the road was in fairly good condition. One Captain slowed so the Commander and the Rabbi could catch up to him.

"Commander, we are about to come to where the road is in poor condition and very hilly. I sent the other captain ahead to find a spot where traveling with the wagon would slow us down too much. He is to mark the spot where we should turn the wagons around and have them wait there until we lead the two families to the wagons. Once the scout has marked a spot for the wagons, he is to ride another fifteen minutes toward the farm to scout that area and then report back to me. Once I get his report, we can tell when we are getting close enough to the farm to be detected if they have any guards"

"Thank you Captain."

They continued their steady pace toward the farm, until they found the marker where they were to have the wagons wait. The Captain directed the drivers where to put the wagons. They decided the best way to proceed from here would be to have only the captain and Rabbi Boni go on horseback to the farm. The less people going from here on meant there was less chance they would be detected by anyone on the farm. Once they got near the farm, the Captain would stay with the horses and the Rabbi would walk in and wake everyone up, get their things, say their goodbyes and they would be headed to the wagons.

The Captain mounted his horse and said to the Commander, "My partner should have returned by now with his scouting report. I'm going to see what is holding him up."

Going at a full gate, the Captain covered about a half a mile when he saw the other Captain coming as fast as he could toward him. Instead of stopping, the Captain charged past his partner and motioned for him to follow. Reaching the wagon turnaround area, the horses were brought to an abrupt halt in front of their startled companions.

"What has happened?" the Commander demanded. The captains had ridden so hard they could not get their breath so they could not answer the Commander's question. The Captain that had been scouting held a finger up, indicating please give me a moment. The other captain pointed to the breathless Captain and shrugged his shoulders, indicating he had no idea what was going on.

"They're coming."

"Who's coming?"

"The families."

"What families?"

By this time the cavalrymen had mounted their horses and were prepared to attack whatever the scout had seen.

"Commander, the family we have been looking for. I was riding so fast I almost ran over them."

"How do you know the people you saw were Devas' and Ezra's family?"

"I ran my horse off the road to miss them. A little way off the road was a deep drop off. My horse managed to stop before the drop off, but I didn't. When I stopped rolling, three men climbed down to see if I was hurt. While we were climbing back up to the road, they told me their names were Devas, Ezra and Legion. When we got back to the road, they asked me where Rabbi Boni was and how far away were the two wagons. I told them I would get Rabbi Boni and send him to meet them."

Rabbi Boni mounted his horse and headed to meet his friends. What a reunion. There were hugs for everyone. When he saw Delaeh, the Rabbi could not take his eyes off him. He could not believe what he was seeing.

Devas came over, took the reins from the Rabbi and arm and arm they started walking again toward the waiting wagons.

Rabbi Boni said, "How did you know we were coming for you? You even knew we had two wagons with us."

"That's what I need to talk to you about. Bird and his father received messages about the outpost Commander, six cavalrymen, two wagons and you were coming to get us. The Jewish underground followed your every move and kept Bird informed of your every move. Bird's father did not want the Roman military people anywhere near his farm. He suggested that we meet you before you got near the farm. We would have left the farm sooner but we weren't sure which way you would take to the farm. There is one more thing; no one is to know that we knew you were coming for us or that we knew your every move. Our story is that we decided to head home and just happened to run into you and the men from the outpost."

"As far as I knew you just happened to run into us. But I don't understand how they followed our every move. These men are seasoned soldiers, they were constantly checking to see if they were being followed."

"Think about it. Most of the road you were on runs next to the sea. There were two boats following your every move and sending homing pigeons to the Bird farm."

They had so much to talk about that the time flew by. Soon the wagons and men were seen through the trees. There was a short period of introductions and the assignments of who rode in which wagon. The Rabbi and the Commander both had to be in Hippos before the Sanhedrin Committee arrived, so they decided to ride on ahead of the others. The four cavalrymen were assigned to follow the last wagon and the two captains were to lead the procession and alternate scouting duties.

The two wagons were filled and the order was given to mount up. The soldiers had performed this maneuver many times. On the order to "mount" the riders placed there right foot into the right strap and when the order "up" was given the riders smartly slung their left leg over the saddle and with this one move landed on the saddle in an erect posture.

The maneuver was completed perfectly for five of the soldiers, but one soldier lay on the ground with his right foot still in the strap and his body lying on the ground. He was able to get his foot free and stand up. He tried to get his right foot off the ground again but he could not reach the strap. The head long catapult over his horse's head, flight through the air and crash landing along with a long roll through trees and rocks were more than his young body could stand. When the other captain and Delaeh got to him, he was under the horse with both arms wrapped around the horse's neck and he was trying to climb into the saddle.

"Just help me get on my horse, I'll be all rig____."

He passed out before he could get the words "all right" out of his mouth.

The Captain and Delaeh lowered him to the ground and began to examine him for injuries. His chest and stomach had cuts and bruises everywhere. There were three large lumps along the right side of his rib cage and his breathing was becoming labored.

Ruth and Esther took one look and said, "This young man needs a doctor right away."

The Captain told the wagon drivers to clear one of the wagons and to make a bed with anything they could find that was soft. The Captain was carefully placed on the bed. The two drivers on the other wagon were instructed on how to administer first aide to the fallen captain and to get to the outpost infirmary as soon as possible.

The Captain made the following suggestions. If Ezra and Devas would drive the remaining wagon, that will leave room in the wagon for Ruth, Esther, Joshua, Sam, Lydia and Cara. That takes care of everyone but Delaeh and Legion.

Delaeh said, "Could I ride on the other Captain's horse and help you with the scouting duties?"

"If you feel up to it, I would appreciate your help. Now we need to find room for Legion."

"I could walk to Hippos."

"No. The last instructions the Commander gave me before he and the Rabbi rode off was to make sure that all of you got to Hippos safely and as quickly as possible."

The Captain rode to the four uniformed cavalrymen that were mounted and ready to escort the group. When he returned, he told everyone his plan. "I will leave two of the cavalrymen here to walk to Hippos. Legion will ride one of the horses and the other horse will be tied to the wagon. The other two cavalrymen will escort us to Hippos. Don't worry about the cavalrymen we're leaving to walk. As soon as we reach Hippos, the two escorting us will take their horses back to them. I need to keep two uniformed cavalrymen with us because I am wearing civilian clothes and if we are stopped by one of the reinforcement soldiers, they might not recognize me."

Joshua asked, "May I ride on the extra horse?"

"That's a mighty big horse; do you think you can handle it?"

"Yes, Sir."

"Go back to the cavalryman. He will help you on and adjust the stirrups for you."

Everyone took their places and they were off to Hippos.

The closer the little caravan got to Hippos, the more people they saw on the road.

Chapter 22
Back in Hippos

The Commander and Rabbi Boni, after a breakneck ride, were approaching the fork in the road just north of the Hippos marketplace. The left road went around the east side of the marketplace and onto the road that led to the outpost. The right road went around the west side of the marketplace and to the small lane that led to the Synagogue compound. The two had decided to take the quickest route to their destinations. They had thanked each other for their help, said their goodbyes and wished each other good luck before the fork in the road came into sight. At the fork in the road, they split without slowing down, each to their duties and destiny.

The Rabbi slowed his horse so he could make the turn onto the small lane leading to the Synagogue. He had expected to see everyone running around waiting for him to give last minute instructions on what needed to be done to be ready for the arrival of their guests from Jerusalem. What he saw was a neat row of tents outside the meeting building, the grounds had never looked better and he could smell food cooking. Volunteers and a group of workers were sitting around waiting for the arrival of their guest. The Rabbi just sat there, on that beautiful horse, surveying what his parishioners had accomplished while he was gone. This is the way his mind had envisioned everything but he was expecting much less.

He was brought back to reality when a familiar voice said, "Are you going to sit on that poor horse that you almost rode to its death or are you getting off so this young man can take it to the stream for some water."

"I'm sorry, Mrs. Ruby. I was just admiring how much everyone has done since I've been gone."

"You had better get cleaned up. That fancy committee is due here in two hours and you look like you have been rolling in dirt. Be quiet when you go to your house, I don't want you to wakeup Merchant."

"Is Merchant here? How is he doing? How did you get him out of the infirmary?"

"Yes, he is here. He's doing much better. I stayed with him last night and the doctor and I decided he would recover quicker if I brought him here."

On the other side of the marketplace, the Commander brought his mount to a slow trot, just before he reached the road that paralleled the marketplace. The little village was already beginning to fill with merchants, all types of entertainers, Jewish scholars and families that were coming to see and hear what the special committee from Jerusalem was going to say or do.

Before he left to get Devas and his family, he gave instructions on where the security guards were to be placed and how they were to act. First they were not to just stand at a particular location and watch for trouble, they were to mingle with the crowds and prevent troubles from starting. None of the guards in the crowds were to be armed. Inside the outpost gate, out of sight, would be twenty armed cavalrymen that could be signaled if they were needed. Remembering that he was in civilian clothes, the Commander decided to dismount, tie his horse to one of the many hitching posts and walk through the marketplace to hear what the people were talking about and to get the general mood of the people.

Seeing about thirty people standing near the fountain at the center of the market place, the Commander stopped and pretended he was not paying attention to what was being said. There was one man with his back to the fountain that was answering questions that were shouted from the group around him.

"When is that special committee of distinguished priests and their aides supposed to get here?"

"Two rabbis along with four aides just arrived at the Synagogue compound. The rest of them are due in at four this afternoon. I hear that this so called 'secret, select committee' is the laughing stock of the nation. The joke going around is: "How long does it take a committee of Jewish Rabbis to get to Hippos from Jerusalem?"

"We give up. How long?"

"Five days maybe six."

The whole group roared with laughter.

"How is the search for the young man that Jesus healed going?"

"I hear that the Roman Commander and the local Rabbi found them and they are to be in here by ten o'clock tonight. They would have been here sooner, but one of the captains with the group was thrown from his horse and he went down a ravine and he is being rushed back here to the infirmary."

All of a sudden there was the loud sound of a team of horses pulling a wooden wagon with wood and metal wheels on a stone highway at high speed. The drivers were yelling to clear the way.

"That must be the injured captain there."

The Commander had heard enough and walked to his horse, shaking his head as he said to himself, "so much for secrecy." Mounting his horse while still shaking his head, he hurried off to the outpost.

The guards recognized the Commander and snapped to attention, salutes and said, "Welcome back Commander."

He rode to the stable, dismounted and asked the groom to walk his horse around until he cooled down and then give him some extra feed. Walking to the administration building he saw the guards were still keeping everyone away from the building and the two guards were making sure no one was on the roof.

One of the commander's aides met him at the door to the administration building.

He was curious what the aides answer would be so he asked, "What time is the committee from Jerusalem due in?"

"The trip from Jerusalem has been one disaster after another, so the main Rabbi has sent two rabbis along with four aides ahead of the main group. That group just passed the marketplace and should be entering the Synagogue compound now. The rest of the committee is expected to arrive at four today. There is a joke going around that asks how many hours."

"That's all right, I've heard it."

The Commander headed for the interrogation room to see how his aide was doing coaching the three soldiers to play the parts the Sanhedrim requested they be taught. The guard outside the door recognized the Commander and opened the door for him. He stepped into the room and sat in a chair just inside the door.

When the aide saw the Commander, he told the three performers to take a short break while he talked to the Commander.

"How are they doing?"

"Commander, you could not have selected three better soldiers to play the parts. At first I thought they would never understand that they were each playing the part of a person playing the part of another person. When they understood that, they had no problem learning what to say. I have played the part of a judge that asked them questions designed to confuse them and they gave the correct answers every time. They even coached each other on what to say."

"Part of the committee just arrived and the rest of the committee are due to arrive later today," the Commander told his aide.

"I thought they were due in today, I didn't know some of the committee were not coming in until tomorrow. That will give us more time to practice."

"I think you and I were the only people within a hundred miles that didn't know that the main group wouldn't be in until tomorrow. The earliest they will be called on to play their parts will be tomorrow afternoon. Give them the rest of the evening off and see that they get whatever they want for supper. Make sure they get a good night's sleep. Run them through a dress rehearsal tomorrow and have them relax until they are called on."

Chapter 23
Rabbi Abdon Arrives At Synagogue

The sound of two mules slowly pulling an old wooden wagon with wobbling wheels made of wood and metal, making uneven clanging on a stone road, could be heard as the wagon and its riders approached the Roman tax gate near the fishing pier.

"That must be Rabbi Abdon and another Rabbi with four of their aides. I heard that the committee from Jerusalem had so many problems on their trip they sent this group ahead to make sure everything was ready for some sort of a trial to be held when the whole "secret special committee of distinguished priests and their aides" get here tomorrow. Go ahead Tertius, raise the gate. The way that wagon sounds, I'm afraid if they stop they may not get started again."

"All right Longinus, but the rules say we don't raise the gate until we have checked their papers."

"You're right but when you have manned this gate as long I have, you can usually tell who is coming before you see them."

"How long have you been manning this gate?"

"I came here, as a new recruit over six years ago, just as you are now. The first night I was here I was assigned to guard this gate. It was cold, windy and raining that night and I was cold, wet and frightened. No one was around the pier or on the road. I had never felt so alone in all my life. Then I heard footsteps coming from the road to the marketplace. I yelled halt, who goes there? The steps kept coming towards me"

"Who was it? What were they doing out so late at night?"

"Hold on, let me finish my story. I shouted again, who goes there? The steps kept coming. Then a voice called my name. Longinus, Longinus."

"How did they know your name? Who was it?"

"Hold your horses, I'm getting to that. He called my name again and this time I yelled as loud as I could, who goes there? This time a friendly voice told me it was Rabbi Abdon. He told me the Commander had given him the names of the four new recruits and told him where they were standing watch. Rabbi Abdon made sure that he met each new soldier and invited them to come to the Synagogue compound anytime they wanted. I told him that I was not Jewish and he said that didn't matter to him and he was pretty sure God didn't care either. He told me that the older guards played tricks on the new guards by hiding the guard shack on them. He and I found where they hid the shack and we moved it back where it belonged. We sat in the shack for over an hour. He asked about me and my family and we talked as though we had been friends for years. Before he left, he invited me to attend the Mini Olympics he holds every year at the same time as the Greek Olympics."

"Boy, he sounds like a great guy."

The wagon was in sight now and it looked even worse than it sounded. Rabbi Abdon was driving, one of the aides was sitting next to him and the other four men were seated in the back of the wagon.

"Is that you Longinus? How are you? How are your mother, father and sisters?"

'They are all fine. You look great, welcome home."

"This will always be my home. I miss every one of you. Which one of the new recruits are you, son?"

"My name is Tertius."

"Oh, you are the young man from Kavalla, Greece. I love your city and hope we can find time while I'm here to talk about it. I hope you enjoy your time in Hippos."

"Please excuse us for not stopping but I'm afraid we won't be able to get this old buggy going again if we stop."

The mobility challenged wagon started up the road which had a slight upward grade. About one fourth of the way up the hill all the riders except the driver were behind the wagon pushing.

The wagon and its riders made it to the road that ran along the west side of the marketplace. When they reached the small road, about halfway up the marketplace that turned into the Synagogue compound, they heard a crack and a loud screech. Everyone except Rabbi Abdon jumped off the wagon. The Rabbi applied the same law of physics. "If you don't stop, you don't have to start again." The driver and the wagon went another one hundred feet and the rear axle snapped, sending the two wheels careening into the trees on either side of the road and the rear of the wagon onto the ground with a loud thud. Rabbi Abdon tumbled backwards off the driver's seat, rolled head over heels the entire length of the wagon bed and made two more complete revolutions on the ground and then unfurled face down on the road.

Rabbi Boni rushed to Rabbi Abdon shouting, "Are you all right?"

Rabbi Abdon struggled to his feet, began brushing the dirt off his robe and said," Now that's an entrance. Maybe you should include that move in your next Olympics."

"Welcome home," Rabbi Boni said. "I see you still have your sense of humor."

A crowd of old friends and well-wishers gathered around Rabbi Abdon. There were hugs, laughter, kisses and questions asked and questions answered.

"All right, all right. Give the man some room. He has work to do getting ready for that fancy committee that's coming from Jerusalem, if they ever get here. Someone take this Rabbi to his room in the meeting building and someone take these aides to their tent outside of the meeting building."

"Hi, Mrs. Ruby, you're just as pretty as I remembered you were."

"You don't look so bad yourself. Now give me a big hug and then you and this young kid you brought me two years ago can go to the house and talk. Be quiet when you go in, I don't want you to disturb Merchant"

"What is Merchant doing in your house?"

"Come on, I'll tell you all about it when we get there."

Rabbi Boni began by telling what had happened to Merchant. That led to the story about Delaeh's remarkable healing, the Roman Army searching for Devas' and Ezra's families, the rescue team that found them and when they were scheduled to arrive back in Hippos.

"So the young man that was healed in Capernaum was Delaeh."

"Yes"

"You have actually seen him. He can stand and walk and you are sure that this is actually our Delaeh?"

"Yes, and not only can he stand and walk, he can run and jump better than you or I ever could."

The two Rabbis could have talked for hours but they both knew that each had other pressing things to do.

Rabbi Abdon was the first to say, "We have other matters to take care of but I want to tell you what this so called "Secret Committee" is really coming here to do. They are here to stop all this talk about a Jewish Messiah that will free his people and set up His own kingdom. The Sanhedrim is being told by The Roman Empire to get their people under control or they will send in troops to stop all this talk of insurrection. I'll tell you more later but now I need to get ready for the rest of the committee's arrival.

Chapter 24
Back in Hippos
Waiting For
Devas' and Ezra's Family

The merchants were doing a booming business. A traveling theatrical group from Athens, Greece had built a stage near the northern part of the marketplace and the actors were mingling with the crowd, inviting everyone to come to the Greek play tonight.

The man, the Commander saw near the fountain at the center of the marketplace was still there. The crowd around him had grown from maybe thirty to over a hundred. His two cohorts gathered bits of information from people in the crowd and when they found something juicy they pushed their way through the crowds to bring him the latest bit of information. He would then combine the information, embellish it and then shout the latest news to all within ear shot.

Two young boys pushed their way up to the man that was shouting the latest news and began to tug on his cloak.

"Beat it kids, can't you see I'm busy."

"We have some news for you and its real, real good."

"Ok, Ok. Tell me your story."

"Not til you give each of us a coin."

"Beat it you little brats or I'll give each of you something upside your head."

"You'll be sorry, its real good news and if you don't want to be first we'll, sell our news to someone else."

The man reached out, grabbed both boys by an arm, gave them each a coin and said, "It had better be good."

"It is good, it's really good. That boy that lives here that Jesus made walk when he couldn't before, will be coming between those two building over there in three hours."

"Is that the boy the Romans have been looking for?"

"Yes sir. Now let us go."

"What's his name? Tell me everything you know about him."

"That'll cost you two more coins."

"Ok, you little thieves, here are your coins."

"My brother and me aren't thieves "

"OK! OK! Now tell me everything you know."

"His name is Delaeh, he use to run the fishing pier. Everybody here knows him and his family. He is with his father, mother, aunt, uncle, sister and cousin. His grandfather is the senior elder of Hippos."

"Tell me again, who is with him."

"Just say he is coming with his family. Now turn us loose or we'll start screaming."

The barker knew he had something good, so as soon as he got his thoughts together, he started shouting. "Gather around folks! Gather around! My highly paid reporters have just informed me that one of your very own home town heroes will be entering between those two buildings right over there. The one, the only Delaeh! You have seen him at the fishing pier. He was carried to Capernaum, just a few short days ago, on a stretcher where he was healed by that great healer, Jesus, and now within three short hours he will walk, yes I said walk, between those buildings right over there. He will have his family with him. You will see his father, his mother, his sister, his uncle, his aunt and his cousins. The whole Roman army has been searching for them for over a week and they could not find them. But I will bring them to you in just three short hours. Thank you for the small contributions you have placed in my basket for all the information I have shared with you so far. Now I must ask you to clear the area from here to the two buildings over there. My assistants will rope off this area and if you want to see this young boy walk, yes I said walk. I say walk, W A L K, into this area right here. He will walk among you and it will cost you only two denarius. Come back in one hour, get in line to pay the unbelievably small price of admission and be one of the first to witness this historical event."

Turning to his cronies, he whispered, "Get some rope and block off this part of the marketplace. Check with that old man that just walked out of that store. See if he will let us borrow enough rope, or talk him into renting used rope and we will pay him after we have collected from these suckers. I mean these discerning patrons of the finer things."

Grandfather had just walked out of his store to see what all the commotion was about. Two men, he had never seen before, walked up and asked if he had any rope they could borrow for two or three hours.

"What kind of rope do you want?"

"Any kind of rope that will keep the cheapoes out. I mean we want to let only the better people in this area."

"What area do you want to block off?"

"From your shop, across the alley, along your neighbor's store and out to the water fountain."

"What are you doing?"

"Don't worry old timer, you won't bother us, just go on with your business."

"My neighbor and I can't conduct our business if you block the entrances to our buildings."

"You are absolutely correct, why don't you and your neighbor close up for a few hours. For just two denarius you can be one of the first to greet that "home town hero" that everyone has been searching for."

"What "home town hero" are you talking about?"

"The boy that lives here, the one that Jesus made walk about a week ago. His name is Delaeh"

"I don't have rope that you can borrow or rent."

Grandfather walked back into his shop. He had been assured that his family was being protected by the Roman soldiers and that they were going to be brought home secretly. He was startled by the information he had received from the men looking for rope. Grandfather explained to grandmother that he had to warn their grandson, Delaeh and their sons, not to go into the marketplace. He hitched two mules to a new wagon and headed north to intercept his family before they reached the marketplace.

Chapter 25
Grandfather On His Way To Protect His Family

Grandfather was on the western road around the Hippos marketplace, headed north and it was crowded. He knew a path that would make his trip quicker but he was afraid that if he took it, he might miss his family. When he got to the place in the road where the roads that went around the Hippos marketplace met and turned north, he began to worry that his family may have taken the eastern road instead of the western road he was on. He wasn't sure if he should rush back to Hippos or continue on the northern road. Just as he was about to head back into town he heard a voice calling, "Grandfather! Grandfather! Wait!"

He turned around and there was Delaeh riding a horse.

Delaeh dismounted and walked over to grandfather's wagon.

Grandfather counted each beautiful step. He wanted to sit there and enjoy the moment but his mind jumped back to why he was there. "Where is the rest of the family?"

"They are about twenty minutes behind me,"

"Go back and tell them to turn off the road and go west until they see a path. When they get there tell them to turn south. I'll meet you there."

"You mean the old "Midnight Logging Trail?"

"Yes."

Grandfather watched as Delaeh ran to his horse, mounted and headed back to the group he was traveling with. Then grandfather headed to the "Midnight Logging Trail.

Grandfather headed north on the trail to shorten the time it would take to meet up with his family. When he saw them, he turned his wagon around. There was a very brief reunion and shifting some from the crowded wagon to Grandfather's wagon. After slightly over an hour's ride they came to a gate and a "DO NOT ENTER – MADMAN WITHIN" sign. Grandfather stopped the wagon and started to climb down to open the gate. Lydia said, "Are we supposed to go in there?"

The man sitting next to Grandfather turned around and said to Lydia, "It's all right, that madman hasn't been there in over thirty five years."

Grandfather was surprised that this person sitting next to him knew how long it had been since Palti had beaten those four boys that were pestering him on that night so long ago. How Patti's mother and he searched those woods for weeks trying to fine him, but he was gone. Grandfather stared at the man for a few moments and said, "Is that you, Palti?"

"Yes, it is. Let me open the gate. I've wanted to open that gate for years."

The gate was opened to let them through and then it was closed.

Palti climbed back on the wagon and asked Grandfather, "Why do you still have that sign on the gate?"

"When my grandfather took over this forest area for the Roman Empire, he selected this part of the forest to be preserved in its natural state. The trees were never to be cut down. The trees here were the oldest and best trees in the forest and they produced the best saplings for replacing trees that were cut down. Every summer he would pay the young children to gather stones from the fields and build a fence around those forty acres to remind people never to damage this part of the forest."

"Did the fence keep people out of here?"

"Oh. We wanted people to come in and enjoy this beautiful forest; we just wanted them to respect it and not harm it. If we lose these trees, we will never be able to replace them."

"Grandfather," Joshua asked. "Did my father and uncle work on the fence when they were little?"

"They sure did and so did Palti. I know someone else that worked on that fence when they were young and you know them also."

Lydia said, "Who were they?"

"I'll tell you later when Grandmother and I come back tonight. First I'll go into town, find out what is happening and

Grandmother and I will come back later. But now I need to show you where the best camping site is."

"I'll take them there."

"Thanks Palti. I'll be back just as soon as I can get here. Grandmother and I will bring food for a cookout."

Chapter 26
Grandfather Back At
The Marketplace

Grandfather parked his wagon across from his store. He could see the men had found some rope and had cordoned off the area in front of his and his neighbor's stores and all the way to the fountain in the center of the marketplace. There was only one place to enter this temporary enclosure and a man was there taking money from anyone wanting to get in.

The same barker was still there shouting out what he called the latest news. He was shouting out enough facts so that what he was saying wasn't lying but what he was shouting was a long way from the truth. "Come on in folks there's a plenty of room! Don't miss the greatest show on earth! They will walk among you and it will only cost you four denarius!"

"Wait! Wait, Folks!" The barker bent down to listen to the two small boys. After negotiating with the boys and hearing their latest report. He straightened up and began calling out, "Wait! Wait, Folks! My highly paid reporters have just informed me that not only will one of your very own home town heroes and his family be entering between those two buildings, right over there. You will also see the man you have been hearing about all day. The man that saw Jesus made a whole herd of pigs run off a cliff into the sea. He saw it all! Now you can hear him tell the story in his very own words! It will cost you only five denarius! Go away kids get me more news."

"Not til you pay us."

"Here's your coins. What's a matter you don't trust me?"

"No we don't."

Grandfather walked away shaking his head. When he walked through the back door of his store, Grandmother was eagerly waiting for news about their family.

"I took them up to the ridge overlooking the sea in the old forest. They are all fine and you'll never guess who is with them."

"First tell me is…."

"Yes, Delaeh is walking. I could hardly take my eyes off of him."

"Tell me who else is with them?"

"Palti"

"You mean Ruby's boy?"

"Should you have left our family up there with him?"

"Mother, he is the nicest acting gentleman you will ever meet."

Grandfather asked Grandmother to get some food ready to take up to the camp site while he walked through the village and the Synagogue compound to see what was happening.

Grandfather walked out the backdoor, turned right, and walked along the north end of the marketplace until he was beyond all the people between the ropes. He walked between two of the merchant buildings and was now where the travelling theatrical group had built a stage. This group had been here last year and every one in Hippos enjoyed their production, especially the children. This year they had many of the same actors they had last year and were planning to present another Greek play. This was one of Grandfather's favorite traveling groups and he knew the director and most of the actors. Grandfather went up to the director to welcome him back to Hippos and to say he was looking forward to seeing their performance tonight.

Titus, the director said, "You are the only one in Hippos that wants to see our play. No one is buying tickets; they spent all their money to see your family walk back into town. All everyone in this town wants to talk about is how your family took your grandson to Capernaum to be healed by that fellow Jesus and how he was healed. No one wants to come to a Greek Play, so, we have changed all our stage and I have written all new parts for the actors. We are going to put on a play about your grandson. I'm going to the Synagogue later today to see if I can talk to a fellow named Merchant. I've been told he was there when Delaeh was healed and was the first to tell the story."

"When do you plan to have your first performance?"

"Tomorrow afternoon."

"I'll be back in about an hour and will introduce you to some people that can help you write your play."

Grandfather wished them good luck and continued his walk through the marketplace. Then he headed to the Synagogue. The marketplace was crowded but other than the roped off section you could walk without pushing your way through. (Many of the Jewish leaders had come to see and to be seen by the leader of the "Distinguished Committee" from Jerusalem had started leaving the marketplace and were gathering at the Synagogue compound.) The "Distinguished Committee" had arrived earlier while Grandfather was on his family rescue mission. The committee took over an hour to walk through the marketplace on their way to their temporary headquarters. They stopped frequently to shake hands and to talk to anyone wanting to greet them. Many of them were dressed in robes identifying them as holding a position of honor in the Jewish religion.

The Roman soldiers were walking about unarmed, but courteously making their presence known. A soldier that had just reported for watch duty was telling another soldier that the Captain that had been rushed to the infirmary was doing better. He had three broken ribs and was covered with cuts and bruises. The doctor said he would be fine in a few weeks.

Grandfather completed his walk through the marketplace and headed for the Synagogue compound to see what was happening there. Walking down the little lane that led to the compound, he noticed four wagons he had never seen before. He could not resist taking a closer look. Placing his hand on the top of one of the wheels and giving a light pull almost caused the wheel to come off the axel. Part of the side boards were missing and a good part of the floor boards were gone. Scratching his shaking head, he said to himself, "No wonder it took them seven days to get here. I'm surprised they made it at all."

A voice from a little way down the lane said, "It actually took them eight days. You haven't changed a bit; you still can't pass a wagon without checking it over."

"Rabbi Abdon. We sure have missed you."

"I miss all you folks in Hippos, especially your family. Tell me is it true that Delaeh is walking?"

"You have been such a blessing to my family and everyone that lives in our village. We miss you also. I saw him for the first time about five hours ago two miles north of the marketplace. He rode up on a large military horse. When he saw me, he dismounted and walked over and gave me a big hug."

"I can't wait to see him."

"I'll tell you a secret, he is with his family on the ridge in the forest. Grandmother and I are going up there tonight. Do you think you and Rabbi Boni can slip away and meet us there in a couple hours?"

"I'm sure we can. Rabbi Boni and I are to meet with the chairman in fifteen minutes. The chairman has had a hard trip so the meeting won't last long. I'm sure he will be turning in early."

"What is this committee chairman like? He seems to be rather pious and shows no concern for the Jewish people outside of Jerusalem. Some even talk about him as a puppet for the Roman Empire."

"He really is a nice fellow and he is totally dedicated to our faith. He was brought into the Sanhedrin, many years ago, because of his dedication to researching the old scriptures and interpreting them so they have a clearer meaning in today's world. His writings and teaching have guided many a young Rabbi and even some of us older Rabbis. He is the reason I was called to Jerusalem. He told me that he was so involved in juggling the religious interests of Jews and the political interests of Rome that he needed someone to continue searching the scriptures for their true meaning. He told me the Sanhedrin sent him on this trip to find anything to discredit John the Baptist and Jesus of Nazareth. He feels they are more interested in proving someone was not the Messiah than they are in finding out what the scriptures say about the Messiah.

There has been a lot of talk and laughter about the committee taking so long to get here. We did have old wagons and we brought more stuff then we needed, but the real reason we were traveling so slowly was the chairman wanted to talk to people along the way to find out what they were concerned about. When the chairman realized we were going to take so much time getting to Hippos, he told me about the Roman plan to claim that Devas' healing was a conspiracy carried out by the followers of Jesus. The chairman and I have talked about my experiences in Hippos and particularly about your family and he wanted me to get here as soon as I could to find out what was the truth about Delaeh's healing. The Romans have threatened to annihilate everyone that is Jewish before, but this time they are already making plans to concentrate on the opposition around the Sea of Galilee. They are threatening to destroy the Temple in Jerusalem and the entire city. The Sanhedrin is convinced that if we do not stop all this talk about a new King of the Jews the Romans will do what they are threatening to do."

Grandfather left to get Grandmother so they could join the children at their camp site. Just as he reached the end of the lane from the Synagogue, he saw three men hiding behind the last wagon the committee rode in on. Grandfather asked what they were doing and got a sheepish whisper back. "We're hiding from all the people that paid us to show them this Delaeh boy that Jesus healed. When the boy didn't show up, we ran with the money. Will you check the main road and tell us if you see anyone looking for us?"

Grandfather recognized the barker and his cohorts and told them to stay there and he would see if anyone was still looking for them. As he reached the road, he saw several people looking in the bushes. He walked over to them and said, "The fellows you're looking for are over there."

Chapter 27
Campsite In Hippos

By the time Grandfather walked back to his home and business, Grandmother had gathered enough food to feed a small army. Grandfather stopped at the stage and asked Titus, the play director, to join him for a walk in the forest. All the food was packed into a small cart that was pulled by a mule and they were off to the camp site. Entering the gate with the sign that said, "DO NOT ENTER – MADMAN WITHIN", they continued up a small trail that led to the ridge that overlooked the sea. The closer they got to the camp site the more talking and laughter they heard. When they were close enough to see and hear their family, they stopped to enjoy and just watched for a few minutes. When Grandfather and Grandmother walked into the camp site they were greeted with hugs and kisses. Grandmother could not take her eyes off Delaeh.

Grandfather said, "This is Titus. He is a friend and the director of the traveling performing group that is putting on a play tomorrow in the marketplace. After we eat, he would like to ask you some questions."

"Come here Mother I want you to look at this gentleman and tell me who he is."

"Oh. I know who he is. How are you, Palti?"

"I have never been better."

"Have you seen your mother yet?"

"I plan to see her tonight."

Joshua said, "Grandfather you promised to tell us who else worked on the stone wall when they were young."

"Ok. Ok. Everyone have a seat and I'll tell you about building the stone wall around the forest. You know the story about how your Great Great Grandfather came here to locate the forest that had been supplying quality wood needed to build ships for the Roman Empire and how the people that were here before he got here were stealing trees and destroying the forest. Who here remembers that your Great Great Grandfather was a one armed….? All right, All right. Put your hands down. I know I have told you that part of the story before."

"Just tell them who else worked on the stone wall. You don't have to go back to the pyramids."

"OK, Grandmother. I'll start my story. My father told me the farmers were having problems with stones in their fields. Our village had grown where we needed to grow more of our food here in Hippos and the stones were damaging the tools used to prepare the fields. Then he told me he could sure use the stones that were in the fields to build the fence around the forest. This was my father's way of getting something done. He identifies a problem, states a possible solution and leaves me to work out the details."

"Devas was nine years old and Ezra was seven years old and we wanted to get more involved with the young people in our village. We agreed that I would work with the boys and Grandmother would work with the girls. Back then we had not built our Synagogue. We had a few tables and benches in the field where the Synagogue is now. Sometimes we had a Rabbi that would conduct Sabbath services around those benches and when we did not have a Rabbi, on the Sabbath, one of the elders would read from the scriptures. We met every Sabbath with or without a Rabbi. During the week Grandmother and I asked the mothers to bring their children to what we now call the "Synagogue compound" at ten in the morning on Mondays and Thursdays and to pick them up at three in the afternoon. I taught the boys about fishing, farming, tree growing, building and sailing. We built our own sail boats, took trips to see the woodsmen cut trees and many other exciting adventures. Our first project was to have the boys find rocks in the farmer's fields and bring them to where the stone fence was to be built. This helped the farmers and gave us stones we needed for the wall around the forest. Each little boy tried to outdo the other boys by getting the biggest stones. Big stones are good for building a stone fence, but when you put one big stone on top of other big stone you get a wobbly wall. You need some smaller stones placed between the big stones to stop the big stones from wobbling. No matter how hard I tried to get the boys to bring in some smaller stones along with the larger stones, they continued to try to bring in the biggest stones they could find. I guess little boys are going be little boys. I think they were trying to impress the girls."

Grandmother was teaching the girls how to cook, sew, preserve food and some of the girls learned how to clean fish.

One night I told Grandmother about the problem, I was having getting the boys to bring in some smaller stones along with the bigger stones. Grandmother said the girls had shown a lot of interest in what was going on where I and the boys were building the stone wall. I am having a hard time teaching them because they are more interested in what's going on over there than they are in what I'm trying to teach them. She suggested that she could ask the girls to gather the smaller stones from the farms and bring them here.

On the next Thursday morning, the boys were all standing around a large pile of assorted size stones next to the large stones. The boys were pointing at the new pile of smaller stones and laughing and saying things like:

"Who brought them tiny silly rocks here?"

"I bet it was them silly little girls."

One boy turned and yelled to the girls, "You better come get them rocks before the wind blow em away."

That was all the teasing one little girl could take. She strutted over to where the boys had gathered around the rocks, put her hands on her hips and said, "You boys don't know anything about building a stone fence."

"Do to. You girls don't know nothing' bout builden nothing' specially bout stone walls."

"We do so."

"No you don't"

"We do so and I bet we can build a stone wall, better than any boys can."

"OK, next Thursday we will have a contest to see who can build a better stone wall."

"Go ahead Devas, tell her after we beat her building' the stone wall, we'll beat her in a sail boat race to."

"Now that's just plain mean Ezra. You know I'm afraid of the water."

"Everybody knows you're afraid of the water. We all saw

you when your family first sailed into the pier. You jumped off the boat yelling you would never get on another boat again as long as you lived and that they were mean to make you get on the boat this time. If I was that afraid of the water, I would move to the desert."

One of the girls ran over to take her friend back to the girl's side of the field. "Come on Esther; don't pay any mind to Ezra. He's just plain mean."

"Thank you Ruth. You know that boy is so mean and his older brother isn't any better. I don't know how anyone can stand to be around them."

"You're right. Let's never have anything to do with them ever again."

"Grandmother and I made up the rules for the stone wall building contest. First we'll mark a one hundred foot line on the ground where we need the real wall to be built. That way if any of the contest walls are good enough to keep we could leave them there as a part of the real wall."

"The boys would start from the west end of the line and the girls would start from the east end of the line. Each team will have two men to help them move and stack the stones that each team captain choses and place them where they are told to place them. The piles of stones and rocks were located equal distance from the east and west end of the one hundred foot line. Both teams will start at the same time and will be allowed three hours to build their wall. When I yell stop each team will stop and stand behind the wall they built. We will have three of the town's elder to say which team built the best wall. The judges will go to the boys' wall first and measure the height of the wall and the length. After the judges have completed walking around and measuring the wall, the team captain will have five minutes to point out why he thinks the boys' wall is better than the girls' wall. Then the judges will go to the girls' wall, walk around it and measure it just as they did at the boys' wall. Then the girls' team captain will have five minutes to tell why their wall is better than the boys' wall. The judges will make their decision and announce the winner. Are there any questions?"

"Yes, I have a question. When the girls see that we are going to win and they start crying will the judges let them win to stop them from crying?"

"No, Ezra. The judges are only going to judge which wall is better."

"I have a suggestion."

"Yes, Esther, what is your suggestion?"

"I think each team should take the judges to the other team's wall and point out what is wrong with their wall before the judges chose the winner."

"That's a very good suggestion Esther."

The next Monday found the boys busy checking the stone pile, looking for the largest stones and talking about how they were going to show them girls who were the best stone wall builders.

"Grandmother and I agreed to let the boys and girls do their own planning for the big contest, while we made sure everyone knew what the rules were. I was busy marking the one hundred foot line where we wanted the final location of the stone wall. Every time I looked toward the girl's area I saw Grandmother talking to them or walking the fifty foot line where the girls were to build their contest wall. It didn't take long for me to realize she had stopped being a neutral observer and had taken on the position of head coach. I maintained my neutral position as we had agreed." Fifteen girls and twenty boys showed up the morning of the contest. We expected that many children but had no idea at least one hundred parents and all the village elders would be there."

The countdown began…X, IX, VIII, VII, V1, V, IV, III, 1l, I. GO!

Half of the boys ran to the pile of large stones and selected the largest stones. Two boys ran to the fifty foot marker, where they could watch what the girls were doing, and to shout appropriate or inappropriate comments, depending on who you were cheering for. The other boys were busy pointing where the men were to place the stones.

On the other end four girls were clearing the weeds, sticks and small rocks. Four girls followed them digging with tools they had brought from their homes. Two girls were checking the depth of the trench with six inch sticks. Three girls were rushing back and forth, gathering various size stones from the small stone pile and the remaining two girls were selecting large stones for the assigned stone carrying men to be placed in the trench as soon as the measuring girls indicated the trench was ready.

When the trench was twelve feet long and at the right depth, all but the two girls that were in charge of measuring shifted their efforts to forcing small stones and rocks between the large stones until each stone was solidly in place. The two girls measuring the trench put their six inch sticks aside and picked up their precut three foot six inch sticks and continued to show the girls responsible for building the wall, how high to make the wall from the bottom of the trench.

The two boys standing at the fifty foot marker were laughing and shouting things like: "Why you digging, are you building a wall or planting a garden?"

"Does your mother know you're playing in dirt?"

"Grandfather, finish telling your story so we can eat."

"All right Grandmother. The three hours are up. I am starting the countdown. X, IX, VIII, VII, V1, V, IV, III, 1l, I stop and stand near your walls."

The judges measured the height and the length of the boys' wall and announced that the height of the wall was at least three foot tall and at some places the wall was three foot eight inches high. The total length of the boys' wall is forty two feet. The boys and most of the men watching gave a big cheer. The judges asked Devas to walk around their wall with them and tell them why their wall was better than the girls' wall.

"The first thing it is forty two feet long. All of our wall can be seen. We didn't waste no time putting stones underground where you can't see em' We only used the biggest stones. We didn't use them small rocks like them girls did. Did I mention that the boy's wall is forty two feet long?"

The judges walked to the girls' wall, measured the height and the length of the wall and announced that the height of the wall was exactly three foot high. The total length of the girls' wall is twelve feet long. The boys and most of the men watching gave a big cheer. The judges asked Esther to walk around their wall with them and tell them why their wall was better than the boys' wall.

"We put the first six inches underground to make the wall stronger and to keep the dirt under the wall from washing away when it rains. The boys' wall will fall down after a few rains and our wall looks better than theirs.

We made our wall exactly three feet tall and it looks better than the boys' wall. If you bend down, you will note that you cannot see through our wall. That is because we wanted to make sure our wall would not be wobbly so we filled in all the void spaces to make the walls strong and last a long time. I also think our wall looks a lot better than the boys' wall. The stones we...."

"I'm sorry Esther but your five minutes are up."

"Oh, I'm sorry that I took more time than allotted but don't you just love the way our wall looks?"

"Girls, if you will walk to the boys' wall and wait there while the boys come to your wall to tell the judges why their wall is better than your wall."

The boys were pointing at the twelve foot wall and laughing.

"What have they been doing, having a tea party?"

"That's enough Ezra. Now let Devas tell the judges what he thinks is wrong with the girl's wall."

"It's only twelve feet long, ain't that enough? Part of the first stones is underground. That's a waste of stones. You can't see through their wall. Those little silly stones make the wall look sissy. It's only twelve feet long. You remember our wall is forty two feet long, don't you?"

"Thank you boys, now go down and stand at the fifty foot mark while the judges meet the girls at your wall."

"Ok, but remember crying don't count."

"Yes, I remember Ezra."

"Well the first thing I see is how crooked the wall is. The top of the wall curves up and down so much that I almost get seasick looking at it."

"A bowl of water makes her seasick."

"That enough Devas. Let Esther talk to the judges."

"Oh, he doesn't bother me, he's just mean."

"So is his brother."

"Girls you only have one minute left to tell the judges why your wall is better than the boys' wall."

"That's plenty of time to show the judges why our wall is better than the boys' wall. All right girls line up along the boys' wall. On the count of III, do what we practiced. I, II, III, push." The boys' wall came down like the walls of Jericho.

"Come on boys, if they want to play that way we'll show em."

All twenty of the boys got on one side of the girls' wall and started to push. Nothing happened so they tried again. Nothing happened.

After the boys pushed for the IVth time, and the wall was still standing, the girls walked up and said, "Remember crying doesn't count."

"Ok. The food is ready," Grandmother shouted.

"Who won the wall building contest?"

"I'll tell you later Joshua after we have eaten."

Chapter 28
How Grandfather Got To Hippos

Grandfather and Titus walked over to the cliff where they could look out over the Sea of Galilee. The night was beautiful and the sky was filled with stars.

"Thanks for inviting me to come with you tonight. You are truly blessed to have such a wonderful family and a lovely place like Hippos to live."

"I'm glad you came. Everyone is excited to have you here and can hardly wait to watch the play tomorrow. I hope you got all the information you need to finish writing your play."

"I learned a lot about, now Mrs. Ruby and her family got here and how your family helped them get settled. I know the history of the Rabbis that have served here and a lot about the people that live here but I don't know how your family ended up here."

"Let me see, how do I begin?"

"I'll tell you. You can begin by coming over here and saying the blessing so we can start eating."

"O K, Mother, I'm coming. Come on Titus, I'll tell you how we got here while we are eating."

Grandfather loved to tell how his family came to live in Hippos, especially to someone that had never heard the story before. So between bites of food and the many heckling interruptions from friends and family, Grandfather started telling his often told story to Titus. When he came to parts of the story that were real familiar to his friends and family they would chime in, word for word, telling that part of the story. "My family lived in Kavalla, Greece which is a seaport city on the Aegean Sea. Almost 180 years ago, a boy was born to a Greek ship's carpenter and his wife. That baby would eventually become my grandfather. The boy grew up working alongside his father and by the time he was sixteen years old, he knew how to build ships and more importantly he knew how to grow and select the finest wood for building ships.

The Greek Empire had controlled most of the lands around the Mediterranean for well over two hundred years when Grand Father was born. The Greeks were building large metropolitan cities-states throughout the areas they controlled and had brought laws, culture, mathematics and other scientific enlightenments to the people under their control. The Greek political rulers began to lose control of the military leaders. Greek generals and admirals fought each other for control of various parts of the Greek Empire. Before long the Greek Empire was challenged by the Roman Empire and in the year my Grandfather was born the Roman Empire officially conquered the Greek Empire.

The Romans realized if they were going to maintain control of the territories they had conquered, they needed as large a fleet of war ships, as they could get. This led to a period of time, when ship building consumed most of the select wood in this part of the world. By the time Grandfather was eighteen, the Roman Navy was sending him all around the Mediterranean Sea in search of the best trees that could be used to build more ships. By the time he was twenty one, he commanded four ships that did nothing but locate the finest wood and carried it back to Kavalla. Because the demand was so great for wood, he noticed that the wood he had to select from was of less quality than he wanted. The one port, where he knew he could get the finest wood, was Haifa, Israel. The quality was always good, but the quantity was less each time he sailed in to pick up wood.

When they approached Haifa on their next visit, the port master signaled that there was enough wood to fill two ships. The decision was made to send one ship to pick up wood from one of the other ports, while Grandfather sailed the remaining ships into Haifa. He oversaw the loading of the two ships and sent them back to Kavalla. He and a few members of his crew would travel inland to see the forest where the trees were being cut. Once they had obtained horses and a map showing them how to get to the forest, they were off.

The first days ride had been hurried with little time to look around. Their thoughts were on getting as far as they could before the sun set. They had been warned that night travel was not recommended in the area where they were headed. Sitting around the camp fire that night and looking up at the stars Grandfather's mind wondered back to stories that his Grandfather had told him about how their ancestors were a part of the Eastern tribe of Manasseh. He remembered some talked about the Greek army capturing that part of Israel and carrying our people back to Kavalla to work building ships. He laid there with his head resting on a bolder gazing at the stars. That night he spent partly awake, partly dreaming, partly day dreaming and partly recalling stories the Rabbis and his family had regaled him with during his youth. These stories were about God promising this very land, that he was lying on, to Abraham, Isaac, Jacob and Moses. In the morning he awoke feeling rested and refreshed. He no longer felt as though he was a stranger in a foreign land. He had a strong sense that he belonged here.

    They continued their hurried ride to the forest but now he was more aware of his surroundings. The trail began to get steeper and after an hour of steady climbing they reached the top of what their map indicated was Mount Tabor. The view was magnificent. They could see a large body of water straight ahead and slightly to the left and a river directly in front of them. There was a tall hill that looked almost like a horse's head with a tall stand of trees on top. Checking the map they could see the large body of water, was the Sea of Galilee, the river was the Jordan River and the horse head shaped hill indicated where the forest was. The decent from Mount Tabor was steep but when they reached the bottom, the rest of the ride was on level ground.

    Crossing the Jordan River, turning north and keeping the horse head hill in their sight, they rode for about an hour, when they began seeing where a large number of trees had been cut down and there had been no attempt to replant the area that had been cut. In the distance they saw a forest of tall trees. As they got near the standing trees they were confronted by three men that appeared to be in charge of the tree operation. Grandfather identified himself and explained that he would like to go through the forest and inventory the remaining trees. He asked why they were not planting young trees where they had cut the older trees down.

    The lead man said, "We was sent here three years ago to cut down them trees, pull them over there and slide them into the sea.

Someone else comes here, floats the trees across the sea, pulls them out on the other side and drags them to Haifa. We ain't gonna get out of here until all them doggone trees is cut down so we sure ain't gonna plant no new ones."

Realizing there was nothing to be gained by trying to explain to these men how valuable these trees were or how important it was to make sure new trees replaced the ones cut down, he thanked the men and said he would spend a few days inventorying and mapping the forest and they would be leaving.

In order to establish the total size of the property the team rode around the property to locate and carefully plot every property marker. They then plotted the forest areas indicating the size of the areas, the quantity and quality of the trees and whether the trees had been cut. The total property contained four thousand seven hundred acres. The total forested area, including the areas that had been cut within the last three years, was two thousand, three hundred acres. The area already cut was one thousand, one hundred acres, leaving one thousand, two hundred acres of uncut premium trees. Some quick calculations showed that at the rate they were cutting the trees, the forest would be gone in a little over three years. It was also clear that all the cut trees were not being sent to Haifa. There was a trail leading off to the north that was caused by logs being dragged in that direction. The survey crew explored the trails a short way and found large quantities of select trees waiting to be picked up by someone other than the Romans. Apparently the men, in charge of the cutting crew, were selling these logs to someone else and pocketing the money.

The survey crew felt they were being followed from the first time they met the three men in charge of the cutting crew. Now they were sure they had been followed. It was one thing to be accused of using poor forestry practices but to be caught stealing from the Roman Empire meant death.

For the last hour there had been almost no noise. The noise of men hacking away at trees had stopped. It had been awhile since they heard a tree fall or the sound of oxen dragging trees.

Grandfather motioned for his crew to stay on their horses and to ride close to him.

"We need to slowly ride back to the road used to get the logs into the water. Once we are off this northern trail we will stop at the stream, dismount, and give the horses water and time to rest awhile. You men know as well as I do that these men have no intension of letting us get out of here alive. In a couple minutes, I'm going to mount up and start riding slowly back to where we entered this property. When I'm twenty feet down the road, you mount up and follow me. Remember our plan is to break through their lines and get back to our ship. We are not interested in fighting them. We'll let the Roman Empire do that."

The area they were in now was open. The trees were at least fifty feet away on both sides of the road, but up ahead the trees were no more than five feet on either side of the road. The first hundred feet into the narrow path gave everyone an eerie feeling but nothing happened. Then one hundred feet ahead one of the men they met when they arrived, was sitting on a horse with his sword held over his head. Glancing back to make sure his crew was there, he saw the two other men they had met charging up the road behind them with their swords ready for battle. He whipped his horse and motioned for his men to follow him into the forest at the side of the road. A few steps into the forest and they were met by a line of over twenty big woodsmen with axes ready to swing. The five horses reared up causing two of his crew to hit the ground. Grandfather drew his knife and started to jump from his horse to help his fallen crewmen when one of the big woodsmen ran up and said, "Don't get off; we'll help them get back on their horse. Run, tell Rome what is happening here. Please help us."

The captain could see the woodsmen were acting as if they were fighting with the fallen riders, but in fact were holding their horses as they helped them get back on. He hesitated a moment, to make sure his men were on their horses and riding away. He thought for sure they were all going to die right there. The two fallen crewmen joined the other escaping crew members. As Grandfather turned to join them, he saw a flash and felt cold steel slice his arm. One of the riders that had rushed up from the rear raised his sword for a fatal blow, when one of the woodsmen delivered a knockout blow to his head with a piece of wood. The horses, the two remaining crooks were on, were no match for the horses of the fleeing crewmen even with the trail of blood gushing from Grandfather's arm.

Once their pursuers had given up their pursuit, they stopped to see how badly Grandfather was cut. The wound was deep and had nearly severed his arm. A tourniquet was placed on his arm, the wound was cleaned and dressed as best they could.

In a weak voice he said, "I can't keep up with you and it is important that what we have found out gets to Kavalla. Two of you go to the ship. Tell the Harbor Master that I had some other business to take care of and will be there in two days. Act as though nothing has happened and tell no one what we have found out. When you get there, complete loading the ship and anchor out in the harbor. Post guards and let no one come on board for any reason. If we are not there in two days, take the ship to Kavalla and give our report to the Admiral.

The five shipmates stayed together until they reached the base of Mount Tabor. When they were sure they were not being followed, two of the fleeing riders rushed back to their ship in Haifa and sailed for Kavalla. The remaining three riders started their slow ascend up Mount Tabor. The other riders staying with Grandfather could see that he was getting weaker. The bleeding had stopped but he was pale and he was warm to the touch. When they reached the top of Mount Tabor, he sat up in his saddle, looked over his reclaimed home land and said, "If I must die let me die looking at the land God has given my people. I have one regret."

"What would that be?"

"I have no children to carry on after me. I feel like Moses as he stood on Mount Nebo overlooking the Promised Land. God allowed him to see the Promised Land but he could not enter it."

"You will be back to walk your Homeland again in peace. We are going to see that you will be well again. Let us help you off your horse. You will feel better after a short rest."

"Please help me off and lean me against that acacia trees so that I may die looking at my land."

His two companions realized their job was no longer getting him to the ship. Their job now was to keep him comfortable until he died. Both man dropped to their knees and prayed. "Oh God only a miracle can keep this man alive to serve you. Please, we pray send a miracle now."

Suddenly a voice said, "I hope we're not too late." The two praying companions almost died of fright right there on Mount Tabor.

"I'm sorry; I didn't mean to frighten you. Two riders stopped us a little way down the road and asked us if we knew where a doctor was that could help a severally wounded man, that should be near the top of Mount Tabor. I am a physician that has served in both the Greek and Roman army and my wife is my assistant. Let me look at the patient."

The physician and his assistant began their examination. He and his assistant conferred a little, felt their patients head with the back of their hand, lifted his eye lids and stood up.

"Can you help him?" Both companions asked at the same time.

"Oh, he is just fine," the physician said.

"What do you mean he is just fine? He is almost dead."

"I mean he is unconscious. For what we are about to do, we prefer he be unconscious and believe he does too."

Once the arm was removed, he was placed in the Good Doctor's wagon and carried to the doctor's home in Nazareth where he could get the attention he needed.

When they did not show up in Haifa by the time they hoped they would, the ship's crew followed orders and set sail for Kavalla. On the morning of the sixth day they pulled into the harbor at Kavalla and dropped anchor. The two men that had been on the trip to survey the forest got into a roll boat and headed for the office of the admiralty. They carried with them all the drawings and notes the survey party had prepared. They were greeted by a young officer who looked up and asked what they wanted.

"We wish to speak with the Admiral."

"What is the nature of your business?"

"Our business is for the Admiral's ears only."

"Do you have an appointment?"

"We ain't part of your regular Navy, we're part of the Merchant Navy. Now wipe that silly smirk off your face and tell the old man we are here."

The Admiral heard the rather loud voice coming from the outer office, got up and walked to the door.
"What's going on out here?" He recognized two of the members of the survey team he had sent to Haifa. "Welcome boys, come on in. Where is that young captain of yours?"

Once the door was shut the Admiral heard the full story, looked at the drawings and read the report including the Captains recommendations. The Admiral pondered a few moments, stood up, patted the two men on the shoulders and said, "Well done men, I'm proud of you and your whole crew. Now let's get those men back here and get this mess straightened out."

He opened the door and told his aide to get his full staff in his office now.

The Admiral started by briefing everyone on what he had just learned about the premium wood forest operation they had started three years ago in Israel. "These brave men have endangered their lives to bring us this report and these drawings indicating the exact location of the forest and its present condition. We do not know about two of the survey team but we believe one of our best merchant captains gave his life making sure we received this report." The meeting ended with the Admiral reviewing the plan decided on in the meeting.

The two merchant sailors that brought the report were each advanced to the rank of captain. One would command the ship that brought the report. On this mission the ship would carry four of the finest Roman soldiers armed with swords and knives and wearing merchant sailor clothing. These men would board the ship at three in the morning. This ship would sail directly to Haifa, pull into port and the captain would lead a five men search party to the forest just as they did before. They would use horses that the Harbor Master kept for people travelling inland. On this trip they will meet up with the twenty soldiers and captain that would be on the second ship in a village called Zippori.

The other new captain would command one of the other wood carrying merchant ships. On this mission the ship would carry twenty of the finest Roman soldiers armed with swords and knives and wearing merchant sailor clothing.

These men along with their horses would board the ship at three in the morning.

This ship would sail directly to a location six miles south of Haifa, where there was an unattended harbor with a pier that would allow the riders and their horses to be off loaded without being seen. The soldiers and the captain would meet up with the four soldiers and the captain in Zippori.

From there they would follow the same route as before but now they would send scouting parties into all the little towns and villages to search for their three missing seamen. When they reached Mount Tabor, the two new captains would lead three of the soldiers down to the forest. The remaining soldiers would follow a short distance behind the lead group. Your mission is to locate the captain and his two ship mates and bring them home. Capture the three leaders we sent there three years ago and bring them back to stand trial.

We are trying something new on this mission. I am sending a man with you that has been trained to handle homing pigeons for the last year. He will be carrying six trained homing pigeons with him and six pairs of pigeons that will be the start of a system that will allow us to communicate with that area.

The trip to Haifa and the abandoned port just south of Haifa went as planned. The five men going ashore in Haifa obtained horses from the Harbor Master and met up with the twenty two other companions at Zippori. The closest village was Nazareth so the first search party, looking for the missing captain and two sailors headed for Nazareth. As soon as they began inquiring about an injured man, they were told to check at the physician's home. The doctor's wife told them about finding the injured man on top of Mount Tabor and treating him.

"How badly was he injured?"

"The doctor and I had to amputate his arm. Then we brought him here to nurse him back to health. We almost lost him several times, but he is improving each day."

"May we see him?"

"He's not here now. The whole time he was delirious he kept saying those workers need my help. We kept telling him he needed more time to heal."

"Where is he now?"

"He kept insisting that he had to go to the forest to help those workers. My husband finally agreed to let him go but only if he rode in the wagon and he went with him. He, my husband and the two sailors left three days ago."

The search party thanked the good doctor's wife and rushed back to tell the rest of the group what they had found out.

"Shall I send a message back to Kavalla telling them that we know where the captain is?"

"No. Not until I see him."

The decision was made to ride as rapidly as possible to the forest. They reached the top of Mount Tabor as the sun was setting. They decided the group would take a one hour rest and then quietly work their way to the forest and surprise the people there.

Taking their time going down Mount Tabor, finding the best place to cross the Jordan River, turning north and reaching the beginning of the forest took two hours. They could see a bonfire about one thousand feet away and they could hear some noise coming from that direction. A signal was given to spread out and approach the area where the fire was. The closer they got to the fire the clearer the song they were hearing became.

One captain looked at the other captain and shrugged his shoulders. The other captain whispered, "It sounds like a Greek, Roman and Jewish version of "I've Been Working in the Forest."

By now the soldiers had completely surrounded the bonfire area and were waiting for the signal from the captain to attack. The captain was about to give the signal when he heard, "Let's sing that again. Oh, I've been Work....."

There was his old friend the captain sitting on the back of a wagon using his one arm to lead the singing.

The two new captains dismounted and walked into the bonfire area. The singing stopped and the two companions helped the captain off the wagon to greet their friends.

"Where is that young man with the pigeons?"

"Here, Sir."

"Send the following: captain and two companions are with us and they are alive and well. Situation at forest is under control."

The young man wrote the note, fastened it to the pigeon's leg and released the pigeon. The pigeon circled above for about one minute and then headed toward Kavalla.

The captain asked the pigeon handler to send another note, just like the first note and send it just in case the first pigeon got lost.

"Captain, I'll do what you ask me to do but neither rain, hail, snow or sleet will stop that pigeon from delivering that message."

"You convinced me, don't send the second message. How long will it take for that message to get to Kavalla?"

"I kept a record of the wind conditions on our trip here and I calculate Homer, I mean the pigeon will arrive in Kavalla by one PM tomorrow."

'You're doing a good job young man. Thank you. By the way, what is your name?"

"Everyone calls me Bird."

The captain smiled and said, "What is this world coming to? No telling what these young folks will come up with next."

Chapter 29
Back at the
Synagogue Compound

     The committee chairman finished his last scheduled meeting and decided to take a relaxing walk around the Synagogue compound. Walking out the back door, he looked to the left and saw a few people sitting around a small bon fire. The chairman turned to his right and walked along the stone fence that surrounded the forest. When he came to the gate with the "DO NOT ENTER – MADMAN WITHIN" sign on it, he stopped, sat on the ground, leaned against the fence and reflected on how much had happened since his first visit here over forty years ago. His first assignment as a Rabbi was to go to the rural areas around the Sea of Galilee to identify areas that had enough Jewish families to support a permanent or part time Rabbi.

     One day while he was visiting a little fishing village on the western side of the sea he remembered meeting a fisherman that offered to bring him here. Now it was all coming back to him. He remembered how enthusiastic the fisherman was about the future of this little village. He had plans to build a marketplace, a meeting building, then a Synagogue. The Romans were surveying to build new roads. He remembered meeting a young Jewish family that was building a house in a small clearing. The father was in charge of building roads from Bethsaida through here. They had two children.

     Now it was all coming back to him. That's the little house over there and the meeting building and Synagogue are right where the fisherman told me they were going to be. There was some talk about a nice marketplace and the Romans talked about building roads through here. We all knew fresh water was needed if the little village was to grow, but no one even dreamed we would have an aqueduct bring good fresh water from miles away. The pleasant memories flooded his mind. He remembered that he conducted the first Sabbath services right over there where the Synagogue is now.

"Hi. Ben."

The greeting jarred the chairman's mind back to the present. He had not been called Ben in years.

He had no idea who this woman was until he heard his own voice say, "Ruby?" Then as if a dam holding back a flood of memories broke. His mind shifted back forty years, however, unfortunately his body remained in the present.

"Here let me help you up."

"I was so sorry to hear about your husband's death. I saw the fountain named after him when I came through the marketplace. I also saw the sign on the gate. Is Palti still living up on the top of the cliff?"

"No. Some boys jumped over the fence and attacked him about thirty five years ago. Palti tried to avoid the boys but they caught him. When he defended himself, two of the boys were seriously hurt. He ran to the gate just as I had told him to do if anything was wrong. I told him to run to the north to the first place we had stopped on our way here. I told him to stay there and I would find him."

"Have you seen him since he ran away?"

"Yes. Every four weeks I carry clean clothes, vegetables and reading materials to him. His sister does the same thing every four weeks so he gets what he needs every two weeks. At first we would sit and talk to him, but the demons got so bad that he asked us to leave the supplies near his camp. He was afraid he would hurt us if he lost control while we were there. I told him, when he was well, to come to the gate, I would be watching for him. I can see the gate if I sit in my house and look out my window. Every Rabbi that has served here wants to move my clothes line from the front of my house to the back but if I did, it would block my view of the gate. I went to deliver supplies to him last week but he was gone. I have no idea where to look for him. I was watching for him when I saw you sitting here. His sister and her family are searching for him, and if they find him, they will let me know where he is."

Rabbi Abdon and Rabbi Boni decided to walk up to the camp site in the forest. As they approached the gate they saw the chairman talking to Mrs. Ruby.

"Hello Mrs. Ruby, would you like to go with us to see Devas' and Ezra's family at the camp site on the cliff?"

"Thank you boys but I'll stay here. Ben, I mean Chairman, you go with them. We'll talk more tomorrow."

Soon the three Rabbis walked into the camp site. The greetings continued for several minutes. When everyone had greeted everyone else, things began to settle down. Everyone was seated around the fire. Joshua walked to Grandfather and reminded him that he never told them, who won the wall building contest.

"We'll get to that soon, first I would like to let the chairman talk to us for a few minutes."

"Thank you Grandfather. I know most of our people think the Sanhedrin has no idea what life is like outside of Jerusalem and they are correct. I wish I could have brought all seventy one of the Sanhedrin with me to see what a wonderful, devoted group of followers there are outside of Jerusalem. The fact is, we are not an independent nation as we once were. The Roman Empire allows us some freedom that other conquerors did not give us. We may live where we choose. We have the freedom to worship as we choose. Some Jewish men serve in the Roman Army. We can choose to be farmers, fisherman, merchants, tax collectors or any other career.

"Rome is very concerned about the areas around the Sea of Galilee. Look around your village. Within the last two weeks Rome has sent over one hundred army soldiers to reinforce those already here. They have added more than one hundred troops in Capernaum. I believe Jesus did healed Delaeh and that he drove the demons from our dear friend Palti. The Romans are not concerned about the good Jesus or John the Baptist are doing but they are concerned about all the talk about a new kingdom. Two of my aides will go to Capernaum tomorrow to locate Jesus and try to set up a meeting between the two of us, so we can try to avoid trouble with the Romans, but tonight is a time for rejoicing. I want to meet the young folks here and to renew old friendships with those I met many years ago. There is one more thing I need to tell you. Come up here Joshua and stand by me. I don't know what your Grandfather told you about the fence contest but I bet I know why he didn't tell you who won. He was waiting to put me on the spot as he did many years ago. I'm sure he told you about the boys building forty two feet of wall and the girls building twelve feet of wall. He probably told you that the fifteen little girls pushed the boy's wall over and that the twenty boys couldn't push the girl's wall over."

"Yes he did but he never told us who won."

"Who do you think won?"

"Well, it was a contest to see who could build the best wall and a forty two foot wall is better than a twelve foot wall. The boys should have won."

"Sam, please come up here. Who do you think should have won the stone wall building contest?"

"The girl's wall was better because it was stronger and looked prettier. The girls should have won."

"Well, let me tell you what really happened when the judges could not agree on who had won. All the ladies that came to watch the contest were yelling that the girls had won. The men were yelling that the boys had won. When your grandfather realized the judges were not going to choose a winner and how determined the crowd was that their side should be declared the winner, he walked to the center of the field, raised a stick over his head and stood there waiting for the crowd to settle down."

"We call that his Moses stance."

"Thank you Sam."

"We were all waiting for him to choose the winner. When everyone was silent, he paused a moment and in a loud, clear voice he announced that our visiting Rabbi would pick the winner. When I walked up to your grandfather, I asked him, "Why are you putting this responsibility on me. His answer was, "Because you get to leave and I have to stay here". I announced that the girls had won and then I got out of town."

After a few cheers and boos everyone broke out in laughter. Every one continued enjoying each other's company, except Palti. Palti left the camp fire and walked through the woods that he had not been in for over thirty years. When he came to the stone fence he turned left and followed the fence toward the gate. The first building he saw was the Synagogue. The last time he was here they were using the Meeting Building and the Synagogue was just a dream for the future. He could see the Meeting Building and he continued to follow the fence toward it. When he got half way between the Synagogue and the meeting building, he stopped, put his hand on the fence and said, "I knew it would still be here. This is the best looking twelve feet in the whole fence."

Looking over the fence he saw the memorial stone marking his father's grave. He thought of the many nights his sister, mother and he would sit on this fence and talk about his father. Continuing to walk along the fence, he came to the fenced in area where his mother kept her mule and next to that he saw his mother's vegetable garden. Oh, how he loved to get the vegetables his mother brought to him from that garden. Again, talking to himself, but this time out loud, he said, "There it is. Oh how often I have thought about meeting my mother at that gate and going through it free of the demons."

"You don't know how often I have wanted you to come through that gate. Welcome back son."

Palti opened the gate and rushed into his mother's arms. They started to walk toward the house when Palti said, "Wait a minute." He went back to the gate and removed the sign.

Everyone at the camp watched as Palti walked away from the fire and headed toward his mother's home. Everyone wanted to run through the woods, so they could be near the gate to watch what they knew would be a beautiful reunion, but no one moved.

Grandmother turned to Grandfather and said, "It's getting late and tomorrow is going to be a busy day."

"You're right. Let me see if Titus has all the information he needs for the play he's writing."

Grandmother started gathering the empty bowls and containers she brought the food in and placed them in the cart.

Titus was talking to Ezra about watching Merchant tell the villagers about Delaeh's healing the night they arrived back in Hippos. "Now, you say he stayed in his wagon the whole time he was telling the story and some of the villagers stood around the wagon until he lay down on the seat and stood up. When the villagers heard that Delaeh stood up and walked, they all left to tell the other villagers about Delaeh being healed."

"That's exactly how it happened."

Grandfather waited until there was a pause in the conversation and then asked Titus if he were ready to head back to the marketplace.

Titus thanked everyone for sharing the wonderful stories with him and said he was ready to go.

Just as they were ready to leave the camp they saw four people walking through the woods toward the camp. They could see Mrs. Ruby and Palti but the other two people were walking slowly and one seemed to be helping the other.

Grandfather hugged Mrs. Ruby and told her how happy everyone was that Palti was home.

Grandmother said, "Who do you have with you, Ruby?"

"The base Commander walked through our yard while Palti and I were sitting at one of the tables. He told me he wanted to go up to the camp site on the hill and welcome everyone back to Hippos. He planned to get here earlier but he had to take care of some business before he could get away. When Palti and I decided to go with him, Merchant called to us and asked if he could go with us. He was able to walk part of the way by himself but now the Commander is helping him."

Merchant was helped to a bench that was near the fire and then he was carefully helped onto the bench. Merchant's body appeared to be half the size it was the last time they saw him. After he rested for a minute he looked up, smiled and waved to everyone. His smile and bright eyes assured everyone that he would soon be the same old Merchant.

The Commander stepped to where everyone could see and hear him. "First I want to tell you how wonderful it is to see this great family safely back in Hippos. I'm sorry I could not get here sooner, but there were a lot of matters I had to attend to before I could leave the outpost. I know you want to get back to your homes as soon as possible, however, I would like to request that you stay here for a couple of days. I make this request because I have reasons to be concerned about your safety. If Grandfather has no objections I would also like to assign two guards at each gate to the forest and eight additional guards to patrol around in the forest. When I asked for volunteers every soldier under my command volunteered for these assignments. There was something said about Mrs. Ruby's vegetables. If Rabbi Boni does not object, I would also like to have ten of my Jewish soldiers, in civilian clothes walking around the Synagogue Compound for the next couple of days."

One of the Commander's aides walked into the camp site and whispered in his ear.

"This young man just informed me that a representative from the Chinese caravan is waiting for me at the outpost. The representative's name is Chuma. I understand you all know him. I wish I had time to help Merchant back to Mrs. Ruby's home."

"Don't worry Commander, I'll help him. He has sure helped me enough times."

"Thanks, Delaeh."

The committee chairman followed the Commander to the edge of the camp site and said, "Commander I won't need the soldiers you were asked to train as witnesses."

"Thank you, Mr. Chairman. They have been trained as the message I received instructed me to do. I'm glad you won't need them."

"I'm also glad we won't be using them. I argued against using false witnesses but Chief Priest Caiaphas ruled that we should have witnesses ready that will say what we want them to.

Chapter 30
Commander Back At The Outpost

The Commander and his aide walked through the forest, went through the gate in the stone fence, walked around Mrs. Ruby's house, down the lane from the Synagogue Compound, crossed the road running along the west side of the marketplace, went between the vendor's buildings and into the marketplace. A few merchants were sitting near their merchandise; the touring theatrical group was working on the stage and backdrop for their play. There were three men leading their camels toward the fountain. They were dressed in colorful robes and wearing head dress that looked almost like crowns. The Commander and his aide stood watching the three men.

The aide said, "I have never seen men dressed like that. Where do you think they are from?"

"They are wise men from the east, most likely from Persia. They are astrologers and their pilgrimage here must have some religious significance. They have seen something in the stars, otherwise they would not have taken the trouble and risk of travelling so far."

"You seem to know a lot about these men."

"I grew up hearing stories about the wise men. It seems that they appeared in Jerusalem when Herod the Great ruled in Jerusalem about thirty years ago. They wanted to know where The King of the Jews was to be born."

"Is that the Herod that rules there now?"

"No. The Herod that rules there now is his son."

"What happened then?"

"I'll tell you more when we have more time but now we need to get to the outpost."

The Commander and his aide continued their walk across the marketplace and before going between the vender buildings the Commander stopped for one more look at the wise men. "They are an interesting group and I wish I knew more about them."

The men continued between the vender buildings and turned right onto the road that ran on the east side of the marketplace and led to the gates of the outpost. Standing with the two guards at the gate was a man he assumed was Chuma.

"Are you Chuma?"

"Yes, Commander. Thank you for meeting with me."

"I have heard wonderful things about you and the way you handle your caravan. The horses you provide us are truly wonderful animals.

"Thank you for such kind words."

The message I received said you were looking for the pig farmer that has his pig farm north of here in the country of the Gerasenes. You must be looking for the farmer whose pigs ran off the cliff into the sea, about three weeks ago."

"That's the one."

"Come with me and I'll take you to him but first, where is your horse?"

"I rode him hard to get here. The guards said that I would have to wait for you before they could let me into the compound. Your guards were nice enough to have a stable man take my horse to the stables and see that he was taken care of and fed."

The Commander asked his aide to see the guard for the forest and the gates was assigned and placed as soon as possible and that the Jewish soldiers that were to be in the Synagogue Compound were in place by morning light. "Please come to the guest house, when you have taken care of the guards."

When they reached the guesthouse, the farmer was standing in the doorway, talking to the guards. The guards snapped to attention when they saw the Commander.

"As you were gentlemen. I'm glad to see that you have been keeping our guest happy."

"Oh, they have treated me like I was someone important."

"You are important. The information you gave us helped bring some wonderful Hippos citizens safety back home."

"Chuma, what you doing with the Commander? Are you in some kinda trouble?"

"No, I'm here to see you."

"Well I ain't got no more pigs. They were all kilt by that Jesus fellow."

"That is what I want to talk to you about. You have been providing us one hundred pigs every month for the last ten years. Our customers like the quality of the pigs you have been providing us and would not buy the emaciated pigs we had to buy from other pig farmers. Their pigs are so mean that five of our men were bit and the pigs refused to walk so we had to put them in wagons while our ladies and older people had to walk."

"Them farmer don't know nothing about raisin no pigs. I wish I had some pigs, I'd show em."

"I bought all their pigs, including all the breeding stock, from two pig farms and they are being delivered to your farm now."

"I ain't got no money to pay you for them pigs."

"We don't want you to pay us money. Here is what we think is fair. We will put three hundred young pigs at various ages and twenty-five sows and five boar hogs on your farm. What we want is this. Every time we buy twenty two pigs from you. You will give us three extra pigs at no cost. At the end of five years, you will owe us nothing."

The farmer's eyes rolled upwards, his brow wrinkled a bit and his index finger moved as if he were writing on an imaginary wall, as he ran the proposal through his mind. After about twenty seconds of calculations he announced, "That sounds like a good deal to me. When do we start?"

"The wagons are bringing the pigs to your farm now. How long will it take for you to get back to your farm?"

"It took me a day and a half to walk here, so I should be able to be there in a day and a half."

The Commander told the two guards that had been watching over the pig farmer, to have the stable man prepare three horses for a trip to the pig farm. "They are to be ready to leave with the farmer in two hours. Once the farmer is safely at his farm, the guards are to stay at the farm for three additional days and then return with the three horses and give the Commander a report on how the restocking of the farm is going."

The Commander and Chuma walked back to the stable where the stable man was told to see that Chuma was fed and that he had provisions for his trip back to his caravan.

"Thank you Chuma. Have a good trip."

Chapter 31
First Full Day After Devas' And Ezra's Families Returned Home

"Didn't you get any sleep last night, Cara?"

"Good morning, Delaeh. I've only been here about fifteen minutes. I love to watch the sun come up over the sea and I wanted to see how many fishermen were going out this morning. I left a full week's schedule on the pier the evening before we sneaked out in the Chinese caravan, but that was almost two weeks ago. I hope someone has updated it to match the merchant's schedule or we will have more fish than we have carts to deliver to the different cities."

"I don't know what would have happened if you and Sam had not been there to do my job, when my health was so bad."

"Cara, it looks like we are the only ones up this morning."

"No, I heard your mother and mine talking about going to the meeting building and helping the volunteers start cooking breakfast. You know how they are. It drives them crazy if they aren't busy."

Ruth and Esther were shocked when they heard someone say, "Who goes there?" Then they remembered the Commander was going to assign some soldiers to patrol the forest. Once they identified themselves each soldier told them how glad they were that their family was back home. When they got to the gate, the guards there had orders not to let anyone into the forest unless they had permission. Nothing was said about letting anyone out.

"Maddi, you know who we are. Now open that gate and let us through."

"Yes, Mrs. Esther, I know who you are and I'm sure glad you and your family are back in Hippos but my orders are not to let anyone into the forest unless they have permission."

"We don't want to go into the forest, we want to go out of the forest."

"I'm sorry Mrs. Esther but…"

"What's all that noise so early in the morning?"

"Mrs. Ruby, my orders are…."

"Maddi, listen to me. Let those ladies through that gate. If anyone wants to know who told you to let them through, tell them to see me."

The three ladies headed to the meeting building to help with the preparation of breakfast but the aroma of bread baking, figs boiling and fish cooking on an open fire let the ladies know volunteers had already been busy for hours. When they got closer, they could see at least a dozen ladies fully engaged in the preparation of breakfast and one large man with his back toward them, bent over placing dough in the stone oven. He had an apron on over his robe and there were hand prints on his rear where he had wiped the flower off of his hands. When he had the fire just right and the bread spaced correctly in the oven, he stood up, wiped his hands again and turned around. When he saw Ruth, Esther and Ruby, the Chairman said, "Good morning ladies! What a wonderful day the good lord has given us."

There was no need to announce that breakfast was ready. The aroma had permeated the Synagogue Compound and the forest letting everyone know it was time to eat.

Rabbi Boni said, "Let's send someone up to the ridge to let everyone up there know we are about to eat."

"No need to do that, we are all here." Devas shouted.

"Oh, lands. I'd better get to the gate before Maddi and his companion guards have a stroke." On her way to the gate, a courier on horseback, approached her and asked where he could find the Chairman of the committee sent by the Sanhedrim?

Mrs. Ruby called one of the plain clothed soldiers and asked him to take the courier's horse to the stream. "Come with me young man, I'll take you to the Chairman."

Rabbi Abdon blessed the food and gave thanks for the safe return of Devas' and Ezra's family and for the return of Palti.

Mrs. Ruby waited for the blessing to be completed and then continued to take the courier to the Chairman. "This young man has a message for you."

The Chairman took off his apron, dusted off the seat of his robe and stood up.

The courier asked if he were the Chairman of the committee sent by the Sanhedrim.

"I am."

"I am to give you this message and to wait for your written answer. I will require one hour getting my horse ready for my return trip to Jerusalem."

"Thank you courier, I will have my answer ready within the hour."

The Chairman walked to his room where he could read the message in private.

Chapter 32
The High Council
Of The Temple of Jerusalem

Be it known that the review commission of which you are chairman, consisting of four distinguished priests and their aides, and ten additional persons, were to have completed their review of the situation in the region around the Sea of Galilee and reported back to this High Council over a week ago.

Herod Antipas and Pontius Pilate are demanding that I give them your assessment of conditions in the region where you were sent. This communication is being sent by Roman Courier and is to be delivered to you personally by Thursday morning.

Your instructions are as follows:

You and Rabbi Abdon are to return to these chambers after the Sabbath is completed. Saturday morning you and Rabbi Abdon are to report to the Roman Outpost in Hippos at eight in the morning where you will be provided horses, supplies for the trip and two military escorts for your protection.

The remaining members of your review commission shall return with the wagons and horses assigned for the trip to Hippos. You are to report to my chambers as soon as you arrive in Jerusalem.

High Priest Caiaphas

While reading the message, the Chairman began to slump in his chair and by the time he had completed reading, he looked and felt every one of his sixty-five years. Forcing himself to get up, he began to pace the floor trying to walk off a few of his years. Why did Caiaphas use a Roman courier to deliver this message when we have better and quicker ways to communicate? Herod Antipas and Pontius Pilate must be pressuring the Sanhedrim. What do they want? What are they planning? After debating with himself for several minutes, he realized that he needed to get himself composed. After a few deep breaths, five deep knee bends, half a minute of rolling his shoulders and facial exercises, he began to regain his positive attitude and appearance. Seated at the table in his room, the Chairman placed the message he had received on the table. Next he placed a blank parchment next to the message so he could address each item in the message. Once he had written the lengthy standard greeting and thanked the high Priest for trusting him with the chairmanship of such an important committee, the Chairman picked up the parchment he had been writing on, read what he had written, leaned back in his chair, rubbed his chin and said, "That should blow enough smoke up his robe. Now how do I tell the old goat, if he would buy some new wagons, we would have completed our trip as planned."

    The Chairman addressed everything in the message he received and signed off by thanking the High Priest for providing military escorts for them back to Jerusalem. The reply was placed in the courier's pouch and sealed. The Chairman opened his door to find his aide to have him tell his committee to meet him in back of the meeting building in one hour.

    His aide had followed him back to his room and was dutifully waiting outside his door should the Chairman need his assistance. "Should I have the committee meet you back here in one hour?"

    "Yes, thank you"

    By the time the Chairman got back to the field in front of the meeting building and the Synagogue, he was surprised to see so many people were there. Rabbi Abdon and Rabbi Boni were waiting for the Chairman as he came out of the meeting building.

    "Chairman, can we help you with anything?"

    "Yes, as soon as I give this reply to the courier, I would like to have a private talk with both of you."

    Soon the Roman courier arrived, received the reply and departed for Jerusalem with the Chairman's reply.

Rabbi Boni said, "Let's go to the Synagogue, we can talk there."

The Chairman, reviewed the message he had received and his response. Then he explained the struggles that had occupied the Sanhedrin's time for over a year. "Now, John the Baptist has openly criticized Herod for marrying his brother's wife. In Jerusalem, if Herod isn't happy, nobody is happy."

The Chairman placed his arm on Rabbi Boni's shoulder and said, "Son, you and young Rabbis like you will be the backbone of our faith in a few short years, if not sooner. You have proven to me and others that you have all the qualities to lead our people in these changing times. Rabbi Abdon and his generation can and will offer you guidance, support and encouragement, but you are going to be challenged by world events the likes of which men have never seen. I want you to attend the meeting with my committee behind the synagogue. Let's go to that meeting now, we will talk more later."

The Chairman told his committee that he and Rabbi Abdon were heading back to Jerusalem early Sunday morning. Each committee member was assigned tasks such as getting the wagons in condition for the trip back to Jerusalem and working with the Hippos congregation to prepare for the Sabbath services. One aide was to get a message to the members that were sent to Capernaum telling them to return to Hippos immediately. The Chairman thanked everyone for their help and adjourned.

The Chairman and Rabbis Abdon and Boni walked around the meeting building and saw Mrs. Ruby and Palti talking to some of the plain clothed soldiers in front of Mrs. Ruby's house. Many of the people in the compound were gathering along the lane in front of Mrs. Ruby's house.

Rabbi Abdon asked one of the ladies what all the excitement was about.

"Mrs. Ruby is having her clothes lines moved from the front of her house to the back of her house."

"Why after all the years, I have tried to talk her into moving them to the back of her house is she having it done now?"

"Don't you men know anything? If she had clothes hanging in the back yard they would have blocked her view of the gate to the forest."

"So what? That gate isn't that pretty."

"I swear you men don't know anything. She has been watching that gate all these years to see her son when he came back. If clothes were hanging on the line, how was she going to see him?"

"What's all the discussion about?"

"Palti and those soldiers are trying to talk Mrs. Ruby into just putting lines between trees to hang her wash instead of putting poles in the ground."

"What's wrong with that?"

"Trees have leaves, leaves block the sun, sun and fresh air makes clothes feel and smell better. Beside birds hang around trees and even men know what birds do. I swear, when I get married, I hope I get a smart one."

The Rabbis began to walk away and Rabbi Abdon said under his breath, "I don't think that is going to happen."

The Chairman walked over to Mrs. Ruby, placed his hand on her shoulder and whispered in her ear, "It's time."

"When and where?"

"I'm going to talk to Grandmother and Grandfather now. I'll let you know more after I talk to them."

"What about number one?"

"I talked to him about a month ago. He was sailing to Rome and planned to be back by now."

The Chairman walked out the lane to the market place, worked his way through the crowds to Grandfather's building at the north end of the marketplace. He waited for Grandfather to finish talking to a customer. There was a friendly greeting and then Grandfather asked the Chairman to come inside where Grandmother was busy writing something in a ledger.

The Chairman softly said, "It's time."

"Are you sure?"

"Yes."

"When and where and where is number one?"

"I talked to him a little over a month ago. He was going to Rome but he should be back by now. He said he would meet us in Hippos when he returned from Rome. I was asked to tell you that if we agree that the time has come, we should do whatever we feel is right. I told Mrs. Ruby and she is waiting for me to tell her when and where."

Grandfather thought for a while and then said, "We need to make sure that no one knows anything about our meeting and it must be held in a secret place where no one can see us."

Grandmother said, "The Hide and Seek Trail. We can walk across the Synagogue field one at a time, take the path that leads to the back of Devas' house. The hide and seek trail is about half way down that path. There is a little clearing where the children used to play where no one would see us."

"That's fine, Mother, but how do we get the Commander there?"

Ruby goes to the base infirmary every day to check on that captain that was hurt when they were trying to get Devas' and Ezra's family back to Hippos. While she is there, she can come up with a plan to get the Commander to walk with her to the fishing pier. When they are at the curve in the road to the pier, Ruby can tell the Commander about the meeting we are having."

"I'll go back to the Synagogue compound and tell Ruby our plan. You all should wait an hour before you come to the compound."

The Chairman told Ruby the plan and she left for the Base Infirmary.

Chapter 33
From the Base
To the Hide and Seek Trail

Walking down the lane she thought to herself, "It does look better with my clothes line behind the house."

When she started up the hill to the two big gates in the wall that surrounded the outpost, a group of guards were coming down the hill going to replace the guards that had been on duty. They all said, "Hello, Mrs. Ruby." Mrs. Ruby called them all by their names. A quick walk through the infirmary, checking on the patients and a chat with the doctor, reassured Mrs. Ruby that everyone was getting the correct treatment.

She walked to the Commander's Office and was met by guards that she knew. One guard told her the Commander had a visitor and could not be disturbed. The other guard was standing there holding the reins of a beautiful horse that had been ridden hard.

"Are you going to take that horse to the stable and have it cooled down properly?"

"Mrs. Ruby, I can't leave my post until I'm relieved."

"Give me that horse, I'll take it to the stable while I'm waiting."

The stable man looked at the horse Mrs. Ruby was leading and said, "Oh, please don't tell me the courier is back."

Mrs. Ruby rushed back to the guards at the Commander's Office and asked her two friends what the man that was riding that horse looked like."

"He's tall and an older gray haired man. I know he is a Roman courier but he never wears a uniform. He comes to see the Commander about once a month, and stays for an hour or so and then he is gone."

"Boys, I need you to get me one of the Commander's aides"

One guard walked to the door, tapped lightly on it and stood there talking to the aide. Occasionally he pointed to Mrs. Ruby and turned his palms upward and shrugged his shoulders.

The aide walked over and said, "Mrs. Ruby, the Commander is busy now. Is there anything I can do for you?"

"Yes, Tarus. You can go to the Commander's personal aide and tell him that I am here and need to talk to him."

"Tarus, you and I both know that Markus has been with the Commander longer than you have and will not get in trouble, if he interrupts a meeting. Please get Markus for me."

"Yes, Mrs. Ruby."

Markus greeted Mrs. Ruby and asked if he could help her.

"Yes, you can. Knock on the Commander's door and tell him that you have a message for the courier. Then tell the courier, it's time and then tell him that I am at the front door."

The aide went to the Commander's door and softly tapped once, opened the door only far enough to put his head in and said,

"Excuse me, Commander, I have a message for the courier."

"Come in Markus."

"Sir, I am to tell you, 'It's time'. I'm also to tell you that Mrs. Ruby is at the front door."

"Thank you Markus. Would you tell Mrs. Ruby that I will be right there?"

"Excuse me. I'll be right back. This must be important."

"Hi, Ruby. I agree. It's time. Where and when?"

"As soon as we can get the Commander to join us at the Hide and Seek Trail. The committee will be there in one hour. You go down this road and…."

"I know where the Hide and Seek Trail is."

The courier walked back to the Commander's Office.

"I hope Mrs. Ruby brought you good news."

"I need to ask you to do me a favor."

"You know that I will do anything for you."

"Good. I need you to tell your aides that you are going to walk around the marketplace and then to the pier. Tell them you will be gone for about two hours."

Out the gate and down the road to the marketplace, the two old friends talked as though everything was as it had always been. In fact the courier was going over in his mind how to tell his friend what he knew he must tell him and his friend was thinking why he doesn't just tell me what he is thinking. Their vocal conversation continued unabated while one of their minds' searched for words to explain what he needed to say and the other mind was juggling thoughts that might explain the unusual trip to the Hide and Seek Trail.

Walking through the vendor's buildings at the marketplace and looking to the north, they could see a crowd had gathered at the fountain. Approaching the fountain, they could see three men dressed in brightly colored robes with hats consisting of different colored cloth and a jewel inlayed crown. Each man was holding the reins of a camel. The crowd was no closer than thirty feet from the three men and their camels. There was no sound coming from the people gathered around watching.

The Commander and the courier watched in silence, as the camels drank from the fountain. The camels kneeled preparing for their riders to mount when two little boys stepped out of the crowd and asked, "Where are you going?"

"We are going to continue our mission."

"Who are you?"

"We are known as wise men. Who are you?"

"Oh, we ain't no body, just me and my little brother."

"Oh, you both are indeed some body. You will do great things and you will lead others to do even greater things. We will remember you as long as there are stars in the sky. Tonight I want you to come back to this spot, look up in the sky and each of you pick a star and the star you pick will be yours forever and no one can take it from you."

The last wise man mounted his camel, the crowds moved aside to let the three wise men through and after they cleared the crowds, everyone returned to where they were standing before the wise men came. The marketplace again was abuzz with talk about things that were important in their daily lives. The talk was as if the wise men had not been there.

"Boy, weren't they great?"

"What are you talking about, kid?"

"The wise men and their camels were right here and the camel drank from the fountain."

"What wise men, what camels? We don't allow no camels to drink from that fountain."

"They were just there. They talked to my brother and me.

"Go away, boys. We have more important things to do than listen to your foolishness. If there were any camels there, we would have seen them and told them to go away."

The little brother looked up at the man that had been talking to his brother and said, "I saw them too. They told us that we were some body and that we were going to do great things and lead others to do even greater things. They also said they will remember my big brother and me as long as there are stars in the sky. One of the wise men told us to come to this spot tonight and we can each pick a star and the star we pick will be ours forever and no one can take it from us. I wish you would have talked to them, they would have let you pick a star for yourself tonight."

Big brother took the hand of his little brother and said, "Come on, let's go tell our friends and parents what we saw. We know what we saw."

"Yes, we do and we're coming back tonight to pick our star."

When the boys came near the Commander and the courier, the grown men crouched down and said, "We saw them too."

"We're glad you did. Weren't they wonderful?"

"They sure were, and so are you."

There was a quick walk to the Hide and Seek Trail. Standing in the middle of the small clearing was Grandfather, Grandmother, Mrs. Ruby and the Chairman. There was a hurried but friendly greeting and then all but the courier sat down on one of the rocks surrounding a well-used fire pit.

The courier began by telling the Commander that everyone here had known him since he was a small baby and each person here swore years ago not to divulge to anyone what he was about to hear today, until they all agreed that the time had come to tell you. We all agreed that the time to tell you is now.

"What is it you want to tell me?"

"Your father was a Captain in the Roman Army."

"I know that he was a road and aqueduct builder. He was killed saving his crew from an avalanche not far from here over thirty years ago."

"NO. Your father was a Captain but he was assigned to the outpost in Jerusalem about thirty years ago during the reign of Herod the Great. His Commander was directed by Herod the Great to send his best man to lead a group of soldiers to the little town of Bethlehem. They were to follow the three wise men, also called magi, and report what they did, where they went and to make sure the wise men came back to Herod as they told him they would. He and his team followed the magi through the richest section of the town, looking for the child that was born King of the Jews. The star continued to move until it led to the poorest part of town and to the smallest house near where the baby was born. The magi went into the house, carrying three containers and in less than an hour they got back on their camels and left. Instead of going north toward Jerusalem they went south away from Jerusalem. Your father followed them for one day and when it became clear they were not going to go back to Jerusalem he sent one of the men to his Commander to tell him what they had seen and ask if they should take the magi prisoner. The messenger took a day to get to the outpost in Jerusalem, and two days to get back to your father with instructions. The instructions were to return to Bethlehem and take the Baby and its parents to Herod."

"When they returned to where they saw the family four days earlier, the house was empty and no one knew where they had gone. Your father and his men went back to Jerusalem and reported to his Commander what they saw, where the house was located that the magi had stopped and what the magi gave the family as gifts. That night the Commander called your father to his office and told him that he was to lead one hundred soldiers back to Bethlehem to kill all the Jewish boys that were two years old and younger. Your father told the Commander that he was sure the baby Herod was looking for was gone. One of the people told your father that the father, mother and baby left Bethlehem and were going to Egypt. Your father told his Commander that it was wrong to kill the babies. The Commander told your father that Herod doesn't care and if Herod doesn't care neither does he. You are to be ready to leave at eight in the morning. Your father went to the barracks and told the men to be ready to leave at eight in the morning in full battle dress. He then went to your home off base and put your mother and you in a wagon and headed north to find a safe place for you and your mother. When I heard what Herod had ordered the soldiers to do and who was to lead the slaughter, I headed for your house. I reached your house just as your father, mother and you were leaving. I stopped your father and told him that I knew what his orders were and I knew he would never carry them out. I asked him what he planned to do. He said he was going to warn the people about Herod's plan and then head to Hippos where he knew the Rabbi there would hide his family. I told your father that he did not have time to go to Bethlehem to warn the people and then escape before he was found missing. I offered to go to Bethlehem to warn the people and for him to leave for Hippos now."

Your father said, "No, it was his duty to warn the people." He asked for my horse and asked me to take the wagon and get your mother and you to the Rabbi in Hippos. I agreed but your mother said if she went with your father, they could warn twice as many people. Your mother and father kissed you, handed you to me, said God bless and before they rode off your father said, "When he grows up tell him I picked a star for him." "That was the last time I saw your mother and father."

"Here I was sitting on one of the strongest horses in the Roman Empire with this tiny baby in my hands, not knowing what to do with it, so I took out my largest courier pouch and treated you like you were a package to be delivered to Hippos as quickly as I could get there. I don't remember the ride to Hippos, but I'm sure my horse remembered it for the rest of its life. As I recall that horse didn't have to remember that ride too long. By day break I arrived in Hippos. Wanting to avoid being seen by anyone at the outpost, I went through the gate near the pier and when I was out of sight of the guards, I cut through Grandfather yard. I went through the field to where I knew I could find the Rabbi. I delivered my package, as I would deliver any package. The Rabbi opened the pouch, took out the screaming contents and looked at you like he was looking for instructions on what to do with you. The noise I made and your yelling brought Ruby running. At that time she was just called Ruby, not Mrs. Ruby and she could still run."

"You keep adding to the story like that and I'll show you I can still run. Land's, Commander, it's a wonder you lived through that ride. Later that day we buried that pouch along with that horse and I don't know which one smelled the worst. Courier didn't smell much better. We should have thrown you in with the pouch and the horse. By the time I got you cleaned up and a little goat's milk, Grandfather and Grandmother came running to see what all the commotion was about. By midday we were getting messages about the dreadful things happening in Bethlehem. Then a message came later that day telling about a rumor that the child the wise men visited had been taken to a little fishing village called Hippos. We knew the large outpost in Capernaum would have a search party here by morning and it was possible that the outpost here was already looking for the child. At that time, this post was more for collecting taxes and seeing they got to Jerusalem. Grandfather you tell what happened next."

Grandfather stood up and waited for Mrs. Ruby to be seated.

"Go ahead, tell what happened next. Everybody is listening."

"I know Grandmother, I'm just getting the facts straight in my head. As I recall, we all agreed that we had to get the baby out of Hippos. That baby was you, Commander."

"We all know that, now get on with your part of the story."

"I know the courier doesn't like for anyone to know how rich and powerful he and his family are and we felt that the safest place for the child was with courier's family in Italy."

"OK. I'll continue. The safest place would be as far from Hippos as possible. The only two people in our group that had total freedom to travel were the courier and Mrs. Ruby. Now as I recall, Mrs. Ruby said she didn't have any special privileges to travel. I asked her to get the papers that she was given after her husband's military funeral. When she returned with the papers, I turned to page two and started to read."

The widow of this honorable deceased member of the Roman Empire military that gave his life in the execution of his duties and by his action saved others in the service of the Roman Empire is granted all the rights and privileges granted to its most honored members of the Roman Empire. These privileges are also hereby granted to the deceased Captain's son named, Palti, and his daughter named Elizabeth.

"Now let me see if I can find the right page where all the privileges are listed."

The courier said, "That's, OK Grandfather, I know what those privileges are and you are absolutely correct. Grandfather let me look at those papers a minute. Each of your children has their own copy of these papers and they are all signed and dated correctly. Palti's first name is given, but his age at the signing of these papers is not given. On Palti's documents there is no date of his birth or the date of your husband's death." The courier thought for a moment and then said, "Mrs. Ruby, if you are willing we can be in the Port of Tyre by tomorrow and sail to my home in Italy where we can make arrangements with my sister to see this child is taken care of.."

"My son is not likely to ever use these privileges and I am happy to go with you for the sake of this child."

"Mrs. Ruby, the child and I sailed for my home two days later and arrived eight days after sailing. When I told my sister and her husband about your mother and father, they were thrilled to have you to raise as their son. Your new parents provided you the best education and the fact that you had the paper conferring most honored members of the Roman Empire, you attended the finest military academies the Empire had. The five of us have watched you grow into the fine person you are today."

"What happened to my real parents?"

The Chairman stood up and said, "They saved many of the baby boys in Bethlehem and they tried to reach Hippos, but they were captured and Herod sentenced them to die as traitors. I was able to see them before they were executed and told them you were safe and well taken care of."

"Why are you telling me this after all these years?"

"Because we are getting old and feel you should know about this part of your life."

"I can never repay you for all you have done for me but there must be some other reason you have chosen to tell me now."

"Let me answer your question. A little over a year ago I received a message from my sister asking me to come home as soon as possible. When I got there, she told me that a close family friend and high ranking member of the Roman Empire Military came to her home for a visit.

During the visit he leaned over and whispered, "Congratulations, it looks like your son is going to be promoted to legate of all Roman troops in Judah and Galilee. The announcement will be made after the usual background checks. The next day my sister checked around and found out what she was told was true."

The Commander said "That explains the reason for some of the visitors telling me they were just in the area and stopped to say hello."

There were a group of historians looking at the stone marker next to the fountain in the marketplace. I watched them from my shop for a while and then walked over to see if I could help them. They had placed pieces of parchment on the stone and rubbed it with charcoal. The writing on the stone showed up on the parchment and they called them rubbings. They asked if I remembered anything about the Captain's children. I told them I did remember the children. They asked if the captain's son was younger than his sister. Before I realized why they asked that question, I said, "No, he was older." They asked if his wife was with child when the Captain died. I now knew what they were trying to find out, so I said, "I think she was." They left the memorial fountain and went to the marker at the Captain's grave and did a rubbing there.

"I knew when Herod found out his Commander in Hippos was the son of the man that disobeyed Herod's father's orders to kill all the Jewish male children two years or younger in Bethlehem thirty-two years ago, he was going to be furious. We need to get you out of Hippos before you are arrested."

"I am not concerned about myself. I'm concerned for all of you that have risked your lives to protect me. Herod will not be satisfied until he has every one of you."

"What do you think we should do?"

"Grandfather, when were the historians here? I did not see them."

"They were here three days ago."

"That's when Rabbi Boni and I had gone to get your family at the Bird's farm."

"I know how slow these government investigating committees work. We have at least two weeks before they have their report to Jerusalem. By the time the report is reviewed by Herod's staff that's an additional week. Once Herod gets the report, we have about the amount of time it will take him to get five hundred of his elite troupers to Hippos."

"What do you think we should do?"

"For the next few days we should act as though everything is normal. Courier, if you could go to Rome and let us know what is

going on there. Chairman, I know that the morning after the Sabbath you and Rabbi Abdon are leaving for Jerusalem with two of my guards. Excuse me, I mean escorts. Grandmother, Grandfather, Mrs. Ruby and I will go about our normal routine here in Hippos.
 I had no idea how important you people had been to me and now that I know, we are going to have a long time to enjoy each other."

The Commander stayed on the road that went around the southern end of the marketplace. Then he took the road that went up the hill to the outpost. His aide was standing at the gate waiting for the Commander's return.

"Commander, you have been so busy and I want to remind you of a matter that requires your personal attention."

"Marcus, what would I do without you? Tell me what I have forgotten to do."

"Sir, the three soldiers I have been rehearsing, to play the parts the Sanhedrin wanted them to play, would like to know what you want them to do, now that they won't be doing what they have been rehearsing."

"Marcus, have them come to my office as soon as you can find them."

"I have them waiting in front of your office now."

Sure enough, there they were seated on a stone block in front of the Commander's building and they were wearing civilian clothes. When the Commander and aide walked up they got up and ambled over and each said, "Hi."

"Come on in men."

Once they were in the office they sat down, propped their feet on the desk and asked the Commander if he had a good day?

The youngest soldier that would have played Delaeh giggled.

The soldier that would have played Devas sat up and had a silly smile on his face. Finally the tall soldier, the one that would have played Ezra, stood up and said. "How's that for acting like civilians. Boy you should have seen the look on your faces"

The Commander snapped, "While you are in my presence, you will conduct yourselves as soldiers at all times." Turning to his aide the Commander said, "Take these poor excuses for soldiers to the brig and put them on bread and water for one week. We'll make soldiers of them again."

You could have heard a pin drop as the Commander stood there looking sternly at the shocked three soldiers and his aide.

"Now that's what you call acting. Have a seat, boys. I'm sorry, I couldn't resist. You have done a great job learning your parts. I'm proud of your willingness to try something you have never done before. You almost had me until I remembered the last order I gave you. We were to treat each other as civilians. No military courtesies. You did a great job, but thank goodness you didn't have to play the parts you worked on so diligently. I understand you are playing parts in the play this afternoon. I have talked to the Director of the play and he would like all three of you to travel with the touring group for the next month. I would like to propose the following. You will continue to receive your regular pay for the month you are traveling with the touring group. You will also be paid by the Director the same as the other actors and in each of these coin pouches is a considerable amount of coins just as I told you that you would receive. I expect each of you back here in two months to resume your regular duties. Thanks again."

Chapter 34
The Play

Neighbors and friends started gathering in the marketplace hours before the play was to begin. Most of the vendor's shops were open for business but the vendors, their family and friends were seated around the front of their shop enjoying greeting friends as they waited for the play to start. All around the marketplace, in back of the vendor's buildings were small cooking fires. Each family was preparing their special meal that would be eaten when the players took a break about halfway through the play. The aroma created by pots of boiling meat, onions, garlic, olive oil and fresh vegetables over shadowed the normal smells associated with the marketplace. Bread had been baked at home earlier in the day but still produced that elixir that makes you feel everything is all right and makes you hungry as a horse.

Grandfather and two of his neighbor venders had moved most of their merchandise out of their buildings last night. The neighbors' buildings were being used as dressing rooms for the players and Grandfather's had been cleared so his family could be slipped in so they could see the play and their presence would not cause too much excitement. The Commander's aides posted ten soldiers in civilian clothes to be near Grandfather's building just in case they were needed.

The soldiers that did not have duty that evening were asked to sit in the roped off area away from the stage. A few minutes before the play was to start the Commander walked to the roped off area and was surprised to see the area was empty except for his aide, Marcus. Seeing the look on the Commander's face, Marcus said, "They were all here but we might as well put up a sign saying, COME ADOPT A SOLDIER FOR THE NIGHT."

The Commander looked around and there they were enjoying the company of their new found families.

The Commander stood there looking out over the crowd for a while and turning to Marcus said, "It seems that most of the young soldiers were adopted by families that have young daughters."

A drum began tapping slowly and softly and then it grew louder and then was joined by the sounds of a flute rippling through the audience. The cadence increased and the flute followed the drummer's lead. Then silence. The Director stepped from behind a curtain, walked to the front of the stage. "Ladies, gentlemen and all others within the sound of my voice, welcome. My name is Titus and I am the Director of this traveling theatrical group from Athens, Greece. This is our fourth visit to your wonderful village of Hippos. Our group is joined this year by three outstanding new actors that will be performing tonight in front of a live audience for the first time. You may not recognize them without their uniforms." There was a slight pause and a few giggles. "Come on out boys."

The three on loan soldiers stepped from behind the stage, waved to the audience and bowed.

The cheers and laughter lasted for over a minute.

"Thank you boys….Thank you." The Director was waving his right hand for the boys to leave the stage and at the same time his left hand was behind his back encouraging the audience to continue their applauding. When the audience was silent again a distinguished looking man with a deep and resounding voice stepped to the side of the stage and said, "Our story begins in the town of Hippos, which is located in the southeastern area of the Sea of Galilee, with Devas, a fishermen, saying to his brother, Ezra, at the end of a hard day's fishing."

The curtain parted and there were two of our stars sitting in a boat.

"So few fish….. So much work… Fishing these waters is not what it was when we were children. Our father and grandfather would fill this boat with fish, then clean and salt them before the sun went down. Now we fish for two days and are lucky if we get half a boat load and then that tax collector takes a fourth of what we catch."

"Now Devas, settle down. You and I have fished these waters all our lives. We have had hard times before. This old boat has fed and provided for our families and given us a good living.

Fishing is going to get better, you'll see.... You know, I've been thinking ...there are so many new settlements and towns springing up around the lake that the increased noise and lights may be causing the fish to go farther out where there is less noise and lights."

"My brother, you are absolutely right. I remember the many times when we were young and playing on this same old boat. Our father would whisper in a stern voice, be quiet and put out that lantern... you are scaring away the fish. I think we should set sail tomorrow to a deserted place I know where there are no lights and no noise. We can catch a boat load of fish. Joshua and Sam have been asking to go with us someday, so let's take them tomorrow."

The scene shifts and we see what appears to be the inside of a home with two mothers shaking a finger at their husbands and a two young children smiling from ear to ear. The curtain is closed. The inside of the home setting is moved and when the curtain opens there is Devas and Ezra preparing the net and one child steering the boat and the other pulling the sail tight. Stretched along the floor and part way up the side of the boat, is a blue cloth that is being moved by two men hidden on each side of the stage. The play continues through catching a boat load of fish, the big storm, Peter's boat and Jesus calming the storm. Now all eyes are attracted to the roof of the vender's building at the south end of the marketplace where a small fire, in a container, is covered, hiding the fire from sight and then uncovered to expose the fire. Quickly heads are turned to the stage where the children in the boat are pointing toward the flashing fire and saying, "I see the light." The children began singing:

"Shine the light for Father to see."

Then they were joined by the audience singing:

"Bring him home for mother and me.
Keep him safe while he's away.
In his strong arms I want to stay."

The Director stepped to the center of the stage and announced, "There will be a short intermission."

The crowd in the marketplace erupted with sounds of approval.

Thirty minutes after the first act ended, a drummer from behind the stage began a slow tapping. The sound increased, but the rhythm remained constant. The drummer is joined by a single voice singing,

"Shine the light for Father to see."

The single voice paused and said, "Please join me in this lovely message."

"Bring him home for mother and me.
Keep him safe while he's away.
In his strong arms I want to stay."

The Director walked to the side of the stage and said, "Welcome ladies and gentlemen to the second half of our play. You know this wonderful family that we are portraying in our play better than I do, but remember we will be performing this play in cities as far away as Rome. So please allow me to tell you what I will be telling others in faraway places about your village and the wonderful characters in our play."

Delaeh is the son of Devas and Esther and the brother of Sam and Lydia. He is a healthy eighteen year old young man now, but his health began to fail when he was four years old. His legs were too weak for him to stand unaided. The Director's introductions of the main characters continued and with each introduction, the actor playing the part stepped on the stage. When all the introductions were complete the Director said, "Now sit back and enjoy the second half of our play."

The stage was filled with actors. One was on a stretcher, two were acting like they were blind and two were hobbling. The remaining actors were carrying the stretcher or helping the blind or lame actors to the side of the stage. A curtain is moved, revealing a tall slender man in a plain brown robe with long hair and a beard.

A curtain is moved on the other side of the stage, revealing Devas and Sam standing there. Devas is standing on his toes trying to see what is happening. Sam is jumping up and down, trying to see what is happening and yelling, "What is happening? What is happening?"

Devas bends down and places Sam on his shoulders and says, "What is going on?"

"It is Jesus and he is healing those sick people."

"Are you sure?"

A man runs by Devas and Sam, waving his hands in the air and laughing.

"Yes, that man is the man that got off the stretcher. Let's get Delaeh. I know Jesus will heal him."

There was a slight pause and Devas runs off the stage with Sam on his back hanging on for dear life. They run all the way around the marketplace and by the time they return to the stage, the scene had been changed to a gate in a small fence and a door to a small house. Devas runs through the gate. Sam is yelling, "Put me down father." Sam is placed on the ground and the door opens. There standing in the door is Mother. Her hands are on her hips and the look on her face brings laughter to the audience. Mother begins to demand answers from Devas. Devas shuffles his feet, moves his hands but no words come from his mouth. There is more laughter. Then mother turns to Sam. Sam tells mother about Jesus healing people in the marketplace. Mother goes back into the house. Devas calls Bird. Bird climbs down from the roof. Ezra and Merchant run through the gate. Then all the actors go into the house. There a slight pause. The door swings open and mother comes through the opening with a determined look. She is followed by Sam and then four stretcher bearers carrying Delaeh. They all march around the marketplace and when they return to the stage, the scene has been changed. We now see a boat at the pier. The stretcher and Delaeh are put on the boat. Ezra, Devas and Sam take their place in the boat. Mother stands on the pier looking down at the boat.

Someone from behind the stage shouts, "Get in the boat, Mother." Soon everyone was yelling, "Get in the boat, Mother."

The play continues and we next join them, when Delaeh is being lowered down from the new opening in the roof. On the stage the actor playing Jesus is standing below the opening in the roof. Sam is in the crowd in front of the stage. You can see four men on the roof lowering Delaeh to the feet of Jesus. Sam, looking up says, "Oh, I wish mother could see this." At that time Mother pokes her head through the opening. This brought a reverent laughter from the audience. Delaeh reaches the floor and Jesus said to the paralytic, "Son, your sins are forgiven you."

The announcer in a loud voice says, "Some of the scribes sitting there were reasoning in their hearts, "Why does this Man speak blasphemies like this? Who can forgive sins but God alone?" Jesus perceived in His spirit that they reasoned within themselves. He said to them, "Why do you reason about these things in your hearts? Which is easier, to say to the paralytic, your sins are forgiven you; or to say; arise, take up your bed and walk? But that you may know that the Son of Man has power on earth to forgive sins He said to the paralytic."

The actor playing Jesus says, "I say to you, arise, take up your bed, and go your way to your house."

Immediately Delaeh arose, took up the bed, and walked.

All the actors said, "We never saw anything like this!"

The main curtain was pulled together and the Director stepped to one side of the stage and said, "That concludes our play. Now ladies and gentlemen please show this wonderful family how happy you are to have your friends' home." Delaeh walked out of Grandfather's building, followed by all his family.

All the audience stood and sang:
"Shine the light for Father to see.
Bring him home for mother and me.
Keep him safe while he's away.
In his strong arms I want to stay."

The Commander saw the crowd rushing to the stage and his natural instincts were to protect the family from anyone that might be in the crowd that wanted to do them harm. He turned to give the pre-assigned signal for the gates at the outpost to open and discharge twenty soldiers on horseback to protect the family. The aide said, "Commander! Stop! Look!"

The Commander could not believe his eyes. The soldiers that had been watching the play had gathered around the stage and were controlling who was allowed on the stage. He turned to his aide and thanked him for stopping him from calling out the reserve security troops stationed behind the gates and then asked his aide to remove all the guards from around Devas' and Ezra's homes. The Commander worked his way to the stage where he motioned for Devas and Ezra to come to him. When they came to the edge of the stage he said, "I have removed the guards from your home and you can go home when you want to."

The Commander now had time to decide what to do about the problem the committee of five had told him about. He neared the stone marker at the fountain but the sun had set and he could not see the writing on the stone. He started to go to the outpost, when he heard two small voices saying, "No. You were standing there and I was standing here. NO. I was there and you were here."

The Commander said, "Boys, you were here and you were over there."

"Thank you, mister. I knew I was right. I want to make sure that I get the correct star."

The Commander leaned against the marketplace fountain and watched the boys. Soon the sky was filled with stars. The boys studied the stars and each pointed to a star. The Commander could not believe his eyes, each star blinked and all the other stars stayed steady. The younger boy said, "No. not that one. I wanted the one next to it." The one star stopped blinking and the one next to it started blinking.

The Commander continued his walk to the outpost and all the while he was thinking, boy and I think I have a lot to keep straight.

Once he was in his office building, he thanked his aides and told them he would not need them anymore tonight. He sat down at his desk and for the first time in days he was alone. He placed a sheet of parchment on his desk, picked up a quill and thought about writing his resignation and then just disappearing to some place, where he could not be found. Then he realized when Herod figured out the truth, he would do terrible things to those wonderful people that saved his life and protected him for thirty-two years. He pushed the parchment aside, leaned back in his chair, placed his feet on his desk, cupped his hands behind his head and stared at the ceiling. His thoughts swirled through what he had heard today and how brave and committed his mother and father were. In the dark room he felt a smile on his lips as he thought about the pouch he had been carried in and the way Mrs. Ruby described what happened to the pouch and the horse. He was not fully awake or asleep but his thoughts were relaxing and refreshing. He would have spent the whole night in that position, if it had not been for the slightest tapping on his eye closest to the one window in his office.

It was not a physical tapping like dust falling from the ceiling or small bug lighting on his eye. It was softer, gentler but just as insistent.

The Commander was so relaxed that he resisted opening even one eye, but when he did peep he could see a star flashing outside the window. He walked to the window and saw a sky full of stars, but only one star was twinkling. He knew that moment that was the star mother and father had selected for him when he was a baby. The Commander also saw three camels hunkered down and three travelers seated around a small camp fire in a clearing outside the outpost wall. The Commander watched for a while and then decided to walk over to where the wise men were. When the Commander walked out the door of his building, he was greeted by two guards.

"Commander, Can we get your aide for you?"

"No thank you. I'm just going for a walk."

He walked out the gate to the road that runs along the east side of the marketplace. He could see the small camp fire that he had seen from his window. He started up the trail that led, where the wise men seemed to be waiting for him. As he was about to walk into the site, he heard a voice shouting, "Commander."

The Commander stopped, turned around and saw a sleepy eyed aide running up the trail.

He motioned for the aide to stop and be quiet but the dedicated aide continued until he was standing next to him. The Commander turned to see if the sound had disturbed the wise men and to his amazement they were gone.

The aide said, "Where did they go?"

The two bewildered men walked into the clearing. There were no signs that the men or the camels had been there. The aide walked to the fire pit, bent down to touch the charred wood and said, "The wood is cold as if there had been no fire here in days."

"I know what happened here is confusing, Marcus. Please go back to the outpost and don't tell anyone what happened here. I want to stay here by myself for a while."

The Commander walked to the marketplace, sat on the edge of the fountain, waited, and wondered about all that had happened tonight. While he sat there, trying to make sense of all he had seen, he heard the faint sound of camels hoofs walking on the stone road coming from the grave site of Captain Philip Apollo for whom the fountain was dedicated. The camels kneeled down and the wise men dismounted.

They stood in front of the marker for several minutes and then walked over to the Commander. No words were said, but the reassuring look on their faces gave the Commander a feeling that everything would be all right. One of the wise men stepped forward and handed the Commander a small medallion. The wise men mounted the camels and quietly rode off.

Chapter 35
Day after the Play

The traveling theatrical group was busy packing their props and costumes in two wagons. Grandfather and two of the other village elders were in Grandfather's building counting the coins that had been placed in the five boxes that had been located at each passageway that led from the roads to the marketplace. When the coins in the last box were counted and the contributions totaled and recorded, the elders presented all the coins to the Director. When the business matters were completed, the actors boarded the two remaining wagons and they were off to the next city on their schedule.

The Jewish ladies were preparing their homes and the meals for the Sabbath and the Jewish men were scheduling their work to be home by sundown.

Delaeh was in the shack at the end of the pier long before the sun was up. The charts Cara put on the wall two weeks earlier were still there.

Ezra and Devas were in their boat checking the nets and getting ready to go fishing as soon as the sun popped through the horizon after the Sabbath.

A boat, with the committee members that had been sent to Capernaum, approached the pier.

"Shalom. It's good to see you working again."

"Hahab. How are you? Toss me a line and I'll tie you up."

Delaeh helped the returning committee members onto the pier. They thanked Hahab for sailing them back to Hippos and then headed to make their report to the Chairman.

Hahab motioned for Delaeh to join him in the shack, where they could talk secretly about what was happening in Capernaum before he headed back home. "You and your family are folk heroes to the Jewish people in Capernaum and all the surrounding areas.

When Jesus healed you and you walked out of that building, Jesus' popularity greatly increased and continues to grow each day. Many are proclaiming Jesus to be the Messiah or King of the Jews."

Reports of Jesus' teachings and healings and John the Baptist condemnations of Herod for marrying his brother's wife has caused a great deal of concern and there are concerns that Herod is about to crack down. The outpost in Capernaum is much larger that the outpost in Hippos and although they have the same rank, our base Commander has seniority over your Commander. It's no secret that the Capernaum's Commander is jealous of Hippos' Commander and has tried to have the two commands combined in order for him to become Commander of both outposts."

"If he outranks our Commander, it seems he would have no problems having the bases combined."

"Your Commander's family is very wealthy and powerful and Rome knows that Hippos region is growing faster than the Capernaum region is growing. The Hippos area also brings in more taxes per person than the Capernaum area and the people that live in your area cause fewer problems. There is a new rumor going around that the Hippos Commander is being considered for advancement to General and he would be placed over all of the territories ruled by Herod, Phillip and Pontius Pilate."

"I have to leave now so I can get back home before Sabbath."

"I always enjoy talking to you. Have a good trip home."

"Any trip that I don't run into dead smelling pigs is a good trip."

The members of the committee that had returned from Capernaum were greeted by the Chairman and Rabbis Abdon and Boni.

"What did you find out in Capernaum?"

"The atmosphere there is much different than here in Hippos. The Roman soldiers stand guard in full combat uniforms. When we asked for directions to the Synagogue, we were told to ask a Jew. Everyone seems to mistrust each other. When we got to the Synagogue compound, it was surrounded by a tall wall with a heavy door that was shut. We banged on the door and after a while a small peephole opened and we were asked to identify ourselves and state our business. We were escorted to the Rabbi's office. The people we passed on the walk to the office never looked at us, nodded or smiled. The Rabbis we met were pleasant, but I could tell they were careful about answering our questions. We talked for over an hour and then I asked the Rabbi if he would like to join us for a walk through the marketplace. He said, "Oh. No! And you should not go either. Jews are not welcome there. All of the Jewish merchants' shops have been closed and there are signs that say, "NO JEWS ALLOWED."

As we were about to leave the Rabbi's office, he asked me to stay a moment. He closed the door and whispered, "I'm sorry I could not be more open with my answers to your questions. Capernaum's Base Commander has been here two years and he is determined to persecute all Jews. Herod recommended Capernaum's Commander to become the General over all military in his territories but rumor is that Rome has chosen the Commander in Hippos for General. The only hope the Commander here has to become General is to control John the Baptist and Jesus, but the more he tries to control them the more the people follow them. Now the word is that he is trying to discredit the Hippos' Commander. He has a group of historians and scribes looking into the Hippos Commander's background."

Chapter 36
What the Historians
And Scribes Found

The historians and scribes arrived in the meeting room hours before they were to meet with the Capernaum Commander. They hung on the wall, the rubbings made of the markers at the memorial fountain and grave in Hippos of the deceased Captain. One stack of parchments contained all the papers pertaining to the captain's widow. Included were the following papers:

Condolences from the General of the region.
Proclamation of Captain Philip Apollo's heroic acts.
Letter proclaiming "most honored members of the Roman Empire" status to Ruby, his widow, Palti, his son and Elizabeth, his daughter.
Receipt for one year's pay.
There was a stack of parchments for each of the Captain's children that contained the same records.

The Capernaum Commander walked into the room, went to the rubbings hanging on the wall, studied the rubbings, looked around the table with several stacks of parchments on it and then sat in a large chair in the center of the room. Turning to his personal historian he asked, "Have you been briefed on what these man have found out about the Hippos Commander?"

"Yes, sir."

"How long did it take them to explain what is included in those papers?"

"Sir, I have been working with them for three days."

"I don't have three days to sit here, while they tell me what is in all this stuff they have on the table and hanging on the wall."

"Sir, I know that but give them two hours and you will be surprised what they have found."

"Very well, have them start."

"These parchments are copies of all the records we found in Rome that recorded the heroic deeds of Captain Philip Apollo. They include the following:
>Condolences from the General of region.
>Proclamation of Captain Philip Apollo's heroic acts.
>Letter proclaiming "most honored members of the Roman Empire" status to Ruby, his widow, Palti, his son and Elizabeth, his daughter.
>Receipt for one year's pay."

"I know, Commander, Palti has the title of the "most honored member of the Roman Empire". I've watched him advance in rank quicker than his academy class mates and now he may be given the position that should be mine. If this is all these historians have found, there is no need to continue this meeting."

"Commander, you need to hear what else they have found."

"OK, let them continue."

One of the scribes went to the rubbing of the grave marker and began to explain what was written on the marker.

>MEMORIAL TO
>CAPTAIN PHILIP APOLLO
>WHO GAVE HIS LIFE IN THE SERVICE
>OF THE ROMAN EMPIRE
>BORN 4185 DIED 4221

The other scribe followed by explaining what was written on the marker at the fountain.

>THIS FOUNTAIN IS
>DEDICATED TO THE MEMORY OF
>CAPTAIN PHILIP APOLLO
>ON MARCH 20, 4223
>HE GAVE HIS LIFE IN THE SERVICE
>OF THE ROMAN EMPIRE
>ON JULY 16, 4221

The historian walked to the table and said, "From the information on these rubbings we know the Captain was thirty-six at the time of his death and from his military records, we are able to establish the following:

He entered the army at the age of eighteen.

He was assigned to Capernaum in 4206.

He led the survey and construction team on many road projects from 4212 to 4219

Was married in 4208

He was assigned to construct the aqueduct to Hippos in 4219 until his death.

His military records indicate the Captain had a son and a daughter but does not give the dates of their birth.

Assuming the youngest child was born no later than nine months after the Captain's death, the latest the child could have been born was March, 4222.

From a ships manifest we know that the Captain's wife and his infant son boarded a ship for Italy where they left the ship eight days later. Also on that ship, traveling on, "most honored members of the Roman Empire status" was a Roman courier. The only name given for the courier was Courier. We found that this ship usually carries twenty passengers on each voyage but on this voyage the only passengers were the widow, her son and the courier. For the next two months no one without special privileges could travel. We found records in Jerusalem."

"Hold it there! I want everyone except my historian and you to leave the room."

Once the room was cleared, he turned to the shocked historian that had been presenting his report.

"Have you told anyone, including the staff that worked with you, about your conclusions after you studied these documents?"

"No, sir. Your instructions to me were quite clear. I was to be the only person to study all the documents. My staff was to only have access to the information that they personally obtained."

"Good. Well done. Now I want you to go out and tell your staff that I am furious. Tell them that I said their work was trash. There is nothing they found that was not common knowledge. Also tell them I have threatened to strip them of their scholastic status and put them to work on the road gangs. Tell them you suggest they go away and never mention this humiliation to anyone. Then you come back in here." The dumbfounded historian opened the door just as the Commander shouted, "I better not see or hear about any of you again."

In about two minutes the door opened again and the befuddled historian returned to the room. "Sir, I'm sorry that I have failed you."

"Don't be silly, you have done a great job. Now go on and explain what you have found."

Just as the historian walked to the table covered with parchments, the door swung open and a guard shouted, "Stand for his excellency."

Herod led by two of his guards and followed by his historian entered the room.

"Well, my soon to be general, do you have the information I need to convince Rome that their choice for general is not worthy of such a high position?"

"Your Grace, we do but I think only you and your historian should hear what I have found out."

"My guards are always with me, so tell me what you have found."

Commander told his now nervous historian to continue his report.

"We found records in Jerusalem that the father of Herod Antipas. I mean your father placed travelling restrictions because he was searching for a child that some wise men told him was to become the King of the Jews. As you know your father liked to refer to himself as King of the Jews and when the wise men left Jerusalem to search for this new born King of the Jews, he sent troops to follow them. When it became clear the wise men were not going to return to tell your father where the baby was born, the Captain sent a messenger to Jerusalem asking for instructions. Three days later the messenger returned with orders for the Captain to return to Bethlehem, get the father, mother and child and bring them to Herod. When he arrived at the house where the wise men had found the baby, the house was empty. The troops that were sent to get the family rode to Jerusalem and reported that the family was no longer in the house and they were told the family left during the night for Egypt."

"I remember my parents talking about the same Captain being ordered back to Bethlehem with hundreds of troops with instructions to kill all the Jewish baby boys two years old and younger. Instead of killing the babies, he and his wife warned the families to hide the young boys."

"That is correct, your grace. The records indicated the Captain and his wife had an infant baby boy that was less than two years old and no one knows what happened to him. When Emperor Tiberius Caesar heard what Herod, I mean your father, was doing, he sent orders demanding he stop the slaughter and report to Rome immediately. Everyone thought Herod was going to lose his position, but he survived and spent the rest of his life trying to cover up what he had done."

"There was an attempt to remove all records that referred to this event but we found some official references to the horrible order Herod gave. They may have tried to cover up what happened, but I can assure you the Jews will never forget what happened."

Herod's historian walked to the rubbings, studied them for a while then he studied the parchments on the table. Turning to the historian that compiled this report he said, "So everything in these documents is from official records."

"That's correct."

"I know we historians will only report what we can prove with documents. Did you find anything that you heard but could not document?"

"Yes. Our interviews with many people that knew the Captain that died as a hero said they remembered his son, Palti. They all said he was a strange boy that beat up many of the boys in their neighborhood."

The Commander said, "That's nothing. I beat up boys in my neighborhood when I was young boy too. Everyone in my home town knew I was a bully."

"This boy was more than a bully; he was possessed with evil spirits. Based on the interviews this boy would have been at least ten years old at the time the infant named Palti was carried on board the ship. We found no records that could verify the boy's age but we know he was older and not an infant at the time the Captain's widow and infant boarded the ship. "

"Is there anything else that you think I should know?"

"Yes. We found the message to Emperor Tiberius Caesar telling him Herod's father was having Jewish babies slaughtered in Bethlehem. When the historian in Jerusalem saw the document I was reading, they snatched it away from me and told me to forget that I saw that message and not to use the information in any way. I did see that the message was sent by carrier pigeon and was signed Courier."

A knock on the door and a voice saying, "Your Grace, I need to talk to you."

Herod recognized the voice of his trusted aide. "Come in."

The aide walked over to Herod and said, "I need to talk to you in private."

The look on the aide's face revealed his concern.

"I'll need this room. I want everyone, but you Commander, to go outside and wait in the hall."

"Your Grace, A courier is here with a message from Rome."

"What did the message say?"

"The courier's instructions are to give the message to you personally and to wait for one hour for you to send a reply back, saying you received the message and that you will comply with the all the instructions."

"Get him and bring him here now."

Soon the aide returned with a young courier.

"Give me the message."

"Are you Herod?"

"You have brought me messages before. You know that I am Herod."

"My instruction is to ask if you are Herod."

Herod's face became red and he was about to explode with rage when his aide stepped to Herod's side and whispered, "You know the rules, just tell the courier that you are Herod."

"I am Herod."

"This message is for you. My orders are to wait one hour for you to read the message, for you to write your reply that you understand the message, that you will follow the instructions in the message. I will wait outside that door for you to give me your reply."

Herod snatched the message from the courier and began to read. The more he read the madder he became. Turning to his aide

Herod said, "Get parchment and write the following."

"Your Grace, I will do whatever you tell me to do but the law states that a courier is to be treated with the same respect you would give to the sender of the message. This courier was sent by the Senate of the Roman Empire. You need to write your reply that you understand the message and that you will follow the instructions in the message."

"You're right, give me that parchment." Herod wrote his reply and handed it to his aide to take to the courier.

"Your Grace, you must personally hand your reply to the courier."

"Give me that message and get that courier to get in here."

"Here is my reply."

Once the courier was gone, Herod told the Commander he was leaving in one hour for Fort Machaerus and that he wanted the Commander and his historians to join him there tomorrow.

Chapter 37
Meeting with Herod
At Fort Machaerus

Two days later the Commander from Capernaum and the historian that headed the team that gathered the information about Palti are in a room at Fort Machaerus, waiting for Herod to come in. The two rubbings are hanging on the wall and a table is covered with parchments.

The door opened and two large men came into the room. They looked more like gladiators that were ready for mortal combat than guards. The Commander jumped from the chair he had been seated in and snapped to attention. The Commander's reaction was not due to his military training, it was his response to the frightful appearance of these men.

"Stand there," demanded one guard. "His Excellency will be here in a moment."

Herod walked through the door, followed by two additional guards that were more threatening than the first two and his personal historian. Herod looked around the room and then dismissed the guards. When the door was closed behind the guards and the Commander could breathe again he said, "Your Excellency it is good to see you."

"It's good to see you again. I hope you brought everything I need to discredit the Commander in Hippos. I don't want him to be my legate, he's too soft on the Jews. The Jewish soldiers under his command have a Jewish cook prepare all their meals. They have their own pots and pans and they do not have assignments on their Sabbath or their holidays. I need someone like you that doesn't care about the soldiers under your command. The very idea of Rome not taking my recommendation for general in my own region is very disturbing. OK. What have you found that I can use against Rome's choice for legate?"

"Your Excellency, the rubbings hanging on the wall and the parchments on the table prove beyond a shadow of doubt that the Hippos Commander is not who he claims to be. In fact, he is the son of a traitor to the Roman Empire."

"Are you sure anyone that looks at all this information will come to the same conclusion you and your historians came to?"

"Yes, I'm sure"

"Good. I had you meet me here instead of Jerusalem for several reasons. My new wife, Herodias and her daughter, Salome, are staying here until I get some things taken care of with my old wife, Phasaelis. Herodias has planned a birthday party for me tonight and there is a prisoner here that I want to talk to. If your historian can convince my historian that we have enough documents to prove the Commander is the son of a traitor and he has been using someone else's 'most honored members of the Roman Empire' status for years. I will go to Rome with this information when I return to Jerusalem."

"I am absolutely sure that anyone that reviews this information will agree with our conclusions."

"Good. If my historians agree with you, I'll see that this information is given to Tiberius. Now I need you to help me with a situation that I have to handle."

"Your Grace, I'll be happy to help you."

"Good, come with me while the historians stay here. I'll explain what is happening. You know that I was married to Phasaelis for many years. Her father, Aretas IV is the king of Arabia. My ex-wife, Aretas' daughter has gone home to her father. I have been told that her father is planning to attack me as soon as his army is ready. The message brought to me by the courier told me that Rome is not happy about this situation because Aretas has been a faithful ally for years. Rome has told Aretas and me that they consider this to be a dispute between two families not between Rome and Arabia. I have been told that I may use my personal guards and hire mercenaries in this matter but no Roman soldiers may be used. I have fifty personal guards to confront Aretas' army. I need you to train these men to get them ready for combat and then to lead them into battle."

"I will be glad to train these men but you said that Rome will not let anyone that is in the Roman Army participate in this battle."

"What Rome doesn't know won't hurt them."

"Do you know when and where the two armies will meet?"

"Their army is forming at Petra about forty miles from here. We are in a very strong position here, so I think we should wait for them to attack us here. His family is the one that feels offended because I divorced his daughter. I'm not offended. I don't care if I ever see that woman again. When they have had time to consider the risks they are taking just to defend their daughter's honor, they won't attack me."

"Let me meet with two of your best men in the morning and I will start preparing a plan to defend the fort."

"Good. Tonight is party time. We can worry about Old King Aretas and his army tomorrow."

The Commander had about six hours before he had to get ready to attend the big party, so he decided to walk around the outside of the tall walls that surrounded the fort. He saw steep drop-offs on three sides of the fort that only leveled off at the bottom of deep ravines over three hundred feet below. The one road that led up to the only entrance to the fort was guarded by a large, heavy wooden gate. The road up to the gate is serpentine to make the climb less steep but at the same time it makes it much longer.

The Commander's military training and the many battles he had been in triggered his brain to start developing a plan for defending the fort against any army, even a large well trained army trying to enter this fort. To defend the fort against a small army of less than two hundred mercenary soldiers would be simple. The Commander found a seat at the top of the winding road to the fort entrance and watched as the guests left their wagons and drivers at a clearing where the long winding road began. The guests would then get in ox drawn wagons for the ride to the gate. After observing the road to the entrance for a while, the Commander felt he knew how to secure this road from an attacking army.

Food was cooking on open pits, the sun was setting and the staff was lighting torches around the court yard. Guests that would be staying for a few days had been assigned to their quarters. The fort was beginning to take on a festive atmosphere except for the dungeon.

Herod, surrounded by the same four guards, walked into a room in the dungeon where prisoners were brought to be questioned. John the Baptist was chained to a wall. He was a small, skinny man. The hair on his head was long and disheveled, his beard was matted, and the garment he wore was made of camel's hair and he wore a leather belt around his waist.

"I am Herod."

"I know who you are and I know what you have done."

"What do you know about me?"

"You're divorcing your wife, Phasaelis, and you broke the law by marrying, Herodias, the wife of your brother, Philip I."

"Moses permitted a man to write a certificate of divorce and send her away."

"Moses wrote that commandment, but from the beginning of creation, God made them male and female. For this reason a man shall leave his father and mother and the two shall become one flesh, so they are no longer two, but one flesh. What therefore God has joined together let no man separate."

"You seem to be a good man that is well versed in the Jewish laws. I would like to talk with you more but now I must attend a party. I will instruct the guards to separate you from the other prisoners and to make you comfortable for a few days. After all my guests are gone, I will meet with you for a while and then you will be taken back to your home."

Herod and Herodias were reclining on several large cushions placed on a raised platform. Party guests had eaten to their fill and the servers saw that no goblet was empty. There was a steady flow of well-wishers approaching the newly married couple. All brought elaborate gifts and placed them at the feet of their host. The gifts were quickly viewed and the givers were acknowledged. Servants carried the gifts to a room where they would later be evaluated by Herodias. The evening's entertainment had been continuous and was performed by the most popular and talented entertainers in the world. Now the guests in the hall seemed to be content with relaxing and talking to old friends. The musicians were returning quietly to their station. A young girl walked up to Herodias and whispered,

"She is ready."

Herodias stood, walked to the edge of the platform, raised her hands and shouted, "Ladies and gentlemen! Thank you for the way you have welcomed me. Your kind words are appreciated and I look forward to seeing you all back in Jerusalem. We are not here to welcome me. We are here to celebrate my husband's birthday. Now sit back and enjoy my gift to the love of my life."

The drummers began with a soft slow beat. A curtain at the entrance to the hall parted revealing four big, brawny men carrying a large jewel encrusted container resting on top of two long poles. Each man's arm was by his side and his hand held one end of the poles. The men wore loincloths; their bodies were tanned and covered with oil. Trumpeters blended in with the drummers, as the men began marching around the room. When they cleared the entrance to the hall, they slowly and effortlessly raised the poles high over their heads. Their first walk around the room was slow but military in its cadence and precision. The second time around the hall, the rhythm became more syncopated and each man's march became more of a swagger. The only sound in the hall came from the instruments. All eyes were fixed on the enticing performance. The excitement and anticipation increased with each step and drum beat. When the mysterious package and monstrous quartet were in front of Herod, the drum beat and the team of carriers stopped. Slowly the poles were lowered to the floor. Each man moved to the jewel encrusted container where the top of the box was removed and carried away. The drums began with a slow rhythmic beat, string instruments began a low whine. Fingers pointed toward the box as a figure covered in beautiful flowing veils began to emerge.

"Ladies and gentlemen I give you my daughter, Salome, performing the dance of the veils."

The full orchestra struck up a tantalizing composition as Salome bowed to Herod. Her body then joined the rhythm of the drummer. Bare footed and wrapped in veils she twirled, leaped and provocatively worked her hips and shoulders as she covered the center of the hall. Her movements were so perfectly synchronized with the music that one could not distinguish, if she was being led by the orchestra or they were following her movements. The veil around her face was partially removed revealing sparkling eyes, bright teeth and a flirtatious smile. Each youthful movement brought sounds of appreciation from the guests as she glided around the hall. The musical accompaniment was light, pure and flighty. Slowly and hardly perceptible, a drummer slightly increased a sub beat. Soon the full orchestra followed the lone drummer's lead. The guests left their lounging positions and formed a circle around the area where Salome was performing. The dance to this point revealed the talents of a beautiful young girl that received the loud approval of the guests. From this point on the only thing revealed was the girl and the guests were shocked into silence. At the end of her performance she stood there waiting for approval from the audience. There was not a sound, it was so quiet you could have heard a veil drop. The young girl waited a moment and then ran to the arms of her mother and was quickly covered with a robe.

Herod motioned for Salome to come to him. The robe she had over her shoulders and wrapped around her dragged the floor and the patter of her bare feet could be heard above the silence. Herod placed his arm over her shoulder and said, "Your talent exceeds all others in my kingdom and your beauty exceeds all others in the world."

The first response from the guest was a deep breath. It seemed that no one had taken a breath in five minutes. Now that Herod had given his approval, they each tried to outdo the other guests with their shouts of approval.

Herod held his hand up and the hall became silent again. "This is the finest birthday gift I have ever received and I am lucky to share it with my friends." In his drunken condition he promised to give Salome anything she desired, up to half of his kingdom.

A simple thank you would have pleased Salome but her mother wanted more, so much more. The mother nodded to the girl and whispered, "Go ahead."

Salome stood on her toes and whispered, "I want the head of John the Baptist on a platter."

Herod stood there, shocked by the young girl's request. Then he realized the dance and this request were all planned by her mother. He had promised to give her anything she desired. How could he go back on his promise even if it were made while he was drunk? So he reluctantly agreed to honor his promise. John was executed in the prison. His head was cut off and delivered to Salome on a tray.

As soon as the severed head of John the Baptist was carried into the hall the guests scurried to get out the gate and down the hill to where their wagons were waiting to take them home or anyplace other than where they were.

Herod did not walk out on his balcony the next day until after two in the afternoon and by that time all the guests were gone. In the light of day and with a clear head, Herod realized what he had done. Not ready to face the problems he had created, he went back to bed.

The Commander was up at the first ray of light. He woke two of Herod's guards and asked them to ride with him to survey the areas at the bottom of the mountain. After two hours of riding, they met a group of men camping near a stream. The Commander dismounted and walked into the camp. A guard stepped from behind a bolder and said, "State your business."

"I seek the services of men to defend a fort from attack."

The leader of the group walked from the camp site and said, "Commander what are you doing so far from Capernaum?"

"Do I know you?"

"Let's just say that our line of work has brought us in contact with each other before. We are mercenaries that take on the causes of people that pay us more than their enemies are willing to pay us."

"What are you doing here?"

"We are returning from a dispute in Mesopotamia and are headed back to our homes."

"Are you available for an assignment?"

"We might be. Tell us what you would have us do."

The Commander and the leader of the mercenaries engaged in a conversation that covered King Aretas' threat to attack his daughter's ex-husband, Rome's refusal to allow Herod to utilize any Roman military to defend himself against King Aretas and Herod only had his fifty personal body guards to help defend the fort.

The leader of the mercenaries said he needed to check with his troops and he would be right back.

The leader came back in ten minutes and told the Commander he had sixty men that would be available and what it would cost for each man and the means of payment. The Commander agreed to go back to Fort Machaerus to meet with Herod to get his approval. The leader of the mercenaries said he would send two of his men to Petra to find out when and where King Aretas planned to attack. The Commander and his two companions left to tell Herod about finding a group of mercenaries, headed to their homes after completing a successful battle, how much it would cost and many of the same things the Commander and the mercenary leader had covered. Herod wanted to know how many soldiers he would provide.

The Commander said, "The mercenaries have a little over one hundred men with them now. The mercenaries could provide sixty men now but the remaining men must continue on to their base to deliver the spoils from their last conquest."

They agreed that at the end of each day Herod would give the leader enough gold to pay each man twice the wages of a Roman soldier and Herod would provide all meals, drinks and dwellings for each man.

Herod was pleased the Commander had found a solution to his concerns about the threats from his ex-father-in-law. The price was reasonable and last night's mass exodus left more than enough food and accommodations to provide for sixty mercenaries for several days.

Commander rode back to the camp and told the leader that Herod agreed with their conditions and wanted sixty mercenaries and the leader must be included in the sixty men.

The mercenary leader said, "I agree but there is one other thing you need to understand."

"What is that?"

"My men will be allowed to keep all spoils of the battle."

"I agree. Herod does not want anything that belongs to his ex-wife's family. He just wants them out of his life."

The Commander and the leader of the mercenaries spent the next day planning how to defend the fort. No one in their right mind would try to climb up the steep cliffs leading up to the high walls surrounding the fort. Any army trying to charge up the steep winding road to the one gate that would allow entrance to the fort, could be cut down with arrows or rolling boulders down the road. The need to store food and water is the only weakness the fort has. Any attacking army would try to keep the fort from replenishing the food and water supply which would force the fort occupants to leave the security of the fort to search for food and water. The Commander assigned Herod's body guards the task of moving large boulders from the valley to the fort wall and smaller boulders to the top of the wall. The mercenaries were assigned to fill all the water containers in the fort and to hunt for game in the area.

The two men that had been sent to spy on King Aretas rushed up to the fort and reported to the mercenary leader that King Aretas' army was about one day ride away from the fort. The two men had infiltrated King Aretas' camp and found that he was sending one hundred and fifty of his soldiers to attack the fort. Their plan was to set up camp so that they would block access to the creek and at night they planned to send the smallest soldiers up the road, just out of the range of Herod's archers. The scrawny looking soldiers would call out insults, daring Herod's body guards to fight. They knew about Herod's big and burley body guards and that they were rewarded their position because they had killed at least ten of their opponents in gladiator fights in Roman arenas. These trained fighters would not be able to stand being taunted for long before they would come out to eradicate these pests. When they came out to fight, the advanced taunters will back away and the body guards would be drawn into the range of their archers.

"To prove we infiltrated King Aretas' camp we took one of his flags."

"Thank you. I understand your message. You have done a good job."

The mercenary leader found the Commander in the fort checking the water supply.

"Our spies are back and they said King Aretas' army is one day away. His army consists of one hundred fifty soldiers."

"Good, we are ready for them. My guards, I mean Herod's guards have carried boulders to the wall and stacked them so that four of my men can remove a few stones and the rest will cascade down the slopes destroying anything in their way."

"We should tell Herod what we have found."

"Don't worry. Herod depends on me. I'll tell him when I see him. You go back to your men and make sure they know what they are to do."

As soon as the leader went to his mercenaries, the Commander headed for Herod's chambers.

"Your grace, my spies have reported that Aretas' army is a day's ride from here. Under my direction the mercenaries have filled all the fort water storage containers and have shot four deer and five goats. Your guards have brought large boulders to the fort walls and I have designed a way to place the boulders, so when a few rocks are removed the large boulders will roll down the mountain crushing anything in their path. I will continue to prepare the fort for your safety."

"I don't want to hide up here like a frightened mountain goat. I want you to develop a plan to defeat them within three days."

"Your Grace, my job is to protect you."

"No! Anyone that wants to be my General will defeat my enemies, not hide from them and hope they will go away."

The Commander met with the leader of the mercenaries and informed him that he had decided to attack and defeat Aretas' army as soon as they arrived.

The leader of the mercenaries said, "While we have time, I want to send my men down to the creek and have them climb up the road to the gate as fast as they can, so I can time how long it would take an army to climb up to the gate. I suggest you have your guards go to the top of the walls, where all the smaller boulders are stored, so they can watch my men climb back up the road. I'll stand a little way down the road and signal my men to start running up the road."

The Commander said," I was about to suggest the same thing, except I will send my guards down to the creek. . You have your guards go to the top of the walls, where all the smaller boulders are stored, so they can see how fast real men can climb back up the road. I'll stand a little way down the road and signal my men to start running up the road."

"I'm sure your plan is better than mine. My men will learn a lot by watching a great Roman Commander such as you lead these superior men in this exercise."

The Commander yelled, "Guards form in a column four abreast." Before leading his men out the gate, he led the column around the court yard and past the balcony off of Herod's chambers. When Herod, Herodias and Salome walked onto the balcony, the Commander shouted, "Salute your King. Your Grace, if you, your lovely wife and her talented daughter would like to see my men train to defeat your enemies, go to the platform above the gate and you will be truly amazed. Guards, continue to march around the court yard, while I escort your King and his family to the seats of honor above the gate." When the Commander returned to the guards, he marched them through the gate and led them one hundred yards down the steep road. At that spot the Commander stopped and the guards marched around the Commander and continued down the road. When the troops reached the bottom of the road, the Commander shouted, "Halt, and prepare to rush the fort."

The Commander smartly turned around to make sure Herod could see him. What he saw was the leader of the mercenaries standing behind Herod and three men walking along each side of the gate.

"Get those men away from those rocks! If they're not careful they will start an avalanche. Herod, make those men get away from those rocks!" Turning to his men at the bottom he yelled, "Rush the fort! Rush the fort!"

The Commander started running toward the gate. He looked up and saw the leader of the mercenaries waving a blue, white and green flag behind Herod. Still running he yelled, "Whose flag is that?"

The last thing the Commander saw and heard before he was hit by the first stone was, Herod shaking his fist and shouting, "It's King Aretas' flag, you idiot."

The muscular gladiators were no match for the thunderous boulder. The dust cloud and noise created by the rampaging boulders covered the site of the mayhem and screams from the falling warriors. In less than two minutes there was total silence. The sound of the cascading boulders stopped but the cloud lingered. Everyone on the fort wall strained their eyes and ears to see or hear the results of the released boulders. No sound came from the dust cloud until a faint clip, clop, clip, clop. The sound grew slightly louder. Then everyone recognized the sound of a horse trotting on the stone road leading to the fort. The cloud lifted revealing the horse's hooves. The horses continued to slowly trot toward the gate until the horse and rider stopped twenty-five feet from the gate. A gentle breeze slowly disbursed the last of the remaining cloud. Herod could not believe his eyes, the rider was King Aretas, his ex-father-in-law.

"So we meet again, you little weasel. I came to kill you and reclaim my daughter's honor."

"Please don't kill me! Don't kill me. I'll get rid of this woman and take your daughter back."

"I'm not going to kill you. Letting you live will cause you more pain than ending your miserable little life now. My daughter is glad to be rid of you and I didn't want her to marry you to start with."

"I will give you all the gold and jewels I have in my fort if you and your men will just leave."

"I don't want any of your gold or jewels, but you did agree to let these mercenaries take all the spoils of victory when you hired them. These men are great soldiers and they're even better at finding anything that has value. You have already given me more than I could have ever hoped for."

"I have given you nothing."

"Oh yes you have. Your adulterous affair with that woman has opened my daughter's eyes to what a scoundrel you are and she has returned home. You have also given me laughter. When the two riders, that your Commander thought were sent to spy on me, told me that you had hired some of my mercenary to defend your fort, I almost died laughing. I cancelled everything I had to do and immediately rode back with the messengers to join my mercenary troops. I had to see this for myself."

By this time the mercenary troops that had been camping out of sight walked up the road and were standing behind King Aretas.

"It took a long time for my men to tell me about the meeting with your Commander. The more they tried to tell me, the more we laughed. One of the men was in Hippos a few days ago, where he saw a travel troop of actors put on a play about a young crippled boy that Jesus healed. The crowd loved the story and the Director said he was not going to perform old plays any more. He told the audience that from now on he was going to put on plays about real people in real life situations. He called it "a reality show." I have sent for my scribes to come here to interview everyone that has been involved in this future "reality show.""

King Aretas asked the leader of the mercenaries to have Herod's flag removed from the top of the fort and brought to him. Then Herod, Herodias and Salome were told there was an oxen drawn wagon waiting for them at the bottom of the road. Herodias asked to go to their quarters so that she and Salome could get some of their clothes. They were told they could not get anything except what they were wearing. Their clothes would be sent to the Director of the travelling acting troop to be used in future plays.

Herod, Herodias and Salome walked through the gate and started down the road. The leader of the mercenaries walked up to King Aretas and told him that three of John the Baptist followers were here to get their leader's body.

"Tell them to pull their cart up the road and into the court yard. Have some of your men help them get John's body."

"What about his head?"

"I saw one of the servants carry his head out of the hall shortly after it was brought to the girl but I have no idea where it was taken."

"We saw a rider leave the fort in a hurry last night. One of our men caught up to him and asked him where he was going. He said he was carrying a package to Capernaum so we let him go. I assume he had the head."

Herod, Herodias and Salome were shown the wagon they were to use,

Herod said, "Where is my driver? Who is going to help us get into the wagon?"

A large mercenary said he had been assigned to see that they had all the help they needed to get started back to Jerusalem.

"Thank you. You are the first person here to show me the respect I deserve. I will remember you when I get back to Jerusalem."

"Oh, I'm glad to help you and I'm sure you will remember me. This is how this is going to work. Do you see that whip on the wagon's driver seat? Well, if you swat the ox on its rump it will start heading to Jerusalem."

"Young man, that's most helpful information."

"You're welcome. Now I have some more helpful information for you. If the three of you are not on that wagon and headed to Jerusalem by the time I count to ten, I'm going to take that whip and start beating anyone that is not on the wagon. One! Two! Three!" Herod jumped into the driver's seat and without looking back started whipping the ox. By the count of five, Salome was standing in the back of the moving wagon holding her mother's hand and yelling, "Jump, mother, jump!" By the count of ten, the ox was running as fast as Herod could get it to go. Salome was holding on to her mother for dear life and Herodias was covering ten feet each time her feet hit the ground. By the count of ten, the fleeing trio were headed for Jerusalem and fading into a cloud of dust.

"Have a nice trip home and remember me! I was the one that helped you get started!"

Three of John's disciples placed his body in the cart and one of the guards placed a cover over it.

The guards followed the cart to the gate. Outside the gate, the mercenaries stood at attention, all the way to the bottom of the road.

Chapter 38
Hippos

Hippos is not a large metropolitan area nor is it still the small, isolated fishing and lumbering village of years past. The citizens here are busy working, raising their children and are more concerned with what is happening in and around Hippos than what is happening in cities like Rome, Athens, Jerusalem or Damascus. They get most of their news from the merchants passing through or traveling entertainers. Some of the news has been so embellished by the people spreading the news that it is hard to determine fact from fiction. Then you have people like Merchant that will only tell you what they know to be factual, leaving out what they are not sure of. When the Chinese caravan is in town, they bring stories about people and places, most of the people that live in Hippos will never see but the ladies do look forward to hearing about the latest fashions and the latest gossip from afar.

By now everyone in Hippos had heard about Herod having John the Baptist's head cut off, placed on a tray and given to his step daughter, Salome. They had just started getting some of the sorted details about Herod's talking to John the Baptist a few hours before the birthday party and finding John to be a smart and spiritual man. One of Herod's guest said he heard Herod tell a guard to separate John from the other prisoners and to make him comfortable for a few days. Herod was also heard telling John, when all his guests were gone, he would meet with John for a while and then John would be taken back to his home.

Stories about some of the guests running out of the hall right after seeing the head of the poor man and leaving the fort without getting their things from their rooms were beginning to be spread by some of the servants of these guests.

A Roman courier rushed into the outpost. He brought his horse to an abrupt stop in front of the administration building, dismounted, and rushed past the guards and headed straight to the

Commander's office. There were no greetings. Just a simple, "I was in Rome when the Senate received news about what happened at Fort Machaerus. Later that day we received your message telling Rome that you had sent fifty of your troops and one of your aides to assist them in running the Capernaum post, until Rome decided who would be replacing the deceased Commander.

I left Rome eight days ago with instructions to meet with Herod to see what was going on. The Senate was furious when they heard about Herod divorcing his wife and marrying his brother's wife. Now that he had this Jewish fellow named John the Baptist's head cut off there is talk about replacing Herod.

"Has Rome decided who is going to replace the Commander in Capernaum?"

"That's your decision to make now that the Senate has selected you to be the new general."

"What about the matter of who my father was?"

"A Senate military committee received a rambling message from Herod about you. The committee chairman reported that the message was full of foolishness and it was not worthy of consideration. That matter is over. I am going to meet with the rest of our committee of five and give them the good news."

The courier and the new to be General walked to the marketplace to find the other committee members and to see the work going on to increase the size of the marketplace.

The Roman survey team had marked off where the Eastern road around the marketplace would be relocated farther to the East of the marketplace and the village men had established the limits of the extended marketplace. The western side of the marketplace will not change and the existing Eastern road will remain in use until the new road is completed. So even though there will be some inconveniences, traffic will still flow and part of the marketplace will remain open. All of Hippos was excited that the traffic problems were finally going to be improved and the new and larger marketplace would give the citizens of Hippos and their visitors new and improved facilities.

For those of you that do not live in our little parallel village of Kempsville, we have a similar project going on here as I am writing this story. When our project is completed we will have better traffic control, more marketplaces and additional recreational areas. Each time I drive through our construction area, my mind takes me back two thousand years to the project in Hippos. By the way, if you get a chance come to Virginia Beach to visit our expanded marketplace. We're a lot closer than Hippos, Israel.

I wrote in my introduction of this book, "the beginning of a story is usually just the continuation of other stories." We are the continuation of these stories, just as the people and events I wrote about were the continuation of the life stories of people and events before them. This book has taken you into the life story of many characters and tells how they interacted with each other.

Author's Note;

I hope reading my book, has given you a better picture of what life may have been like around the time Jesus came to earth as a child and throughout His ministry. The Bible tells the wonderful story of Jesus much better than I could, so I wrote about the people that were much like you or me. The disciples' caught up in the storm and Jesus walking on water is recorded in the scriptures, however, there must have been others at sea during that storm and there were anxious people in Hippos worried about their children, husbands, sons and grandchildren. My story is about people like those folks. I have been very careful not to add or delete anything written in the bible.

Now that I have gotten a little older, there are many people and events in my life that I realize played a part in helping me write parts of this story. Some of these influences were so small and seemingly insignificant at the time they occurred, that it has taken many years for me to fully appreciate their importance. I also realize that fancy programs planned to reach out to children or to anyone for that matter, can never replace the individual effort you make to simply invite someone to be a part of your community, church family, scouts and friends.

In the first chapter of this book, I confessed, that I love to watch the expressions on peoples' faces as a story takes them on a journey. (That's one of the many great joys a Grandfather gets.) Many of these faces belong to the wonderful children that attended Carrow Baptist Church's Vacation Bible School held each summer. These children come from homes throughout our little village. It has been my pleasure to be one of the storytellers at our Vacation Bible School. Over the many years I have enjoyed each class that listened so eagerly. During story time, some of the children appear as though they were right in the middle of the story. I know this is what Jesus meant when He said, "except you become as a little child you shall in no way enter into the Kingdom of Heaven."

Preparations for telling my stories start in the same way each year. My wife provides me a bed sheet that she no longer needs. I go to the garage and with the help of a large tub and some Ritz dye, I turn the sheet into a garb that approaches what might have been worn during the time of the story I would be telling. Somewhere around the house, I find something that can be used as a headpiece, and along with a fake mustache and beard, I'm pretty well set.

One of the main imaginary characters in this story is Devas. This name came about because of a simple question that was asked by Mrs. Rita Berry. Rita has taught Sunday school and Vacation Bible School at Carrow Baptist Church for many years. One Sunday several weeks before Vacation Bible School, Rita asked how she should introduce me when I came to her class to tell my stories. I asked her to let me think about it and I would let her know the following Sunday. Anyone that knows me knows that I'm a doodler. Give me a piece of paper and a pencil and before long I have written, drawn and sketched all over the paper. Rita's question kept bugging me. What seemed like a simple request kept me pondering for most of the week. I tried a combination of words. Nothing seemed to be suitable for the name of a storyteller. I tried looking up Hebrew words that had special meaning, such as the Hebrew word for storyteller.... Follower... Teacher and many other words. Then it came to me. A name written backwards might help the children remember the story I was telling that day. The first story I was to tell was about salvation. I doodled SAVED on my paper, and having just tried writing names backward, I wrote Devas and realized that the story I was telling first was about someone turning their life around. Now I could tell Rita how to introduce me to her class. I wanted to be introduced as Devas

The first thing I did in each class was to write my newfound name, Devas, on the blackboard. At the end of each class the children were asked what happens when the name DEVAS is turned around. They understood that by writing DEVAS backwards the letters became SAVED. All that week the children were calling me Devas. As a matter of fact every once in a while I still get a, "Hi Devas," or I'll hear a child tell their parent or friend, "That's Devas."

The chapter I call "The Village" in my book has special meaning to me. Even though I am writing about a town that is six thousand miles away and events that happened over two thousand years ago, I was picturing the area where I have lived with my family for over forty years. It's not really a village. It's a section of Virginia Beach called Kempsville and more specifically Carolanne Farms/ Arrowhead/ Huntington. There is no large body of water in our village, but there is a small branch of the Elizabeth River that looks like the Jordon River and a small lake called Turtle Lake. You may be wondering what similarities this area has with the region in my book. Well, I'll tell you.

    First, the little branch of the Elizabeth River that runs along one side of the property on which our little church, Carrow Baptist, sits is about the width of the Jordan River at high tide. One of our elementary schools, Arrowhead, is on the property adjacent to our church, just like the Synagogue and the Meeting Building (school) in our story.

    The homes in our area are occupied by a wonderful group of people. Many of them have ties to Carrow Baptist Church, Arrowhead Elementary School, Carolanne Swim Club, Scouts, Vacation Bible School, or Civic League activities. They are students or graduates from Arrowhead or just play on our property. A lot of families have lived in our village for many years and we are seeing second and third generations returning to the neighborhood to raise their family where they grew up. Many a father has watched his child catch their first fish in Turtle Lake and whispered, "Be quiet or you'll scare the fish away."

    In Chapter 4, when grandfather was addressing the elders, he talked about how the Romans had built aqueducts to carry fresh water to Hippos. Virginia Beach does not have a Roman aqueduct, but we do have a pipe that runs underground from Lake Gaston, that is about one hundred miles away from here that provides the water needed in our village. We are very proud to say that one of our village elders (I'm going to get in trouble for calling her that) led the battle to get that needed water source to our village and she and her family have lived and grown up in our village and are cherished members of our village. Meyera Oberndorf served the city of Virginia Beach as mayor for twenty one years and she and Roger attend many functions held in our village.

    Most of the friends my family and I have made over the years lived in our little village, attended our church or have had children attend Arrowhead or Point O View Elementary School.

In short, our little village is a quiet, caring community where you know you can count on your neighbors to be there in times of need, just like in my story. If you have lived through a hurricane in our area, where the average land is about ten feet above sea level and the ocean is just eleven miles away, you have no problem imagining a storm such as the one in this story. I have seen the concern neighbors have for their neighbors and the way the whole community pulls together to help each other pick up and make repairs after a storm.

This community not only responds in times of emergency, but during normal times, the community takes on a wonderful life of its own. Neighbor meeting neighbor at the annual Easter egg rolls in the church yard, the Fourth of July parade on Susquehanna Drive, Arrowhead Elementary School annual carnival, PTA meetings, Civic League meetings, playing sports in the Arrowhead Park & Recreation programs, Carolanne Swim Club, live Christmas manger scene, decorating homes for Christmas and Halloween trick or treat.

We do not have an official town crier; however, our civic league uses face book to keep us informed.

Our church met in Easton Elementary School's gym while our building was being constructed. Much like my story, life in our community revolves around the church (synagogue), school, home, ball field and the marketplace, Our marketplace is not quite the same as I pictured the marketplace in my story, but if you want to meet your friends and neighbors, go to Food Lion, Rite Aid Pharmacy, El Gran Rodeo Mexican Restaurant, Pizza Hut, Dollar General or Bobbie and Helen's annual dance recital.

So even though Hippos is separated by 6,000 miles geographically and 2,000 years chronologically from our little community, this little story becomes more realistic because the reader can see and feel some of the same things the people in this story have experienced.

Many of the imaginary characters in my story took on some of the characteristics of people in our community.

I'll not reveal every literary cloning I did, but there are a few I would like to mention. I think you might recognize some of the characteristics in people you know.

When Devas was running, with Sam on his back, to get Delaeh and Mother confronted him at the front door, no one else could better play that part than Bill Burns. Bill is a worker, not a talker.

The character of Bird took on the physical and personal qualities of Bruce Jackson. Long, lanky and dedicated to his work just like a bird. I have watched Bruce as he has taken on many responsibilities in our church and Village and he has performed every task to perfection.

In this story, the merchant that carried away fish and returned with the needed rope, canvas and other repair items was never given a name, other than Merchant. When asked to help carry Delaeh's stretcher and go on Mother's great sea adventure, Merchant went beyond the call of duty. While I was developing Merchant's characteristics, I was picturing one of our longtime villagers, and friend, Charlie Temple. Charlie is retired now, but before retiring he was a sales representative for a large firm and his job required that he travel throughout the United States. If you are planning a trip, Charlie can tell you the best route to follow. He is likely to take out a piece of paper and draw you a map, just like Merchant did for Devas and his family when they decided to walk home from Capernaum.

I set the number of children in Devas' and Ezra's family at a total of five, because I have five grandchildren. My oldest grandchild is Robby. He is a healthy young man twenty years old. He has no physical ailments but because of his alert, analytical mind and his abilities to get along with almost anyone, I used Robby's characteristics to develop the character of Delaeh.

The outgoing nature of Samantha (Sam), her determination not to be left behind and her keen awareness of what is going on around her are traits I see in Robby's sister, Lauren. The main reason I picked Lauren is the devotion she has for her brother Robby.

My youngest grandson, Tyler, was twelve when I first started writing my book. I took the literary liberty to portray him as a teenager when I developed the character of Joshua in my story. Even at his young age, he is a determined young man that is very serious about whatever he does. He would have manned the sails or steered the boat on his first fishing trip as well as an adult would.

My oldest granddaughter is Cara. I pictured Cara climbing to the top of the tower at the end of the pier to tend the signal light that guided her father, brother, uncle and cousin home during the storm. When I continue to develop this story in another book, she will be running the pier.

Jennifer is my youngest grandchild. In this story she was Lydia. I liked the part in Chapter 16 where Chuma and Lydia have the following conversation. Chuma says, "Your family will be here in a few minutes. I'll meet them because no one is allowed into the camp unless I escort them."

"May I go with you?" Lydia asked.

"Sure. Come on let's go meet your parents, brother and sister, I know you have not seen them for several days."

"Oh. I miss them, but I can't wait to see my brother walking. I have never seen him walking before."

Hand in hand the two headed to the edge of the camp. There was no conversation between the two of them. Chuma used his free hand to wipe the tears from his eyes.

"There they are! There they are! He's walking! He's walking!" Lydia let loose of Chuma's hand and started to run toward her brother. A guard stepped out to stop her. Chuma motioned the guard to let her through.

The guard says, "But your instructions are…"

"I know. I know. This is a special occasion." Chuma was careful not to let the guard see his eyes.

The teachers that brought their class to see Jesus in the marketplace could have been none others than Mrs. Joyce Allen and Mrs. Linda Crawford. They have taught the young children in our church faithfully for many years. I envisioned Joyce and Linda leading their class across the marketplace to get them as close to Jesus as possible. Joyce has gone on to be with her Lord, but her Sunday school class continues under the leadership of Linda Crawford, Bonnie Jackson and Angela Gilley.

While writing this story, I pictured Mother as a rather large woman.

Now my wife is small, but that is where the dissimilarities end. There is not one trait that Mother showed in this story that does not fit my wife to a tee. She is meek and low-keyed as anyone can be, but stay out of her way when anyone or anything crosses the protective barrier she has so lovingly constructed around her family. When confronted, she can rattle off a list of potential dangers and why not's as long as your arm. Stopping a wild horse like Devas, as he was running home to get Delaeh, and then turning this large determined man into a little boy who had just been caught with his hand in the cookie jar, would be no challenge to her. When I wrote about Mother's feelings about going out on a boat, I had a very clear picture of my wife.

Our church has had a Vacation Bible School every year for over forty years for the children in our neighborhood. For two years we were blessed to have Central Baptist Church from Athens, Tennessee come to our church and conduct the Vacation Bible School. They came with dedicated adult teachers and a youth group that simply won the hearts of all the attending children and the Carrow Baptist Church members and guests. They put on a wonderful program both times and they did all this out of the goodness of their heart. Now you know why I selected Athens for the home base of the touring group in my story. Anyone of the adults in their group of leaders could play the part of Titus, the director of the touring group in this story.

Writing about the Chinese caravan was easy. Several years ago we started sharing our church building with the Family Bible Church. Most of their members are Chinese. Our churches have combined services several times a year, but normally they have their worship services while we are having our Sunday school. When it is time for us to head to the sanctuary and for them to head for their Sunday school we meet in the hallways. I'll not try to name all the individuals I cloned to be in the caravan in my story but I think they will be able to guess.

In Chapter 24 I wrote about two young boys that brought news to the barker in the marketplace and later they saw and talked to the Wiseman. While writing about them and every time I read what I wrote about them I pictured Joey and Kyle Moore. They are polite, attentive and their eyes have just the right amount mischievousness in them. I'm sure there is a special star in the heavens that will lead them to do great things. Their Grandmother, Judy Dunn, is one of the hardest working and most faithful members of our church.

I came to Norfolk, Virginia as an eighteen year-old sailor in 1953. One evening, while standing at the corner of Freemason and Boush Street a lady came out of the basement door of Epworth Methodist Church and asked what I was doing. I told her I was waiting for a bus to take me back to my ship, the USS Corry DDR 817. She said, "No you're not, you are coming down to our youth group." That lady was Frances Briscoe. She was working with the youth group at the church. I met a great group of people there and returned each time my ship was in port. One young lady named Joyce Silcott caught my eye and in 1956 we were married in Epworth Methodist Church. I mention Frances for many reasons, but I'll give you four right now. One is to point out how little things can change your life. Two, I liked to imagine the look on her face when she reads this. Three, to say, "Thanks for what she has meant to my family and me. Four is to point out that you do not need to wait until your church comes up with a program to invite someone into your church. Your individual act of simply inviting someone to come in will get the job done.

    This pretty well completes my story. I thank you for taking time to read it and my notes. I know my wife will read all of this before it is published and she always says that I'm long winded, so I'll stop here.

    This book laid the ground work for other stories. Make up some of your own stories. Remember, we are not changing any part of the wonderful truths in the Bible; however, let your mind wonder about the possible effects the Bible stories had on the people that were around when these stories happened.

    Thanks again.